Managing Mergers, Acquisitions and Strategic Alliances: Integrating People and Cultures

Second edition

Sue Cartwright and Cary L. Cooper

Manchester School of Management
University of Manchester Institute of Science
and Technology

BUTTERWORTH
HEINEMANN

Butterworth-Heinemann
Linacre House, Jordan Hill, Oxford OX2 8DP
225 Wildwood Avenue, Woburn, MA 01801-2041
A division of Reed Educational and Professional Publishing Ltd

℞ A member of the Reed Elsevier plc group

OXFORD   AUCKLAND   BOSTON
JOHANNESBURG   MELBOURNE   NEW DELHI

First published 1992
Second edition 1996
Reprinted 1997, 1999 (twice), 2000

British Library Cataloguing in Publication Data
Cartwright, Sue
    Managing Mergers, Acquisitions and
    Strategic Alliances: Integrating People
    and Cultures – 2Rev.ed
    I. Title II. Cooper, Cary L.
    658.16

ISBN 0 7506 2341 1

Composition by Genesis Typesetting, Rochester, Kent
Printed and bound in Great Britain by MPG Books Ltd, Bodmin, Cornwall

PLANT A
TREE

BTCV
British Trust for
Conservation Volunteers

FOR EVERY TITLE THAT WE PUBLISH, BUTTERWORTH-HEINEMANN
WILL PAY FOR BTCV TO PLANT AND CARE FOR A TREE.

Contents

Acknowledgements

With particular thanks to Jenny Ellison for her patience in typing this manuscript and Joe Jordan for his research contribution to the international material included in this volume.

1

Introduction: mergers, acquisitions and strategic alliances – a people issue

During the 1980s, mergers, acquisitions and other forms of strategic alliance, dominated the business and financial press, especially when they proved unsuccessful:

- 'An Engagement is Broken – The Collapse of a Dutch–Belgian Banking Merger'

  (*Financial Times*, 19 September 1989)

- 'Marriage brings woe for Wedgwood – Broken dreams: shares nose dive since the "perfect" marriage in 1980'

  (*The Mail*, 25 March 1990)

This preoccupation with the incidence and outcome of such organizational marriages was hardly surprising for, in the 1980s, mergers and acquisitions (M & A) became a worldwide growth industry. The global value of M & As has risen rapidly from £60 billion in 1984 to £355 billion in 1990. Thirty-seven per cent of the 1990 figure relates to cross-border international M & As. This occurred despite the seemingly high risks attached. For, although the opportunity to merge or acquire is presented to shareholders as a strategy for wealth creation, it is estimated that more than half of all mergers and acquisitions prove financially unsuccessful.

As the business world entered a new decade and the gloom of global recession, the merger mania of the 1980s seemed to have lost its impetus. M & A activity began to decline as many organizations moved to 'downsize' rather than 'upsize' their operations. However, managerial predictions, suggesting that the potential growth benefits to be gained from M & A would continue to exercise a persuasive and seductive appeal to organizations, have proved accurate. Recent upturns in the economy have caused a resurgence in business confidence, and M & A activity has started to pick up once again. In the first six months of 1993, the number of US M & As showed an increase of 30 per cent compared with the same period in the previous year (*New York Times*, 1993). The value and frequency of cross-border deals has steadily risen between 1991 and 1993, with a marked increase in joint ventures (KPMG, 1994). A recent survey (Cartwright, Cooper and Jordan, in press) of almost 500 senior European managers suggests that the upward trend is likely to continue. The survey found that 50 per cent of managers considered that it was highly likely that they would make acquisitions within the next three years. Forty per cent indicated that they expected to become involved in a joint venture/ strategic alliance, while 10 per cent expected to merge, within the same period. Therefore, there are powerful indicators to suggest that M & A activity is likely to continue to be an important feature of organizational life throughout the 1990s.

As, historically, mergers and acquisitions have been considered exclusively the domain of economists, market strategists and financial advisers, the financial and strategic aspects of the activity are well appreciated and have been extensively addressed and debated in the management literature. In contrast, although mergers and acquisitions are something which happens to people in organizations rather than to organizations in any abstract sense, the human aspects of the phenomenon have received relatively little attention. Indeed, 'people' are largely ignored or dismissed as being a soft or mushy issue by those who initiate or guide the merger decision. Consequently, people have come to be labelled the 'forgotten or hidden factor' in merger success.

There are a number of reasons why managers need to recognize the importance of human factors to any inter-organizational combination.

1 There has been a phenomenal growth in M & A activity in the 1980s which will continue

The financial importance of mergers and acquisitions is blatantly obvious, as indicated by the size of the reported bid prices and the high cost of broken or incompatible organizational marriages. But beyond the headlines – what Harry Levinson (1970) terms 'the hoopla and the glamour' – there is a human side to merger, whereby the lives of millions of employees are likely to be changed with the stroke of a pen.

In the United States alone, it is estimated that 25 per cent of the workforce has already been affected by merger and acquisition activity during the 1980s (Fulmer, 1986). It has been estimated that if the level of the activity were to continue at its current pace, by the end of this decade every public company would be under new ownership and/or management (McManus and Hergert, 1988). As the trend seems likely to continue, no manager or worker can consider themselves to be immune from the likelihood that their organization will be taken over or merged with another in the future. Or alternatively, that they will be charged with the responsibility of managing a merger or acquisition, and implementing or perhaps handling the consequences of sudden and major organizational change at some time in their career. It is highly likely that many of you who are reading this book will have already been affected in some way by merger and acquisition activity, or been involved in other less dramatic but equally important forms of inter-organizational combination, such as joint ventures.

2 Merger and acquisition activity has increasingly become 'people intensive', and concerns cultural change or integration

The recent boom in merger and acquisition activity differs from previous waves, not only in terms of its increased scale and geographical spread (discussed in detail in Chapter 2), but also in terms of the type of organizational combinations it has spawned. It is usual to consider mergers and acquisitions in terms of the extent to which the business activities of the acquired organization are related to those of the acquirer as falling into four main types: (a) *vertical*, (b) *horizontal*, (c) *conglomerate* and (d) *concentric*.

(a) Those of a *vertical* type involve the combination of two organizations from successive processes within the same industry, e.g. a manufacturer may acquire a series of retail outlets.
(b) *Horizontal* mergers and acquisitions involve combinations of two similar organizations in the same industry.
(c) *Conglomerate* refers to the situation where the acquired organization is in a completely unrelated field of business activity.
(d) In *concentric* mergers, the organization acquired is in an unfamiliar but related field into which the acquiring company wishes to expand, e.g. a producer of sports goods might acquire a leisure-wear manufacturer.

In the last major wave of merger and acquisition activity in the 1960s, most combinations were of the conglomerate type. When an acquiring organization makes an acquisition in an unrelated area, it is unlikely that it would seek to change, other than perhaps minimally, the way in which the acquired company transacts its business – at least until it has learnt the 'logic' of its new appendage, when it may move to integrate it more fully within its own activities. Consequently, conglomerate mergers and acquisitions tend not to have any large-scale impact on the working lives of the vast majority of employees. The previous domination of the conglomerate type merger or acquisition is reflected in the existing literature which has not tended to extend beyond stressing the importance of the buyer–seller relationship.

In contrast, the current wave of activity is dominated by combinations between companies in similar rather than unrelated business activities. Consequently, the fusion or integration of some or all of their human resources is required, and success becomes heavily dependent on human synergy. It has been suggested (Porter, 1987) that related acquisitions and diversifications tend to have a greater probability of financial success than unrelated acquisitions. This is primarily because they have the advantage of transfer of product knowledge and expertise, and offer more potential economies of scale.

The growing trend towards related combinations has had important implications for merger and acquisition management in that the successful outcomes of such combinations have increasingly become dependent on the wide-scale integration of people, as well as the imposition of external financial control and accounting systems. Whereas in the past acquiring organizations may have been more content to adopt a 'hands-off' approach, the management of mergers and acquisitions today is definitely more interventionary and 'hands on', which brings its own set of problems (Cartwright and Cooper, 1993b).

Most acquisitions in the 1980s and 1990s have been made with the intention of changing the way in which the acquired company transacts its business. Even if it is already performing successfully, the high level of investment which the acquisition represents means that shareholders will expect it to do even better in the future. Many organizations borrow heavily to make an acquisition which has the effect of substantially increasing their gearing ratios, thus increasing their own vulnerability to takeover. In an accountancy-led economy, dominated as it is by 'short termism', the pressure 'to turn a company round' and integrate it into core business activities as quickly as possible is likely to be extreme.

Because mergers and acquisitions are associated with large-scale and often sudden organizational change, they have come to represent the challenge *par excellence* for the management of change. As the organizational title changes hands, so too does the ownership and control of an entire workforce. Company logos are revamped, often together with the organizational chart; management changes; and so inevitably does the style of work organization. Changing the way in which the organization conducts its business – its managerial style, systems, procedures and the symbols of its identity – means changing its people and their organizational culture.

3 Human factors are increasingly being held responsible for merger and acquisition failure

Because financial and strategic factors dominate merger and acquisition selection decisions, the diagnosis and analysis of merger failure has traditionally tended to adopt a similar focus. Mergers and acquisitions are considered to fail for rational economic reasons, e.g. economies of scale were not achieved of the magnitude anticipated, the strategic fit was poor or ill-matched, or there were unexpected changes in market conditions or exchange rates.

It is true that mergers and acquisitions do fail for reasons of a rational financial and economic nature; but making a successful merger or acquisition, as many organizations have learnt to their cost, is more than just a matter of 'getting the sums right'! Many have also come to recognize that a compatible and successful organizational marriage depends upon characteristics of the partner, which extend beyond the suitability of the strategic match. Financial advisers may guide merger managers in suggesting the broad areas in which economies of scale might be achieved, but they do not have to translate them into practice, and physically implement such decisions.

Readers who have already experienced the trauma of merger and acquisition activity, are likely to be well aware of the multitude of 'people problems' and issues which inevitably arise, many of which involve non-routine managerial decisions, e.g. who to lose and who to retain. Nobody comes through the experience entirely unscathed or without a tale to tell, as evidenced by the many anecdotal reminiscences which make up the folklore of a company, and regularly appear in popular management journals. As one manager, speaking on the basis of his own experience, suggests: 'those who underestimate or ignore the human factor do so at their peril!' Although his particular organization, a large multi-national, merged over three years ago, it is still considered to be experiencing human merger problems, and a rate of staff turnover in a difficult recruitment market which is uncharacteristically high compared to that pre-merger.

As the inadequacies of traditional, rational economic explanations of merger and acquisition failure are increasingly being recognized, more progressive companies are coming to realize that what happens to the employees involved, and their organizational cultures, cannot be considered as separate and distinct from what happens to the organization. There are, therefore, two important human factors to merger and acquisition success which determine the speed and effectiveness with which integration can be achieved. They are:

● The culture compatibility of the combining organizations, and the resultant cultural dynamics.
● The way in which the merger/acquisition integration process is managed.

The importance of organizational culture was well demonstrated in a now classic study of over forty highly successful American organizations carried out by Tom Peters and Bob Waterman (1982). The message of *In Search of Excellence* was loud and clear: consistently outstanding financial performance was the outcome of a strong, dominant and coherent culture. This link has subsequently been supported by research in the UK (Goldsmith and Clutterbuck, 1984). Organizational culture has also been linked to market strategy (Piercy and Peattie, 1988) and managerial style (Sathe, 1983). The experiences of organizations operating in a highly mobile job market and changing external environment suggests that a strong coherent and unitary culture injects stability into the workforce and reduces labour turnover.

The issue of cultural compatibility and its implications for subsequent integration is important in the context of any inter-organizational combination or collaboration. Cultural differences and the concept of cultural distance can inhibit and positively obstruct management attempts to create a cohesive and coherent organizational entity. Such problems are unlikely to be confined to domestic M &. A activity. Certainly, combinations between two organizations within the same country are likely to result in a greater degree of physical and procedural integration than cross-border collaborations. However, in order to be successful, international M & As and strategic alliances will also, at least minimally, require certain groups of key individuals to work together and to establish a shared or joint understanding of common objectives and strategy. In the context of international combinations, the integration issue is further complicated by national cultural differences.

The implications for mergers and acquisitions are clear. The type of culture of the combining organizations, the resultant cultural dynamics and the extent and speed with which a unitary and coherent culture emerges, will play critical roles in determining the eventual outcome of any inter-organizational combination or joint venture. Indeed, a survey carried out by the British Institute of Management (1986) concluded that managerial underestimation of the difficulties of merging two cultures was a major contributory factor to merger and acquisition failure. Interestingly, despite evidence to suggest that UK acquirers typically pay on average a 40 per cent premium over pre-bid stock market valuation, cultural compatibility was rated by managers as significantly more important than price paid. For those who still remain unconvinced that merger is an essentially human activity, involving the fusion of organizational cultures, in the course of this book we will present further and more recent evidence to support this proposition. On the basis of recent research undertaken by the authors, which draws on the experiences of both successful and unsuccessful combinations, we will demonstrate how the cultural dynamics of mergers and acquisitions influence both organizational and individual outcomes.

4 Managing people more effectively in mergers and acquisitions requires a proactive approach

A considerable amount of managerial time and energy is expended in negotiating and completing a merger or acquisition deal. Recent evidence on the pattern of acquisition activity in this country (Hunt, 1988), suggests that having made an initial identification of a potential acquisition target, it is usual for a predator to stalk its prey for a period of two years before making a bid. Then, having made a bid, the subsequent negotiations are likely to lengthen the process. It is not uncommon for such negotiations to last several years. During this period, the acquiring organization is likely to have become extremely well informed as to the financial health of the acquisition – but little more beyond that! Typically, it is only when 'the ink has dried', and the initial euphoria has begun to wear off, that the question of what happens next is raised or given any serious consideration. On the basis of our research, we were left with the distinct impression that acquisition/merger success was more a matter of 'good fortune' than the outcome of any well-conceived management strategy. From the time the deal was signed, what subsequently followed then became something of a journey into the unknown.

Most organizations are ill prepared for the scale of problems that they invariably have to face. In the absence of any human merger audit, or carefully formulated human merger integration plan, most organizations muddle through the merger process, moving from one organizational crisis to another, rather than proactively managing people and anticipating and confronting problems before they get out of hand. Indeed, current merger management is characterized by an *ad hoc*, reactive 'firefighting' approach, particularly in terms of the Anglo–American model.

Although cultural compatibility and the way in which the merger integration process is managed are to some extent related, cultural compatibility or fit alone is no guarantee of merger or acquisition success. Combinations between organizations with well-matched and highly compatible cultures will fail to meet expectations if they are insensitively or poorly managed. Conversely, in situations where the cultures of the combining organizations prima facie are highly dissimilar and potentially incompatible, good management can still prove effective.

As the business world continues to demand rapid response to change, organizational survival will increasingly hinge upon the ability to implement and manage that change successfully. For many, this means getting the 'people issues' right.

We consider that this book will make an important contribution to the merger literature in extending understanding in an under-researched and important area of business activity. Most of the literature to date that has addressed the human aspect of the phenomenon emanated from the boom of the 1960s, and is now outdated. We also hope that its implications and recommendations will lead to an improvement in the way in which mergers, acquisitions and other forms of strategic alliance are managed in the future; and that we will move to a more healthy and positive situation, in which mergers and acquisitions are no longer automatically seen as 'win/lose' games, but are approached from the premise that both sides can potentially win.

The book is based on an extensive survey of public information and research, both in the UK and overseas, carried out by the authors in the last seven years. Included in this volume are a number of case studies, all of which involve horizontal combinations in which success is dependent upon the integration of people. They involve combinations within a wide range of business activities in manufacturing and retailing, and within a variety of business sectors including information technology, engineering and financial services. They range in size from small ventures involving less than one hundred employees, to a large UK and pan-European merger involving several thousand employees. They are representative of merger and acquisition activity generally in terms of success, in that about half lived up to initial financial expectations.

In drawing on their experiences and the collective lessons learnt, we have used these studies to illustrate both effective and ineffective managerial integration practices, which have implications not only for inter-organizational combinations, but also for major intra-organizational restructure and change generally.

The book is broadly divided into three parts. Part One (Chapters 2–4) provides a global overview of the topic and a review of the current literature, in which are discussed the commonalities of the merger experience as it affects the individuals involved. In Part Two (Chapters 5–7), we focus on the issue of culture, both national and organizational, and its implications for M & As and other forms of strategic alliance. Several predictive models are proposed, which in the light of our research evidence have already proved their value. Of practical help to managers in formulating a human merger integration plan, in Part Three (Chapters 8–11), we have broken the merger/acquisition process into a series of stages in which we outline the pitfalls and problems specific to each stage.

Throughout the book, we refer to or incorporate material drawn from case studies to illustrate or support various points made in the text. For the interested reader, we have included a more detailed account of a number of these case studies in the Appendices. Although it has been necessary to assign these fictitious names and disguise certain background details to protect their anonymity, they all refer to recent actual mergers or acquisitions.

References

British Institute of Management (1986). *The management of acquisitions and mergers*, (Discussion paper No. 8), Economics Dept., September.

Cartwright, S. and Cooper, C.L. (1993a). If cultures don't fit, mergers may fail. *New York Times*, 29 August.

Cartwright, S. and Cooper, C.L. (1993b). The role of culture compatibility in successful organizational marriages. *Academy of Management Executive*, 7(2), 57–70.

Cartwright, S., Cooper, C. L. and Jordan, J. (in press). Managerial preferences in international merger and acquisition partners. *Journal of Strategic Change*.

Fulmer, R. (1986). Meeting the merger integration challenge with management development. *Journal of Management Development*, 5(4), 7–16.

Goldsmith, W. and Clutterbuck, D. (1984). *The Winning Streak*. London: Penguin Business.

Hunt, J. (1988). Managing the successful acquisition: A people question. *London Business School Journal*, Summer, 2–15.

KPMG (1994). *Deal Watch*. Amsterdam: KPMG International Headquarters.

Levinson, H. (1970). A psychologist diagnoses merger failures. *Harvard*

Business Review, March–April, 84-101.

McManus, M. and Hergert, M.L. (1988). *Surviving Mergers and Acquisition*. Glenview, Illinois: Scott Foresman & Co.

Peters, T.J. and Waterman, R.H., Jr (1982). *In Search of Excellence*. New York: Harper and Row.

Piercy, N. and Peattie, K.J. (1988). Matching market strategies to corporate culture: The parcel and the wall. *Journal of General Management*, 13(4), Summer.

Porter, M. (1987). From competitive advantage to corporate strategy. *Harvard Business Review*, May–June, 43–59.

Sathe, V. (1983). Some action implications of corporate culture: A manager's guide to action. *Organizational Dynamics*, Winter, 4, 23.

Part One

Overview

2

Trends, patterns and motives

In this chapter, we give some indication as to the scale of the phenomenon and outline the motives and climatic conditions which are considered responsible for this sustained growth in mergers, acquisitions and strategic alliances.

The recent and continued growth in M & A activity

M & A activity has been described as occurring in waves. In the UK, the first wave was in the 1920s, the second in the 1960s and the third in the early 1970s. Despite earlier predictions to the contrary and pleas for celibacy (Meeks, 1977), the fourth biggest and most sustained wave occurred in the 1980s. As Table 2.1 illustrates, the level of activity began to fall in the early 1990s. However, it still continues at a sufficiently high level that it is perhaps no longer appropriate to award it the temporary status of a 'wave', but rather to recognize both M & As and strategic alliances as potentially permanent features of organizational evolution in an increasingly competitive and global market economy.

It should be recognized that these statistics understate the true initial financial cost of acquisition activity. This is because they only report the actual transactional share value paid by successful bidders. They do not include associated costs such as fees to intermediaries, advertising expenses, payments to incumbent senior management in the form of 'golden parachutes' or 'golden hellos', or the cost of unsuccessful bids.

With reported fees to intermediaries in the US commonly as high as 10–12 per cent of the bid price, it has been suggested that the real winners in the recent merger boom have been the divesting shareholders and the 'marriage brokers', bankers and accountants who arrange, advise or execute the deals (McManus and Hergert, 1988).

The amounts involved in launching public advertising campaigns to promote or defend a takeover deal are also often substantial. In 1987,

Table 2.1 *Acquisitions and mergers by industrial and commercial companies within the UK from 1984 to 1994*

Year	No. of companies acquired	Total expenditure (£m)
1984	568	5,474
1985	474	7,090
1986	842	15,367
1987	1,528	16,539
1988	1,499	22,839
1989	1,337	27,250
1990	779	8,329
1991	506	10,434
1992	432	5,941
1993	526	7,063
1994		
1st quarter	183	2,720
2nd quarter	184	1,652
3rd quarter	154	2,109

Source: Central Statistical Office: London

BTR made a hostile bid for Pilkingtons. For two months, until the offer was withdrawn, Pilkingtons prepared for battle and launched a massive and expensive public campaign which included the setting up of a twenty-four hour international news agency (Turner, 1987). In the more recent saga of the Dixons–Woolworth takeover, both companies incurred advertising expenses which ran into several millions, perhaps serving further to weaken Dixons' financial position.

Merger mania has not just been confined to the UK, but has occurred on a global scale. In a ten-year period, there have been over 23,000 registered acquisitions in the USA. The financial scale of the phenomenon is reflected in *Fortune*'s annual list detailing the purchase price of the fifty largest US acquisitions and leverage buyouts. In 1985, this represented a collective expenditure of $94.6 billion. This previous record was surpassed three years later in 1988 when, despite the stock market crash of October 1987, the total expenditure on the 'Top Fifty' deals rose to $111.8 billion. The largest acquisition that year was made by Philip Morris, who paid $12.9 billion for Kraft Foods, a figure which represented 609 per cent of the book

Table 2.2 *Cross border deals by number and value ($m)*

Year	Total no.	Value
1991	4,165	86,209
1992	4,036	127,695
1993	3,811	152,273

Source: Dealwatch, 1994: KPMG International: Amstderdam

value. In the same year, on this side of the Atlantic, Nestlé paid a record £1.8 billion for Rowntree–Mackintosh, a figure equivalent to twenty-six times its historic earnings.

Recent figures compiled by KPMG International show the pattern of cross-border transactions, including joint ventures (Table 2.2).
While the USA and the UK have traditionally been the major players in the merger game, both in terms of inbound and outbound activity, social, political and market changes, particularly in Europe, have influenced investment patterns. The USA and the UK still remain popular targets for investment but recent political and economic events in Russia and China have also made these two countries major targets for foreign investment. For example, in the energy sector, 1993 saw the acquisition of Joeganneftegas JV in Russia by Amoco at a cost of $5000 million. In the same year, Wing Merrill International took a 70 per cent stake in China's Jiangsu National Gas Power Station at a cost of $1689 million. Between 1982 and 1992 more than £106.3 billion worth of government assets worldwide went private, providing a

Table 2.3 *Completed acquisitions in Western Europe 1984–1989*

Year	Total no.	Value (£m)
1984	596	7,050
1985	1,138	13,414
1986	1,565	29,045
1987	2,246	36,274
1988	3,361	52,659
1989	5,138	85,759

Source: Amdata/S.G. Warburg & Co.

Table 2.4   *European mergers by sector and type 1983–1992 (June–May)*

Sector	National		Community		International		Total	
	No.	*%*	*No.*	*%*	*No.*	*%*	*No.*	*%*
Food and drink	253	53	159	33	68	14	480	100
Chemicals	256	35	336	47	132	18	724	100
Electrical engineering	167	57	71	24	57	19	295	100
Mechanical engineering	185	61	60	20	59	19	304	100
Computers	16	67	3	12	5	21	24	100
Metals	176	60	88	30	28	10	292	100
Vehicles	72	49	53	36	22	15	147	100
Wood, furniture and paper	184	54	101	29	58	17	343	100
Extractive	66	62	30	28	11	10	107	100
Textiles	64	65	27	28	7	7	98	100
Construction	158	58	105	39	3	3	271	100
Other manufacturing	55	53	21	21	26	26	103	100
Total industry distribution	1,652	52	1,054	33	482	15	3,188	100
Banking and insurance[1]	715	64	232	21	167	15	1,114	100

[1] Refers to 1984–92 only
Source: EC reports on competition policy

substantial opportunity and need for investment and collaboration with continental partners. As Table 2.3 illustrates, in the period between 1984 and 1989, the number of cross-border acquisitions within Western Europe increased almost ninefold (Table 2.3).

Based on data available for the period 1983–1992, Table 2.4 gives some indication of the pattern of European activity by sector and type. It highlights the particularly high level of mergers and acquisitions which has occurred within the pharmaceutical sector.

During the 1980s, Japanese organizations started systematically to acquire British and American businesses. In 1990, Fijutsu acquired the

Table 2.5 *Number of USA acquisitions*
by country of buyer – 1979–1988

Country	Total
United Kingdom	692
Canada	423
West Germany	152
France	132
Japan	120
Switzerland	90
Netherlands	86
Australia	76
Sweden	67
Italy	35
Total foreign acquisitions	2,075

Source: W.T. Grimm & Co. Mergerstat
Review, 1988, p. 65

UK computer giant ICL and Renown, a Japanese-based clothing group, paid £74 million for Aquascutum. Although the UK remains the largest direct investor in the USA (Table 2.5), the high level of Japanese investment in the latter part of the 1980s contributed to mobilize a wide-scale anti-merger movement. This resulted in the formation of a number of political action groups with emotive names, such as the 'Coalition to Stop the Raid on America'.

More recently, resultant changes and tightening in regulations and tax arrangements governing M & A activity and the comparatively high cost of US acquisitions, coupled with Japan's own domestic problems, have substantially slowed down Japanese takeover activity. This has made strategic alliances with US companies a more attractive alternative to acquisition.

Joint ventures and other forms of strategic alliance, more generally, have become an important and necessary feature of European business activity through the 1980s and 1990s. Such ventures are often a prelude to merger or acquisition, as evidenced by the Fijutsu–ICL takeover. Joint ventures have frequently been described as an ill-defined and complex organizational form, in that they involve any organizational partnership to attain some strategic objective. However, they can be considered similar to mergers in two important aspects. Firstly, although it is the high rate of merger failure which has tended to capture public attention, joint ventures have also shown a disappointing success rate. Secondly, the factors which are often held responsible for their poor performance are those also associated with merger failure, for example the selection of inappropriate venture partners, cultural incompatibility and 'parenting' problems more generally.

The high level of merger activity has also caused some European concern. It has resulted in the formation of the European Mergers and Monopolies Commission and a general tightening of transaction procedures. However, such concerns about the high incidence of M & As centre around the financial aspects of the activity and its effects on national and consumer interests. Typically, these concerns do not extend to employee interests.

The enabling climate

As will be discussed later in this chapter, the motives for merger and other forms of alliance are many and various. However, there are specific climatic factors which, individually or collectively, can be considered to have facilitated or promoted activity during the 1980s and 1990s.

Changing market conditions

During the 1980s and 1990s, many organizations have found themselves facing rapidly changing market conditions. Because it is hard to plan ahead when the product market is in flux, organizations tend to be hesitant to commit themselves to the long-term investment of setting up new outlets or developing on greenfield sites.

For many organizations, new and often unexpected global markets have recently opened up. In this respect, the establishment of the Single European Market in 1992 and the ratification of the Maastricht Treaty have been influential. The net result of these conditions has been to stimulate merger, acquisition and joint venture activity as the need to respond quickly has meant that strategic acquisitions and alliances have been the only expedient growth options available. Strategic acquisitions and alliances also provide a convenient means of eliminating competition and controlling markets. In the context of establishing an operational base in a foreign country, because of restrictive legislation sometimes this objective can only be accomplished by merger, acquisition or joint venture.

Increasing availability of capital

Acquisitions can be financed either from surplus funds within the organization or, as is more often the case, by borrowing from financial institutions. The availability of capital and interest rates obviously affect activity. During the 1980s and 1990s, there has been a substantial borrowing capacity and, at present, interest rates world-wide are low.

More companies for sale

In recent years, there has been an increasing pool of potential buyers and sellers. A number of factors are responsible for this. Firstly, as the successful entrepreneurs of the post-war years reach retirement age, an increasing number of companies have come onto the market, either because they have grown so large that they can no longer continue as family businesses or because there is no natural successor within the family.

Secondly, the 1980s was a decade of change. A considerable number of organizations who failed to recognize the need to change lost markets or lost competitive edge and found themselves on the acquisition market. Many small businesses, crippled by the high interest rates or cash flow problems suffered the same fate, particularly during the period 1989–1991.

As the recessionary gloom has started to lift and interest rates have dropped, certain organizations have survived the 1980s to emerge in a rather better state of financial health than others. As the predatory instinct returns there are likely to be numerous bargains around. At the same time, M & A is being increasingly used as a defence against the possible threat of a hostile takeover.

Finally, social, political and economic changes in Europe have generated a considerable number of 'willing partners', particularly amongst the nations of Eastern Europe.

Easing of regulations (e.g. the repeal of the Exchange Control Act)

Merger and acquisition activity is influenced by political climate and the prevailing attitudes and policies of individual governments. The 1980s has been labelled 'the enterprise culture', and the attitude of the British Government has been one of minimal intervention in corporate affairs.

The Mergers and Monopolies Commission is considered by many managers to 'lack teeth', and in any event is only consulted in the case of mega-mergers. A recent analysis of the pattern of US acquisitions (Gartrell and Yantek, 1980) suggests that 'right of centre' administrations stimulate activity. It is therefore perhaps no coincidence that the so-called merger decade has also been 'the Thatcher decade'.

The need to share risk

In capital-intensive industries, and in areas where the cost of research and new product development is high, organizations have frequently moved to combine witli others in response to the need to share risk and technology.

The existence of complex indivisible problems

Many organizations have increasingly faced what have been described as 'indivisible' problems (Aldrich, 1976), often of a technological nature, that are without precedent and are considered to be bigger than any single organization can resolve. As a result, organizations have increasingly felt it necessary to combine their skills and expertise with those of others, either on a permanent or temporary basis.

Merger motives

The stated motives

Mergers and acquisitions are considered to be rational financial and strategic alliances made in the best interests of the organization and its shareholders. The literature on merger motives generally draws the distinction between financial or value-maximizing motives and managerial or non-value-maximizing motives (Napier, 1989) although, in practice, the two are often related.

Mergers are considered to be initiated by financial or value-maximizing motives when the main objective is to increase shareholder wealth and financial synergy through economies of scale, transfer of knowledge and increased control. Managerial or non-value-maximizing motives relate to mergers which occur primarily for other strategic reasons, e.g. to increase market share, management prestige, reduce uncertainty and restore market confidence or perhaps even as a takeover defence or a means of protecting profits from taxation.

Although mergers and acquisitions are overtly presented to share-holders and employees as being justified on rational economic and financial grounds, there may be unrecognized psychological motives behind the merger decision.

The unstated psychological motives

There are times when the decision to merge or acquire is initiated solely to satisfy the needs of an individual or small group of individuals, rather than any wider or longer term organizational interest. *Share*

Some senior executives are motivated to instigate a takeover or merger out of fear of obsolescence (Levinson, 1970). In their view, the managers who survive, or move on to greener pastures, are highly visible men and women of action; people who are recognized as always looking for new opportunities – forever moving the organization onwards and upwards. Consequently, out of a sense of insecurity and fear for their continued *Management* survival, mergers and acquisitions provide a useful means by which they *motives* can enhance or renew credibility, and restore their own self-confidence and that of the board. Making an acquisition or merger can be a good career move for those recognized as having been responsible for that decision, often irrespective of its eventual outcome. For, by the time the financial results are known and the imprudence of the decision is questioned, the executive involved may have already moved on. Even if she or he has remained with the organization, a bad decision may not necessarily jeopardize his or her career. Because decision makers are generally so remote from the actual management of the merger/acquisition process, they can always find lots of other people to blame when things are recognized to have gone wrong!

Others may be motivated by an avaricious and egotistical need to exercise power and flex their muscles by engaging in some empire *Hubris* building. Alternatively, for some, mergers or acquisitions are no more than an amusement. A stimulating and exciting game which the 'big boys' play to relieve boredom, and to keep their managers on their toes. In the course of our research, one senior executive of an extremely acquisitive organization stated that he enjoyed making acquisitions because, in his words, 'it was sexy'.

While British and American executives seem to regard mergers and acquisitions as a game, recent research into Japanese takeovers (Kester, 1990) suggests that Japanese managers hold a somewhat different attitude, which may explain their reluctance to play the merger game. The style of work organization in Japan has been powerfully shaped by the underlying philosophy of corporate paternalism, the company-as-family simile. Kester (1990) suggests that because this simile still persists in the minds of many Japanese managers, even today the idea of selling a company has the unsavoury connotation of 'flesh-peddling'. Consequently, a merger or acquisition is not a particularly honourable activity because it violates cultural norms and is, for the Japanese, therefore more a strategy of last resort. Indeed, the Japanese word for takeover is 'nottori', which is the same word they use for 'highjacking'.

References

Aldrich, H. (1976). Resource dependence and interorganisational relations. *Administration and Society,* 7 (4), 419–454.

Gartrell, K. and Yantek , I. (1986). *Congressional politics and corporate mergers* (Working paper). Academy of Management Meeting, Chicago, August.

Kester, W.C. (1990). *Japanese Takeovers.* Boston, Massachusetts: Harvard Business School Press.

Levinson, H. (1970). A psychologist diagnoses merger failures. *Harvard Business Review,* March–April, 84–101.

McManus, M.L. and Hergert, M.L. (1988). *Surviving Merger and Acquisition.* Glenview, Illinois: Scott, Foresman & Co.

Meeks, G. (1977). *Disappointing Marriage: A Study of the Gains from Merger.* Cambridge: Cambridge University Press.

Napier, N.K. (1989). Mergers and acquisitions: Human resource issues and outcomes. A review and suggested typology. *Journal of Management Studies,* 26 May.

Turner, J. (1987). The Pilkington experience. *Personnel Management,* July.

3

Merger and acquisition p[   ] a disappointing history

'Acquisition strategy has been described as an [   ] corporate strategy where inappropriate mathematical theory and a yearning for greener grass has prevailed over common sense'

(British Institute of Management, 1986)

Assessing merger gains

While the motives for mergers and acquisitions may be many and various, the objective of any organizational combination or alliance is to increase and strengthen its financial health, i.e. to achieve what is commonly described as the '2 + 2 = 5 effect'. Hovers (1973) defines the objective of any acquisition as follows: 'The main aim of every takeover is to produce advantages for both the buying and selling companies compared with the alternative situation in which both companies will continue independently.' In the context of mergers and acquisitions, synergy is taken to mean financial synergy. The expectation is that the combination will result in increased efficiency, economies of scale, widening of markets, greater purchasing power and so to substantially increased profitability. However, despite the continued popularity of this form of business activity, the available evidence on merger, acquisition and joint venture performance is far from encouraging.

There has been considerable debate as to the most appropriate and accurate way in which to assess merger gains, both in terms of the indices used and the appropriate time span over which to judge performance (Lubtakin, 1983, 1987). Consequently, there is a plethora of empirical studies which have examined the financial success of mergers and acquisitions, using various criteria such as managerial assessment, earnings performance measured as the return on total assets or net worth and fluctuations in share prices (e.g. Kitching, 1967; Newbould, 1970; Hovers, 1973; Meeks, 1977; Fairburn and Geroski, 1989).

ial assessments have the advantage over strictly mathematical
ae in that they overcome the difficulties of combining historically
erent accounting procedures and practices. Furthermore, as there may
have been a certain amount of 'creative' accounting or 'window dressing',
especially in the first financial year, the balance sheet may look more
healthy than it actually is. For example, bottom line figures may look
encouraging in the first year, but may represent 'one-off' savings as a
result of rationalization, pension 'holidays' and/or asset stripping. On the
other hand, managerial assessments do have the disadvantage of being
subjective. In terms of time-scale, there appears to be a developing
consensus that M & A performance should be based on performance over
a two-year period (Hogan and Overmyer-Day, 1994).

The high rate of merger failure

Irrespective of the criteria selected, research evidence has repeatedly
demonstrated that mergers have had an unfavourable impact on
profitability. Instead of achieving the projected economies of scale,
mergers have become associated with lowered productivity, worse strike
records, higher absenteeism and poorer accident rates rather than greater
profitability (Meeks, 1977; Sinetar, 1981). It has been suggested that in the
long term between 50 per cent and 80 per cent of all mergers and
takeovers are considered to be financially unsuccessful (Ellis and Pekar,
1978; Marks, 1988a), and in terms of financial return represent 'at best an
each way bet' (Lorenz, 1986). Similarly, studies of joint venture failure
here and in the USA (Killing, 1982; Kogut, 1988) suggest that, despite the
adequacy of the financial backing they receive, they are highly unstable,
with ventures involving research and new product development, or
partnerships between organizations significantly different in size, being
particularly at risk. Kogut (1988), in a study of 148 US joint ventures,
found that over 24 per cent of ventures terminated within the first three
years. Firth (1980), in a study of 434 UK acquisitions, concluded that no
aggregate financial advantage accrued. Evidence provided from a study
carried out by the Department of Trade and Industry, and reported in the
1978 Green Paper, stated that 'in roughly half the cases we examined the
merger had resulted in an unfavourable or neutral effect on profitability'
(Cmnd, 1978).

A later discussion paper published by the Department of Trade and
Industry (British Institute of Management, 1986) found there had been no
improvement in the intervening years, and the merger failure rate was still
running at around 50 per cent. More recent evidence (Hunt, 1988)
continues to report success rates post-acquisition to be in the region of 50

per cent. This particular study was based on a sample of over forty medium and large acquisitions with an average bid price of £70 million.

Although it included many practised acquisitors (e.g. Hanson, ICI), experience was not found to be a significant factor. The 'novices' or first-time acquisitors performed as well, or rather as badly, as the experienced. There are two possible reasons for this. Firstly, acquisitions reflect individual rather than corporate decisions; the organization may have a historical experience of acquisitions, but not the actual decision makers. For, according to Roll (1986), 'although some firms engage in many acquisitions, the average individual bidder/manager has the opportunity to make only a few takeover offers during his career.'

If the high level of merger and acquisition activity continues, this situation may change. However, because acquisition experiences have not tended to be systematically investigated and documented, those managers who may have learnt from a 'bad' experience are unlikely to be afforded a second chance to build on and utilize that knowledge within their organizational lifetime. As mergers and acquisitions have traditionally tended to remain essentially private corporate events, with no effective model to draw upon, acquiring management seem set to continue to make the same mistakes.

Secondly, and more importantly, as we will demonstrate in Chapter 6, different acquisitions are likely to result in quite different cultural dynamics and potential organizational outcomes. Consequently, acquiring management cannot assume that because they were successful in assimilating one acquisition into their own culture, that same culture and approach to integration will work equally successfully with another acquisition.

The financial success rate of the mergers and acquisitions and joint ventures we studied was comparable with existing evidence. On the basis of their financial results in the first year of combined trading, half of these mergers and acquisitions proved successful, and only one out of three of the joint ventures.

The US experience has been similarly disappointing. Farrant (1970) found a negative correlation between profitability and merger and acquisition activity, based on an investigation of 200 large US companies. A similar study repeated by Ravenscroft and Scherer (1989) found that the profitability of target companies, on average, declines after an acquisition. McManus and Hergert (1988) report that, in the first twelve months following a merger or acquisition, companies typically experience a loss in market value of 1–10 per cent. The shareholders who gain most from takeover activity are likely to be the divesting shareholders, who tend to experience an increase in share value at the time of the offer. Asquith, Bruner and Mullins (1983) found that merger bid announcements on average result in a 7 per cent increase in target firm value in the short term. A much quoted study by McKinsey and Co. (McManus and Hergert, 1988; Hunt, 1988) found evidence to suggest that most organizations would have received a better rate of return on their investment if they had merely banked their money rather than purchased another company. Wishard (1985) estimates that two hours productivity per employee are lost per day during the early stages of a merger. According to Wishard, productivity declines because of distracting rumours and gossip which take employees away from the more immediate tasks in hand.

Traditional approaches to merger and merger failure

The process of merger can be said to begin at the decision-making stage, and involves a small number of key negotiators, rarely more than five (Hunt, 1988). According to McManus and Hergert (1988), 'most of the decision makers who initiate the strategies have climbed the corporate ladder through technical or functional disciplines'. Consequently, decisions are essentially led by accountants and lawyers described as 'the paper entrepreneurs' (Free, 1983; Hunt, 1988), and rarely involve the personnel or human resource function.

At this stage at least, a merger or acquisition is conceptualized as being exclusively an association of financial and strategic convenience, which will lead to rapid and substantially increased profitability (Hovers, 1973). The selection of a suitable merger partner is considered to be a rational decision-making process, involving an informed choice with regard to issues of availability, price, potential economies of scale and projected earning ratios (Jemison and Sitkin, 1986).

When what appeared to be a promising acquisition or merger on paper proves disappointing, the same rational economic factors which prompted the initial decision are then called into question. The essence of such an approach of financial reductionism is that financial questions are deserving only of financial answers. In the traditional mode of analysis, disappointing financial results tend to be explained as being the consequence of:

1 Poor selection decisions, in that an over-inflated purchase price was paid – the 'hubris hypothesis' (Roll, 1986) or the companies were strategically mismatched.

2 The potential economies of scale and projected earnings ratios were not
  realized because of financial mismanagement or incompetence.
3 There were sudden and unpredicted changes in market conditions.

Unarguably, such factors are likely to be responsible for or contribute to
poor financial performance but, as Kitching (1967) suggests, 'the mere
existence of potential synergism is no guarantee that the combined
operation will realise the potential'.

In conceptualizing 'the merger' exclusively as a rational financial and
strategic activity rather than a human activity, and ignoring what
Altendorf (1986) describes as the 'mushier' issues, such explanations are
likely to be incomplete. All decisions can be considered to involve two
elements: the *rational* and the *affective*. The *rational* element concerns the
technical content of the decision, based on available knowledge relating to
financial and strategic factors. The *affective* aspects of the decision
concerns the 'emotionality of the decision makers' and the 'organizational
quality' of the decision. *Organizational quality* refers to the acceptability
of the decision to those who have to carry it out, and the commitment
they have to its implementation. As we have already discussed, although
mergers are thought to be rational and strategic decision-making
processes, decision makers are often motivated by personal emotions and
aspirations which tend to override rational thinking, and neglect the
wider organizational implications – though decision makers may be
unaware or unwilling to acknowledge such factors.

The inadequacies of the rational–economic model

Because people are a less measurable organizational asset, less easily
appreciated by a study of the balance sheet than material assets or market
share, they are often overlooked or little considered at the time a decision
to merge or acquire is made. In a survey carried out by the London
Business School and Egon Zehnder (Hunt, 1988) of forty British
acquisitions, all forty companies conducted a financial and legal audit of
the company they intended to acquire. Although some of the companies
(30 per cent) considered the financial implications of employee pension
arrangements, not one made any attempt to carry out an audit of the
company's human resources to assess the indigenous talent they were
acquiring. This is like buying a house when one is satisfied as to price,
title, location and structure, without inspecting the interior; then, having

moved in, finding oneself uncomfortable with the layout and irritated by the eccentricities of the workings of the central heating system.

Harry Levinson (1970) first likened the process of merger to a marriage, whereby the compatibility of the partners is crucial to the healthy growth of the new or revamped organization. In the predominant view of decision makers, compatibility is only a matter of ensuring a 'good strategic fit', and the compatibility of management styles and corporate cultures is a little considered pre-acquisition issue.

Although people are a difficult asset to quantify at the pre-acquisition stage, the depletion or under-performance of this asset post acquisition has a noticeable effect on the balance sheet. Unfortunately this is not usually appreciated or accommodated by the rational–economic model. A recent estimate (Davy *et al.*, 1988) attributed 'employee problems' as being responsible for between one-third and a half of all merger failures. A discussion paper prepared by the British Institute of Management (1986) identified sixteen factors associated with unsuccessful mergers and acquisitions, at least half of which directly relate to people and people management issues:

1 Underestimating the difficulties of merging two cultures.
2 Underestimating the problems of skills transfer.
3 Demotivation of employees of acquired company.
4 Departure of key people in acquired company.
5 Too much energy devoted to 'doing the deal', not enough to post-acquisition planning and integration.
6 Decision making delayed by unclear responsibilities and post-acquisition conflicts.
7 Neglecting existing business due to the amount of attention going into the acquired company.
8 Insufficient research about the acquired company.

A survey of over 200 European chief executives carried out by Booz, Allen and Hamilton (1985) found that 'ability to integrate the new company' was ranked as the most important factor for acquisition success; 'price paid' was ranked as one of the less important factors.

Culture collisions are frequently the outcome of poor integration. The 'friendly' merger of Connecticut General and Insurance Company of North America into CIGNA in March 1982 is a widely quoted example. The merger involved two organizations in which the people held very different cultural values and expectations. According to press reports, the merger resulted in low morale, poor work quality and declining financial performance, in that operating income decreased by 18 per cent from 1982 to 1983.

Walter (1985) suggests that sociocultural integration takes between three and five years. Furthermore, he estimates that the cost of culture collisions resulting from poor integration may be as high as 25–30 per cent of the performance of the acquired organization.

Mergers and acquisitions, as they represent sudden and major change, generate employee uncertainty. Davy *et al.* (1988) suggest that 'the only thing certain about organizational acquisition is that nothing is certain'. This uncertainty is considered to be associated with lowered morale (Altendorf, 1986; Sinetar, 1987), job dissatisfaction and unproductive behaviour, in that a considerable amount of employee time is spent commiserating with others or on unofficial job hunting. In addition, mergers and acquisitions have also been linked with acts of sabotage and petty theft (Altendorf, 1986), increased staff turnover (Unger, 1986), absenteeism rates (Davy *et al.*, 1988) and concomitant stress (Sinetar, 1981; Schweiger and Ivancevich, 1985; Bruckman and Peters, 1987; Hall and Norburn, 1987). This is illustrated by the following comments made by employees involved in the Getty–Texaco takeover (Altendorf, 1986):

- *On petty theft.* 'Employees who would never consider "stealing" from the company began to take plants, stationery, pictures and books.'
- *On productivity.* 'Productivity for eight months was zero or maybe 10%. People didn't work ... they just sat around ... It's one of those things that snowballed. When everyone is down and out and depressed, others get depressed, I don't think any work got done.'

Such effects are likely to have an adverse impact not only on organizational performance but also on the longer term physical, psychological and mental health of employees, which in turn is likely to have negative long-term organizational implications. There are other hidden costs in mergers: for example, one of the mergers included in our research sample reported massive increases in telephone charges within the first six months, as rumours were circulated and exchanged throughout the branches.

Because the positive combination effects or synergy of mergers and acquisitions are only measured by the conventional financial indices which appear on the balance sheets, behavioural indices remain little monitored. By behavioural indices we refer to indicators such as high staff turnover and absenteeism rates, poor accident and safety records, increased recruitment and training costs and the rising incidence of customer complaints, which are often dismissed as irrelevant, unimportant or even inevitable, until such time as these cumulative financial costs impact upon the balance sheet.

The inadequacy of rational economic explanations of merger failure was first demonstrated over twenty years ago (Kitching, 1967). The study, examining the variance in performance of almost seventy US acquisitions, found that analysis of objective results (i.e. statistical evidence relating financial performance to known pre-acquisition factors of size and type) was insufficient to explain success, without integration with subjective results (i.e. the reflective experiences of the top executives involved).

Kitching concluded that the key to merger success was essentially the way in which the 'transitional process' was managed and the quality of the working relationship between the partnering organizations. The study found that in 81 per cent of failed mergers, 'reporting relationships' were said to be unclear or frequently changed.

A more recent and larger scale study (Datta, 1991), along similar lines, attempted to examine the performance of over 700 acquisitions in the US manufacturing and mining sectors. It involved a questionnaire survey of senior managers who had remained within the target company for approximately two years post acquisition. Based on data collected from the surviving managers of 173 acquisitions, the study found a correlation between poor performance and differences in managerial style. Interestingly, differences in managerial style were found to have a negative impact on acquisition performance, even in acquisitions characterized by low post-acquisition integration.

Kitching's article was influential in drawing the attention of the behavioural sciences to M & A activity. It appears to have been less successful in changing the attitudes of decision makers and the direction of most merger research, which disappointingly has continued to focus on the strategic and financial aspects of the activity. While it is generally accepted that complex and important phenomena benefit from a multi-disciplinary approach, there seems to be a continued reluctance amongst strategists and accountants to accept that the behavioural sciences and human resource specialists can play an important complimentary role in organizational combinations and alliances.

References

Altendorf, D.M. (1986). *When cultures clash: A case study of the Texaco takeover of Getty Oil and the impact of acculturation on the acquired firm* (Dissertation). Faculty of Graduate School, University of Southern California, August.

Asquith, P., Bruner, R.F. and Mullins, D.W. Jr (1983). The gains to bidding firms from merger. *Journal of Financial Economics*, 11, April, 121–139.

4

The impact of merger and acquisition on the individual

'A quick fix may work for a machine, but not for an organization.'

(Kilmann, 1984)

M & A activity may be increasing in frequency but, for those involved, it is still an extraordinary and destabilizing life event requiring considerable personal adjustment. The magnitude of that adjustment and its concomitant stress has been universally rated as being equivalent to the gain of a new family member or becoming bankrupt (Holmes and Rahe, 1967). Interestingly, merger has been found to require more social adjustment than major life events such as buying a house, mortgage foreclosure or the death of a close friend. In this chapter, we focus on the impact of merger and acquisition on the individual.

Transactional differences between mergers and acquisitions

Mergers and acquisitions are legally different transactions. Within the literature, the two terms tend to be treated synonymously, primarily because in practice a merger is rarely a marriage of equals (Humpal, 1971). The *Oxford Dictionary* defines an acquisition as 'an outright gain of something (especially useful)' and a merger, less rapaciously, as 'the joining or gradual blending of two previously discrete entities.'

An acquisition occurs when an organization acquires sufficient shares to gain control/ownership of another organization. Takeover bids are generally classified as being 'friendly' (i.e. when the first bid made is accepted), 'contested' (i.e. when there are specific issues which have to be debated) and 'hostile'. It is common for organizations who recognize the inevitability of a takeover to respond to a hostile bid by seeking an alternative and more attractive bidder, or 'white knight'. For example, in

1989, when Jaguar first faced a takeover offer from Ford, the management introduced the possibility of a deal with General Motors. As such responses tend to arise out of a sense of desperation, they are frequently described as 'shotgun weddings'.

Other takeover defences, or 'shark repellents' (Nelson-Horchler, 1987) as they are popularly termed in the US, are often adopted. These may involve the target company itself making a bid for another organization, and so forcing up its own share prices. This tactic has become known as the 'pac man defence'. In the USA, another popular defence strategy is to become incorporated in a state with anti-merger or anti-trust legislation.

The distinction between 'friendly' and 'hostile' acquisitions can essentially only be used to describe the attitudes of the shareholders and the negotiating senior management, rather than those of the acquired workforce. For the latter, being acquired or merging is essentially only a semantic difference in that, regardless of context or the quality of the relationship between the negotiating teams, the merger or acquisition event creates considerable uncertainty.

So called 'amicable' negotiations are likely to be more discreet and less public, so the change in ownership may only be disclosed to the majority of employees when the deal has actually been formalized. This usually occurs in situations where the acquired company is not listed on the Stock Exchange, as is likely in cases where the bid price is £2 million or less.

According to Hunt (1988), almost half of the acquisitions made in the UK are uncontested, and so described as 'friendly'. Although it is hostile takeovers which attract public attention, Hunt suggests that these only account for approximately 10 per cent of all acquisition activity. Further, in the UK, advisers or third parties are likely to be used in hostile negotiations, but excluded from friendly bids. Usually, but not always, the acquired organization is smaller and/or less profitable than its acquirer (Singh, 1971; Meeks, 1977).

Mergers and joint ventures, publicly at least, represent a cooperative agreement, usually between organizations more closely matched in terms of size, etc. Although Pritchett (1985) suggests there are four types of merger – rescue, collaborative, contested and raid – which influence the degree of cooperativeness.

Generally the overt power relationships between parties to an acquisition is likely to differ from that between merger partners – at least at the time of the initial announcement. In an acquisition, there are clear winners and losers; power is not negotiable, but is immediately surrendered to the new parent on completion of the deal (Mangham, 1973), or, as McManus and Hergert (1988) state, 'Those who hold title also hold the pen to draw the organizational chart.'

The acquisition of another company is a visible symbol to employees and the business community generally that the acquiring organization is successful and confident in its future. Similarly, 'being acquired' is likely to be construed as a symbol of failure at the organizational level, and also for some at the personal level: 'Being acquired has traditionally meant a great loss of face', said John Schlesinger, managing director of the investment bank, Salomon Brothers East Asia Ltd (*Financial Times*, November 1990).

As we suggest, a merger is rarely a marriage between equals, but as the parties are likely to be more evenly matched in terms of size, the distribution of power is more likely to evolve over time. Therefore there will be greater and more overt initial conflict and resistance to change within bitterly fought takeovers, particularly if the issue has mobilized the entire workforce, as in the Pilkingtons–BTR battle (Turner, 1987), than in voluntary mergers or acquisitions. In such circumstances, feelings of defeat and powerlessness are likely to be heightened.

The distribution of power has important implications for merger outcomes in setting the scene and the direction of future cultural change. The implications of this are discussed in Chapter 6.

The merger/acquisition process

Mergers and acquisitions can be considered to differ from any other process of major organizational change in three important aspects: the speed of change, the scale of change and the critical mass of the unknown they present for both parties. Marks (1988) describes the mergers process as consisting of three temporal segments – pre-combination, legal combination and post-combination.

Mergers differ from acquisitions in terms of the speed with which change and integration are introduced once the deal has been formalized. Having made an acquisition, it is usual for the acquiring organization to move swiftly to impose its own control systems, frequently freezing bank accounts or changing signatory arrangements immediately on signing the deal. In contrast, it is usual for merger partners to function as separate business entities for some time following the announcement of the legal combination. This pre-integration period is likely to continue for many months, in some circumstances a year or more, before there is any actual physical or cultural integration. The process is likely to be further lengthened in cross-border combinations by the language difficulties faced by the partners. It is, therefore, difficult to place any exact time-scale on the merger or acquisition process, which may be as short as twelve to eighteen months in the case of acquisitions, or between three and five years for mergers.

The impact of mergers and acquisitions on the individual

Understanding the likely effect of mergers and acquisitions on the people involved is a precondition to more sensitive and successful integration management. When reviewing the literature (for a more detailed academic review article see Cartwright and Cooper, 1990), we found that much of what had been written about human resource issues relating to mergers and acquisitions emanated from the conglomerate boom of the 1960s, and was fragmented and eclectic and lacked any well-defined merger paradigm. In the main, the existing literature had tended to focus on the objectives and strategies of the acquirer, particularly during the pre-combination period and the first three months post acquisition. As a result, it has been concerned primarily with the role of pre-acquisition factors such as 'context', 'size' and 'type', as affecting interpersonal relationships between senior managerial groups. Because it was written at a time when most mergers and acquisitions were of the unrelated conglomerate type, it inadequately addressed the wide-scale integration problems faced by most M & A managers today.

Managerial relationships are a well-recognized source of merger problems, but the successful integration of senior management alone is insufficient if the line managers and the rest of the workforce are factious. Employees need not be directly involved in the negotiation or execution of an acquisition to feel its impact, in that it produces a psychological ripple felt throughout the organization. Mergers and acquisitions are about power, differing perceptions, cultures and definitions of the situation and so are potentially conflictual, the social and cultural ramifications of which extend beyond the boardroom. Compensatory payments, or 'golden parachutes', are unlikely ever to become an available or practical solution for the vast majority of employees or even those at the 'marzipan level' (i.e. the middle managers). This is particularly pertinent in the financial services sector, an area which has recently witnessed a considerable amount of consolidation through M & A activity, where goodwill plays a major role in determining the 'marriage values'. Indeed, one might question the increasing practice of senior executives of negotiating substantial compensatory sums in the event of a future merger or acquisition as part of their initial employment contract, and its effect on their commitment and the long-term interests of the organization.

In treating mergers as essential crisis-producing events for acquiring management, there has been a notable tendency to ignore the role of the acquired organization or 'the other' merger partner, and its organizational members. A merger is both a phenomenological and significant life event for the organization and its employees, and a major long-term process of change and integration.

Apart from the anecdotal recollections of senior ex-employees, which tend to focus on personal survival tactics, the longer term and wider scale experiences of integrating employees and the adverse impact of poor organizational fit have been comparatively little considered, particularly in the commercial sector. Such empirical studies as we were able to locate tended to have arisen as much by accident as design, i.e. researchers/consultants just happened to be there doing something else when the event happened. Or, alternatively, studies reported have taken place under simulated or 'quasi' conditions, by which (Humpal, 1971) we mean studies that have addressed the impact of intra-organizational restructuring, or mergers involving voluntary and/or non-profit-making organizations. For example, one study we located concerned twenty-four managers involved in the combination of two divisions of a national community organization (Blumberg and Weiner, 1971); another (Wicker and Kauma, 1974) examined the effect of increased organizational size on organizational commitment as a result of the merger between two religious bodies. Elizabeth Berney (1982) examined the impact of power and culture differences on buyer–seller relationships through a series of simulated group interactions.

More recently, there has been a detectable change of direction from an essentially pragmatic approach, to a longer term, more process-orientated approach, and a change of emphasis from micro to macro level of analysis. Of the small number of later studies, two of these, Graves (1981) and Buono, Bowditch and Lewis (1985) are more relevant in that they concerned mergers within the commercial sector, involved generally larger sample sizes and addressed the issue of combining cultures.

Graves (1981) examined the successful merger of two UK reinsurance brokers – Drake Cecil. Success was attributed to the ability of the merged organization to integrate the two cultures and evolve a new coherent and unitary culture. The study emphasized that successful organizational outcomes are linked to successful individual outcomes. Employee assessments rated the merger to be between 80 and 100 per cent successful in organizational terms, and between 60 and 80 per cent in terms of personal success.

Buono *et al.* (1985) conducted a study of a 'friendly' merger between two medium-sized US savings banks. The study examined the cultures of the two banks pre-merger, the attitudes and perceptions of employees before and twelve months after merger and the emergent culture of the newly formed organization. Post-merger measures indicated that the former employees of the displaced culture (Bank A) were less satisfied and committed than the group (Bank B) whose culture had been retained by the new merged organization. In contrast, prior to the merger, Bank A's employees had held more favourable attitudes towards change than the other group. Discontent was found to centre around subjective aspects of organizational culture, managerial style and behaviour, rather than procedural or material aspects such as reward systems and training policies. Unfortunately, the paper does not report on the financial or managerial assessments of the success of the merger.

On the basis of our own and previous research in this area, there is sufficient commonality of experience to suggest that the scenario of events which immediately follows a merger or acquisition announcement is likely to be typical of all combinations. This we have called the 'five absolute truths' about mergers and acquisitions.

Absolute truths about mergers and acquisitions

Mergers and acquisitions are emotive events which affect everybody

Mergers and acquisitions may be merely financial transactions to those negotiating the deal, but to the employees involved, the vast majority of whom are not cushioned by the existence of any 'golden parachute' or similar compensatory payment, they represent a significant and potentially emotional and stressful life event.

Table 4.1   *The merger process*

Stage	Non-problematic	Problematic
1 Courtship	Voluntary, controlled	Imposed or uncontrolled
2 Marriage	Endorsed, accepted	Unendorsed, unaccepted
3 Honeymoon	Blissful, trusting	Rocky, untrusting
4 Marital allegiance	Fidelity	Open marriage
5 Interdependence	Silver Anniversary (Dependence)	Separation (Independence)

Source: Jick, 1979

Certainly, the imagery and terminology associated with merger is highly emotive, and consistent with that used to describe intimate personal relationships such as marriage or parenting. Jick (1979) has proposed a useful five stage model of the merger process. As Table 4.1 shows, at each stage there are potential problems which may result in the failure of the relationship. Unlike a civil marriage which involves the relationship between two individuals, a corporate marriage involves the relationship between two workforces composed of a large number of interacting individuals.

The following account of a takeover situation taken from a research paper published some years ago suggests such analogies underestimate the emotionality of the situation: 'Marriage, in fact, is too soft a word to describe the situation; it wasn't experienced as seduction it was experienced as rape' (Mangham, 1973).

Others have likened the merger event to the sense of loss experienced following the bereavement of a close friend or relative, or to the distress a child experiences when separated from its mother:

> Whenever a young child who is attached to her mother is separated from her, she shows distress – and should that child be placed in a new environment, the distress is likely to intensify. The way the child behaves in this situation will follow a distinct pattern: At first she protests vigorously and tries by all possible means to recover her mother. Later she seems to despair of getting her mother back but nevertheless remains preoccupied with her. Finally, the child seems to lose interest and becomes emotionally detached from the mother ... Like the child, many employees involved in acquisitions experience a powerful sense of loss when strong attachments are destroyed or changed.
>
> (Schweiger, Ivancevich and Power, 1987)

Professor Philip Mirvis has suggested that the psychological response to merger can be understood within the framework of the Kubler–Ross model of personal bereavement. According to Mirvis (1985) one can expect that employee reactions will pass through four stages.

Stage I – Disbelief and denial

Typically, the individual's first reaction is extreme shock. He or she may deny that the merger or acquisition will ever happen despite circulating rumours or a bid announcement. Even when the deal is actually signed, the individual may strive to convince him- or herself that nothing will change. Often an existing organizational leader is identified as a champion of the status quo who will successfully fight to preserve the established identity and culture of the company.

Stage II – Anger through rage and resentment

As the reality of the situation becomes more obvious, feelings of shock and disbelief are replaced by anger and resentment towards those considered responsible, i.e. the old management, the new merger partner, the state of the economy, etc.

Stage III – Emotional bargaining beginning in anger and ending in depression

As fear and uncertainty about individual job future develops, this anger often turns inwards. The individual becomes angry with him- or herself for not anticipating the event and may come to resent the commitment and loyalty he or she has invested in the company. Often the individual becomes increasingly nostalgic for what is past and may worry that his or her existing skills/areas of expertise are not transferrable to the new company. These feelings may subsequently subside to be replaced by depression.

Stage IV – Acceptance

Finally, the individual comes to recognize that what is past is gone forever, and accepts that he or she must face up to the new situation.

Until there is an acceptance that any attempt to deny or resist the situation is futile and unproductive, a positive approach will not begin to develop. Fixation at Stage I, II or III will result in preoccupation and unproductive behaviour, or cause the employee to leave the organization. Similarly, acceptance may imply behavioural compliance but not necessarily renewed organizational commitment.

Hunsaker and Coombs (1988) have proposed an alternative, but basically similar, nine-stage sequential model of emotional response to merger (Table 4.2).

Although there has been no specific empirical research in this area, the strength of response is considered likely to be related to the length

Table 4.2 *Emotional responses to merger*

Stage	Characteristic response
1 Denial	The 'It won't happen' syndrome
2 Fear	'When will it happen?' 'What will happen to me?'
3 Anger	'We've been sold out' – Resentment towards those considered responsible
4 Sadness	Mourning and grieving for what's past
5 Acceptance	Recognition of futility – positive approach starts to develop
6 Relief	Things actually better than expected
7 Interest	Increasing feeling of security
8 Liking	Recognition of new opportunities
9 Enjoyment	'It is really working out well'

of service of the employees and the degree of their attachment and commitment to their former organization. As illustrated by this comment made by an employee we interviewed (see Appendix 1) following the acquisition of a small family business (Princess Garage) for whom she worked:

I've been here 20 years. When I heard the news I was devastated. I was like that all weekend. I kept thinking why me? What am I going to do? It was like hearing someone you knew had just died. Mr . . . (the owner) was in his seventies. He was old, we knew that this would happen but not so soon. It was still a shock that this can happen and your life can change; everything is turned upside down and there is nothing you can do about it but wait and see.

This comment was fairly typical of the initial response of acquired employees we encountered, particularly in organizations where there was a strongly identifiable figurehead or organizational founder. The comment above illustrates the extent to which acquisitions are experienced as major events considered likely to change an individual's life and, perhaps more important, events over which he or she has no control. In the course of our research, acquired employees frequently reported feelings of extreme shock, disbelief and great sorrow, which resulted in 'behavioural numbness' and inertia in the period immediately following an acquisition announcement.

Whether or not the individual subsequently evaluates the merger as presenting a threat, a personal opportunity or as having little or no impact on his or her future working life, the event in itself will initially be responded to as being of consequential importance by almost everybody. This includes 'acquiring management', by whom the acquired employees are viewed as a major, if not ultimate, test of managerial talent. This is not to suggest that organizations with a large proportion of long-serving employees necessarily make bad acquisitions or are poor merger prospects. Indeed, Costello, Kubis and Shaffer (1963) found that older employees were more favourable to a bank merger than their younger counterparts, who felt their promotion plans were more likely to be blocked.

Although the merger or acquisition event itself is often most shocking to those who have been with the organization for some time, feelings are so volatile throughout the pre- and early integration process, that initial reaction is singularly not a good predictor of attitudes and longer term response. Of greater importance is the way in which the acquisition or merger is presented, the proposed direction and clarity of future change and the acceptability of that change.

Mergers and acquisitions create an expectancy of change and increase organizational cohesiveness

Mergers and acquisitions create an expectancy of change. In that the change is spontaneously associated with the onset of conflict, this inevitably produces an almost automatic 'kneejerk' reaction to close ranks. This was found to occur regardless of context (i.e. whether a friendly merger or hostile takeover), and irrespective of an individual's perception of the likely personal outcome of the combination.

Increased cohesiveness can be said to arise from a temporarily shared sense of loss. For example, never was the British Parliament so cohesive as when it lost the territories of the Falklands Islands to Argentina in 1982. Previous psychological research in the area of 'loss' more generally has repeatedly demonstrated that it produces a conservative and nostalgic impulse in people to hold on to what they have and value. Freud considered that 'collective grief' powerfully maintains a sense of community, and so increases cohesiveness, which arguably makes new cultures and managerial practices even more difficult to introduce. A recent study of the Getty–Texaco combination reports strong evidence of increased cohesiveness post merger, facilitated by what was described as 'collective remembering'. 'Even though there was a "family" oriented culture already, 75% of informants expressed how much more cohesive they were now than before the takeover' (Altendorf, 1986).

We consistently found similar evidence of increased cohesiveness post-combination in our own research. One of our case studies (reported in detail in Appendix 3) involved a friendly Anglo-French merger between Age Engineering Company and the Nouvelle Compagnie. Even though 77 per cent of Age's managers reported that they were initially excited and entirely positive about the merger, considering it to be in the best interests of their organization, an immediate 'them and us' attitude developed, more characteristic of a territorial battle than any cooperative combination. This was clearly evident from the time we first began to negotiate research access, when we found that Age were unwilling to invite the participation of their new merger partner, out of fear of revealing any vulnerability or valuable 'intelligence'. Such a cohesive tendency was found to occur even in organizations in which there was no recognizable team culture prior to the takeover (e.g. see the Fast Car case study, Appendix 1). Mergers and acquisitions are most effective in breaking down communication barriers, and stimulating intra- and interdepartmental interaction in the interest of rumour exchanges. The challenge for acquiring management is to attach that cohesion to a new organizational leader or goal.

Merger or acquiring management are invariably over-confident in their estimation of the speed and ease with which they can achieve integration

A considerable amount of time and energy is devoted to financial planning during the negotiation period, yet, in contrast, most organizations are prepared to complete deals without making any prior appraisal of the indigenous talent they are acquiring or in formulating any human merger plan. It has been suggested (Searby, 1969) that so much energy is often expended at the negotiation stage that the acquiring management is often too exhausted and apathetic to manage the merger effectively.

On the day an organization is acquired, nobody knows less about that organization than the acquiring management. At the time the acquisition is made, knowing or appreciating the culture of the acquired organization is often considered unnecessary, because the acquirer or dominant merger partner is so totally committed to changing it and imposing their own culture, that it seems unimportant and irrelevant.

In making a horizontal acquisition, the assumption that they are 'sticking to the knitting' and acquiring a business they know, confers the acquirer with a sense of arrogance and affirms to them the superiority of their culture. The acquirer often automatically expects its acquired workforce to adopt their culture and do things 'their way', because they have to. In the acquirer's logic, the existing culture of the acquired organization is not worth preserving because it is, by definition, unsuccessful, which is why it has been taken over by an organization with a superior or successful culture.

Unfortunately, the acquired workforce do not always share the same perceptions, changes meet with resistance, and culture change becomes an even longer and more difficult process. This is illustrated by the following comment, drawn from the accounts supervisor of Princess Garage (see Appendix 1), and a frequently encountered reaction in the course of our research: 'Just because they work at Fast Car doesn't mean they will work here. We've never done things like this before. We are used to doing things in our own way – nobody's ever complained before.'

The acquirers who participated in our research all realistically expected difficulties from the outset, but admitted that they had seriously underestimated the scale of the 'people problems' they were to face, and the length of time it would take to integrate systems. Also, they had little accounted for and had not prepared themselves for the possibility of other related crises, e.g. loss of key customers, personnel or UDIs from breakaway managerial groups. Most importantly, they seriously under-estimated the time-scale within which culture change could be achieved, and the amount of managerial time and attention which the acquisition consumed, often at the neglect of their existing core businesses – at a time when, because of increased borrowing, established business units are under acute pressure to perform even more successfully than before.

Changing the culture of an entire workforce within a period of twelve months, the objective of some acquirers we encountered, is an optimistic goal, even if the 'new' culture is perceived as being more attractive than the old. For those charged with the responsibility of initiating that change, the first twelve months are likely to be an extremely demanding period. In a typical post-acquisition year, we witnessed dramatic changes in the mood of acquisition managers from initial confidence and optimism, to desperate frustration and anger, and often exhaustion. The following comments made by one of the acquiring managers of Fill-it Packaging (Appendix 2) illustrate the problems:

- 'I am extremely confident that we will be able to turn this business around and get these people on our side.' *(Day 1 of the acquisition)*
- 'When we acquired this business, Mr C. offered his advice as to who we should keep and who to get rid of. He didn't have a good word to say about most of the workforce. We listened but rejected his advice. His managerial style was different, and we were prepared to give the

people the benefit of the doubt. Now I'm not so sure he wasn't right. We have been very disappointed by the people and their response to us. I'm still hopeful that we can bring these people round, but it's bloody hard work and it's very stressful. I have a financial stake in this business – it's my children's future and I can't let it all go down the pan.' *(6 months post acquisition)*

● 'I was never in favour of acquiring this particular business. The last year has been a continual battle with people. I think we've achieved something, but it's been a slow process. With hindsight, I would never do this again – it's been exhausting.' *(1 year post acquisition)*

Mergers and acquisitions result in unplanned personnel losses

Mergers and acquisitions involve job losses and redeployment, as a result of rationalization and role duplicity. In the course of our research, we found that in order to accelerate the process of culture change, organizations frequently elect to replace people. The senior managers of the acquired organization occupy the most vulnerable position, and tend to be removed from the outset *en masse*, irrespective of their individual abilities and competencies, as illustrated by the following comments made by Carl Icahan, when interviewed about his acquisition of TWA:

At TWA – to make it simple we basically replaced all the top management. That's one of the steps we took in the first few months. We really replaced the whole 42nd floor. There's nobody there on the 42nd floor at 605 Third Avenue who was there before. Possibly there's one, but I think he's leaving. And it had to be done.

Not surprisingly, such actions are frequently seen as insensitive and indiscriminate, and have reverberations throughout the organization, as the currency of organizational loyalty and commitment becomes automatically devalued. With the result that regardless of context, the most common merger concern is fear of redundancy. Apart from early retirements, redundancies and circumstances amounting to constructive dismissal, mergers and acquisitions are associated with high levels of voluntary resignations – what has been referred to as 'the post-acquisition drift factor' or 'the haemorrhage effect'.

In a study comparing senior management turnover rates between fifty-five acquired organizations, and a matched control group of thirty non-acquired companies over the same time period, James Walsh (1988) found there was a significantly higher turnover rate amongst acquired execu-

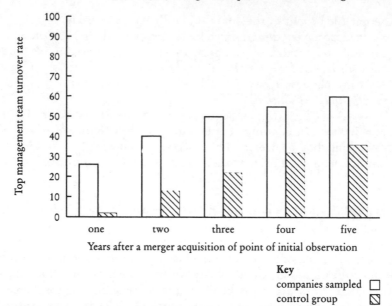

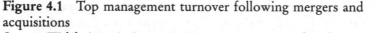

Figure 4.1　Top management turnover following mergers and acquisitions
Source: Walsh (1988), *Strategic Management Journal*, Vol. 9, p. 177

tives. The number of senior executives leaving the acquired organization increased from 25 per cent in the first year post acquisition to 59 per cent (inclusive) in the fifth year. (See Figure 4.1.)

On the basis of a study of 150 large mergers and acquisitions in the US, Harlow Unger (1986) has reported senior executive turnover rates of almost 50 per cent within the first year, rising to 75 per cent by the end of three years. Similarly, John Humpal (1971) has presented data based on the US experience, which demonstrated the 'propensity to quit' was three times higher amongst acquired employees than parent employees. Loss of managerial autonomy is frequently cited as a major reason for voluntary decisions to leave acquired or merged organizations (Hayes and Hoag, 1974) and rated as significantly more important than changes in pay and benefits.

Unplanned personnel losses are not confined to the more senior levels of the organization. In 1981, Graves conducted a total population survey of a UK merger between two reinsurance brokers. From an original pre-merger population of 130, the remaining post-merger population twenty-one months later had reduced by about a third, mainly as a result of voluntary resignations. These occurred even though the merger was

Table 4.3 *Staff turnover*

Organization	Size of workforce		% Old employees	Rate of staff turnover %
	Initially	One year later		
Greenside Motors	290	200	89	35
Princess Garage	88	51	64	61

widely considered by both managers and employees to be successful, in organizational and individual terms.

Staff turnover rates were an aspect of M & A activity we considered in our research. Fast Car, one of the acquiring organizations we studied (Appendix 1), made two acquisitions within the same year. One of these, Greenside Motors, proved to be financially successful, whereas the other, Princess Garage, did not. Both organizations recorded above average rates of staff turnover in the twelve months post acquisition, as Table 4.3 illustrates.

Unplanned personnel losses occurred at all levels. Abnormally high rates of staff turnover and increased absenteeism were recorded amongst blue-collar and shopfloor workers, even though, in actuality, jobs at this level were never under threat.

There had been economies of scale and rationalization at both organizations, which had resulted in job losses. Fast Car had also deliberately chosen to accelerate the displacement of the existing cultures, by replacing a substantial number of employees whom they considered to be resistant to change or unable to 'fit in'. Even so, the number of employees who voluntarily left the organizations outnumbered the planned losses.

According to Charles Handy, a psychological contract exists between the individual and his or her organization, whereby each party knows of and has certain expectations of the other, and whose terms determine motivation and organizational commitment. When an organization ceases to exist or is fundamentally changed, that contract is broken or becomes unclear and has to be re-established or negotiated. The period following a merger announcement or rumour is one of personal risk analysis and self-appraisal, in which an individual decides whether he or she effectively wants to form a 'new' contract with his or her new employer.

As already discussed, one of the most absolute truths about a merger or acquisition is that it is an important event in an employee's working life over which he or she has no control. It is seen as precipitating change for which one has not self-selected. Employees may choose to leave the organization because they consider they will be unable to fit into the new organization, or, particularly in merger situations, in response to an unacceptably prolonged period of uncertainty as to the likelihood or direction of expected future change. This decision may not necessarily be taken out of fear of change itself, but as an opportunity to regain control and exercise choice in one's working environment. It is during this period that competent staff become most vulnerable to 'headhunters' and 'poachers'. Mergers and acquisitions may be seen as an opportunity to get rid of the 'dead wood', but not everyone who leaves the organization will necessarily be those of the acquirer's choosing.

We found that not all departures were unhappy or bitter; one manager at Greenside Motors, in his late thirties, felt that the acquisition had forced him to reconsider the whole direction of his life. As a result he decided to leave and go to the US to open an English tea shop in California.

Mergers and acquisitions are stressful

Bereavement in itself is considered to be a universally stressful life event. However, at the same time that employees may be dealing with feelings of loss, they have to cope with the uncertainty associated with major organizational change, which is also likely to be stressful.

In the course of our research, we interviewed in depth almost 200 managers and their employees affected by mergers and acquisitions. In addition, we have surveyed more than 600 other managers and employees of merged and acquired companies. One aspect of the M & A process in which we were interested was the short- and long-term response of employees, and its impact on their psychological and mental well-being. Three years earlier, an American research team headed by David Schweiger interviewed over 150 employees involved in friendly or uncontested acquisitions, in the period immediately following the combination. In terms of the short-term response of employees, our findings were similar, in that the emotional detachment and attendant uncertainty experienced by employees manifested itself in five immediate concerns. These related to:

1 *Loss of identity.* The acquisition or merger marks the death of the organization as its members knew it. Previous organizational status, loyalty, commitment and hopes and promises for the future no longer count, or are considered unlikely to be honoured.

2 *Lack of information and increased anxiety* – concerning future job prospects, reward systems, changes in role, possible geographical relocation, career paths, staffing changes, alteration in working practices and changes in organizational culture.
3 *Survival becomes an obsession.* Maintaining existing personal status, prestige and power becomes all important and overrides organizational goals, at least temporarily. One of the common characteristics of the merger situation is the fear on the part of managers of exposing any sign of vulnerability, or giving any indication that one is not tough or fit enough for the post-merger organization. For many managers, voicing objections to post-acquisition changes and risking earning the label 'resistant to change', is considered to be a kiss of death for their future career prospects.
4 *Lost talent.* Apart from the disturbing effect of job losses as a result of rationalization, many employees also choose to leave the organization at this time. Those who remain are often angry, resentful or upset by their departure. Mergers and acquisitions also result in increased workloads for those who remain. The departure of competent and committed managers and co-workers may represent the loss of influential role models for the less experienced.
5 *Family repercussions.* Work-related anxieties, particularly if they concern the financial implications of an uncertain job future or the possibility of relocation, spill over into family life. The obsessive need to survive and demonstrate one's personal value to the organization means that managers tend to work even longer hours than they did before, with obvious implications for the quality of home life.

The human and financial cost of occupational stress is increasingly being recognized, with over 10 per cent of our gross national product spent each year in coping with the manifestations of job-generated stress. For businesses in the 1980s, stress in the workplace was ten times more costly than all the industrial relations disputes put together (Cartwright and Cooper, 1994). In terms of sickness absence and premature death or retirement due to alcoholism, it costs the UK a staggering £2 billion per annum. Stress is primarily caused by the fundamentals of change, lack of control and high workload.

The model in Figure 4.2, based on extensive research into occupational stress, conceptualizes potential sources of stress as emanating from six general areas of work-related behaviour. The most common merger stressors, according to Cartwright and Cooper (1994), are:

● Loss of identity/increased organizational size.
● Lack of information/poor or inconsistent communication.

- Fear of job loss/demotion.
- Career path disrupted.
- Possibility of job transfer/relocation.
- Loss of, or reduced power, status and prestige.
- Changes in rules, regulation, procedural and reporting arrangements.
- Changes in colleagues, bosses and subordinates.
- Ambiguous reporting systems, roles and procedures.
- Redundancy and devaluation of old skills and expertise.
- Personality/culture clashes.
- Increased workload.

Major organizational change, such as merger or acquisition, is likely to impact on all these areas, possibly simultaneously. While the financial cost to industry of occupational stress more generally may be well documented, it has been little considered in accounting for merger failure.

Professor Jack Ivancevich (Ivancevich, Schweiger and Power, 1987) proposes a transactional model of merger stress as triggered by two factors: (i) the nature of the merger events taking place, and (ii) characteristics of the individual involved. In terms of this model, each individual makes a cognitive appraisal of the situation. This appraisal will vary, dependent upon whether the merger is perceived:

1 As having no effect on the
  individual   IRRELEVANT APPRAISAL
2 As a challenging opportunity for
  the individual   POSITIVE APPRAISAL
3 As having harmed or damaged
  the individual in some way, e.g.
  reduced self-esteem or conferred
  a sense of powerlessness   NEGATIVE APPRAISAL
4 As potentially threatening to the
  individual   NEGATIVE APPRAISAL

A negative appraisal is likely to be experienced as stressful, the intensity of which depends upon the degree of uncertainty and the duration of that uncertainty. Although semantically the prospect of being 'merged' sounds less traumatic than being 'taken over', the experiences of our case studies suggest the reverse. Mergers, as they create greater and more prolonged uncertainty, were found to be more stressful, and have a longer term adverse effect on mental health than acquisitions, for a variety of reasons. Mergers differ from acquisitions in that:

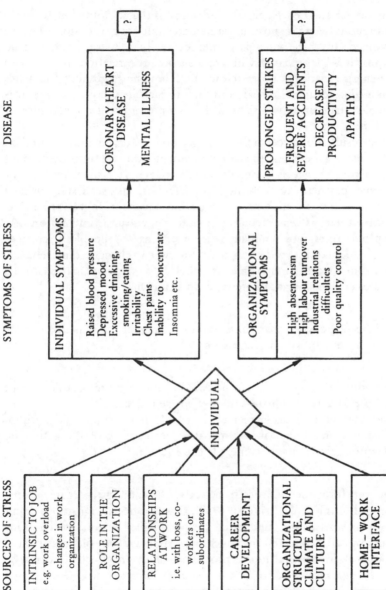

SOURCES OF STRESS

SYMPTOMS OF STRESS

DISEASE

SOURCES OF STRESS

INTRINSIC TO JOB
e.g. work overload
changes in work
organization

ROLE IN THE
ORGANIZATION

RELATIONSHIPS
AT WORK
i.e. with boss, co-
workers or
subordinates

CAREER
DEVELOPMENT

ORGANIZATIONAL
STRUCTURE,
CLIMATE AND
CULTURE

HOME – WORK
INTERFACE

INDIVIDUAL

INDIVIDUAL SYMPTOMS

Raised blood pressure
Depressed mood
Excessive drinking,
smoking/eating
Irritability
Chest pains
Inability to concentrate
Insomnia etc.

ORGANIZATIONAL
SYMPTOMS

High absenteeism
High labour turnover
Industrial relations
difficulties
Poor quality control

CORONARY HEART
DISEASE

MENTAL ILLNESS

?

PROLONGED STRIKES

FREQUENT AND
SEVERE ACCIDENTS

DECREASED
PRODUCTIVITY

APATHY

?

Figure 4.2 Sources of occupational stress

(a) They result in substantially more role duplicity or overlap, which promotes competition and jealousy between organizational members.
(b) The power and hence cultural dynamics of the combination are more ambiguous. Mergers pose an immediate conundrum to most of those involved, in that 'when is a merger really a merger and not an acquisition?' Compared with acquisitions, the relationship between the merger partners is less clear cut from the beginning and takes some time to unfurl. Head counting as each new layer of organizational restructuring is disclosed is an important and popular merger pastime.
(c) They result in unacceptably long periods of 'organizational limbo'. The interval between the announcement and the introduction of any actual change is generally much longer. It is not unusual for merger partners to continue to function as separate business entities for many months, in some circumstances a year or more, before there is any actual physical or cultural integration. As employees respond to their perceptions as to the likely changes which may result, rather than to the actual changes themselves, a 'fear the worst' syndrome is likely to develop; alternatively, employees become apathetic and withdrawn.

It has been proposed that vulnerability to merger stress is likely to be mediated by individual characteristics:

1 Personality variables such as Type A/B behaviour patterns, tolerance of ambiguity, locus of control, and level of self-esteem.
2 Other factors such as perceived level of social support, length of service, personal financial circumstances, availability of alternative job opportunities and previous merger experience(s).

However, from the evidence of a study of major intra-organizational change within AT & T (Ashford, 1988), organizational transitions result in universal stress, little moderated by personality characteristics. This study of approximately 180 employees reported evidence of stress-related physiological and mental health problems, likely to affect performance negatively, continuing up to six months post integration. One suggested reason for this is that because major organizational change is an unprecedented event for most employees, they are unlikely to have developed any effective coping strategy to deal with the stress experienced.

References

Altendorf, D.M. (1986). *When cultures clash: A case study of the Texaco takeover of Getty Oil and the impact of acculturation on the acquired firm* (Dissertation). Faculty of Graduate School, University of Southern California, August.

Ashford, S.J. (1988). Individual strategies for coping with stress during organizational transitions. *Journal of Applied Behavioural Science*, 24, 19–36.

Berney, E.J. (1986). Management decision-making in acquisitions: An intergroup analysis (PhD thesis). *Abstracts International*, No. 86-14199. Ann Arbor, Michigan.

Blumberg, A. and Weiner, W. (1971). One from two: Facilitating an organizational merger. *Journal of Applied Behavioural Science*, 7(1), January/February, 87–102.

Buono, A.F., Bowditch, J.L. and Lewis, J.W. III (1985). When cultures collide: The anatomy of a merger. *Human Relations*, 38(5), 477–500.

Cartwright, S. and Cooper, C.L. (1990). The impact of mergers and acquisitions on people at work: Existing research and issues. *British Journal of Management*, 1, 65–76.

Cartwright, S. and Cooper, C.L. (1994). *No Hassle: Taking the Stress Out of Work*. London: Century Business.

Cooper, C.L., Cooper, R.D. and Eaker, L.H. (1988). *Living with Stress*. London: Penguin Health.

Cooper, C.L. and Marshall, J. (1978). *Understanding Executive Stress*. Macmillan: UK.

Costello, T.W., Kubis, J.F. and Shaffer, C.L. (1963). An analysis of attitudes towards a planned merger. *Administrative Science Quarterly*, 8, 235–249.

Graves, D. (1981). Individual reactions to a merger of two small firms of brokers in the re-insurance industry – A total population survey. *Journal of Management Studies*, 18(1), 89–113.

Handy, C. (1985). *Understanding Organizations*. New York: Penguin.

Hayes, R.H. and Hoag, G.H. (1974). Post acquisition retention of top managers. *Mergers and Acquisitions*, 9, 8–18.

Holmes, T.H. and Rahe, R.H. (1967). The social readjustment rating scale. *Journal of Psychosomatic Research*, 11, 213–218.

Humpal, J.J. (1971). Organizational marriage counselling: A first step. *Journal of Applied Behavioural Science*, 7, 103–109.

Hunsaker, P.L. and Coombs, M.W. (1988). Mergers and acquisitions: Managing the emotional issues. *Personnel Journal*, 65, 56–63.

Hunt, J. (1988). Managing the successful acquisition: A people question. *London Business School Journal*, Summer, 2–15.

Ivancevich, J.M., Schweiger, D.M. and Power, F.R. (1987). Strategies for managing human resource issues during mergers and acquisitions. *Human Resource Planning*, 12(1), March, 19–35.

Jick, J.D. (1979). *Processes and impact of a merger: Individual and organizational perspectives* (Doctoral dissertation). Cornell University.

Kilman, R.H. (1984). *Beyond the Quick Fix: Managing Five Tracks to Organizational Success*. San Francisco: Jossey-Bass.

Kubler-Ross, E. (1969). *On Death and Dying*. New York: Macmillan.

McManus, M.L. and Hergert, M.L. (1988). *Surviving Merger and Acquisition*. Glenview, Illinois: Scott, Foresman & Co.

Mangham, I. (1973). Facilitating intraorganizational dialogue in a merger situation. *Journal of Interpersonal Development*, 4, 133–147.

Marks, M. L. (1988). The merger syndrome: The human side of corporate combinations. Journal of Buyouts and Acquisitions, 18–23, January–February.

Meeks, G. (1977). *Disappointing Marriage: A Study of the Gains from Merger*. Cambridge: Cambridge University Press.

Mirvis, P.H. (1985). Negotiations after the sale: The roots and ramifications of conflict in an acquisition. *Journal of Occupational Behaviour*, 6.

Nelson-Horchler, J. (1987). A catchall parachute: Herman Miller has a silver shark repellant. *Industry Week*, 3 February, 16–17.

Pritchett, P. (1985). *After the Merger: Managing the Shock Waves*. New York: Dow Jones Irwin.

Schweiger, D.M., Ivancevich, J.M. and Power, F.R. (1987). Executive actions for managing human resources before and after acquisition. *Academy of Management Executive*, 2, 127–138.

Searby, F. (1969). Control of post merger change. *Harvard Business Review*, September/October.

Singh, A. (1971). *Takeovers*. London: Cambridge University Press.

Turner, J. (1987). The Pilkington experience. *Personnel Management*, July.

Unger, H. (1986). The people trauma of major mergers. *Journal of Industrial Management (Canada)*, 10(17), April.

Walsh, J.P. (1988). Top management turnover following mergers and acquisitions. *Strategic Management Journal*, 9, 173–183.

Wicker, A.W. and Kauma, C.E. (1974). Effects of a merger on a small and a large organization on members' behaviour and experiences. *Journal of Applied Psychology*, 59(1), February, 24–30.

Part Two

Culture and Performance

5

Differences in corporate culture – awareness and recognition

'Matrimony as the origin of change was always disagreeable'

(Jane Austen)

The motives behind a decision to merge or form a strategic alliance are increasingly becoming a focus of research attention, but in themselves provide insufficient explanation or understanding of unfulfilled merger expectations. According to Jemison and Sitkin (1986), a distinction can be drawn between making an M & A decision and making an M & A work, the former being concerned with the selection process (i.e. recognizing the synergistic potential) and the latter with the management of the integration process (i.e. releasing that potential). In practice, the responsibilities for these two aspects usually lie with different managerial groups.

In terms of selection, the 'goodness' of both the strategic and the organizational fit are considered to be important determinants of the outcome of any inter-organizational alliance. Strategic fit concerns shared or complimentary business strategies and goals. Organizational fit is considered to relate to the degree to which partnering organizations are compatible, in terms of their administrative systems and procedures, managerial style, decision-making approach and preferred control and communication patterns (Bhagad *et al.*, 1990).

During the boom of the 1960s, an article appeared in the *Harvard Business Review* (Davis, 1968) which suggested that 'A successful combination depends at least on compatibility of business styles ... Usually the greater the degree of integration the greater the risk of eventual breakdown of the combination due to differences in business styles.'

According to Davis, 'business styles' are characterized by attitudes towards the following:

1 *Risk-taking* – the degree of risk a company is willing to take in its business.

2 *Investment* – the time an organization is content to wait to realize a gain on its investment, i.e. whether managerial thinking is characterized by 'short-termism' as opposed to 'long-termism'.
3 *Power and control* – the delegation of authority and responsibility within the organization, and the extent to which management participates in the decisions and share in the financial profits of the company.
4 *The importance of organizational functions* – the degree of emphasis placed on various functional areas of the organization, i.e. is the marketing function valued and considered more important than research and development?

This concept of 'business styles', as a collection of attitudes which form the basis for action, would seem synonymous with the broader and now widely accepted concept of 'organizational culture', a now frequently cited reason for merger failure.

It is naive to expect that acquisitions, mergers or other organizational alliances will be made exclusively on the basis of their culture match, but at present it would seem that insufficient consideration is given to this increasingly significant issue. However, knowing and appreciating the culture of your own organization, and that of any potential or newly acquired organization or merger partner, is an important first step in assessing future compatibility and the likelihood of a potentially smooth and relatively unproblematic 'honeymoon period' post merger. In this chapter, we discuss in detail the main types of organizational cultures, their characteristics and the ways in which these can be identified. In addition to including a short culture questionnaire, at various points in the text we refer the reader to a number of case studies in the appendices, which serve to illustrate working examples of particular types of culture.

The origins of organizational culture

The idea that organizations, as mini societies, can be considered as having a culture has its theoretical origins in sociology and anthropology, where the concept is fundamental to the understanding of any society or societal group. Culture is considered to be a powerful, enduring and pervasive influence on human behaviour. Through the socialization process within a culture, individuals learn the norms and expectations of membership of that society, the right and wrong ways of doing things, acceptable and unacceptable forms of behaviour, language, etc. It is through culture that society maintains regularity and order.

Culture is considered to be a collective phenomenon, because it is, at least partly, shared with people who live or work within the same environment, which is where it is learnt (Cartwright, Cooper and Jordan, in press). The core of culture is values. Values are broad tendencies to prefer certain states of affairs over others and act to influence behaviour. Morgan (1986) focuses on the metaphor of culture as a shared sense of reality. Those that do not possess a culture which is compatible, do not share the same reality and, as such, cannot therefore enact reality with each other.

Culture as it relates to business activity can be considered to operate at two levels; national and organizational. National cultures are shaped by tradition, and reflect economic and social history as well as climate and other demographic conditions. Consequently, different nations have different cultures, as the seasoned traveller or international business person comes to appreciate. For example, in Japan, introductions at a first business meeting are invariably distinctly formal compared to the USA, where the informality of first names is the norm. Japanese social etiquette dictates that business and personal lives are kept separate, and so it is considered taboo to enquire about a colleague's family during working hours. In contrast, discussion of such matters in the USA is often used as a means of 'breaking the ice' and establishing rapport.

While national cultures may to some degree influence the style of the work organization and the preferred organizational culture, different organizations as a subgroup within the same national culture have different cultures. They can be considered to differ in terms of the strength, coherence, pervasiveness and type of their organizational culture. The type of culture an organization has is shaped by a variety of factors, namely:

● Its history and ownership.
● Its size.
● The technology it employs, and the nature of its business activity.
● The external environment and product market.
● The people, particularly the founders and leaders.

It has increasingly been argued that culture may not be simply an important variable to be accounted for in the 'managerial equation', but a paradigm in itself by which we can understand an organization. Culture, therefore, is something an organization *is* rather than has.

Within some organizations, particularly large organizations, there are likely to be a number of sub-cultures operating within certain departments or work groups. A multiplicity of sub-cultures may add to the problems of integration, but, nevertheless, their existence does not weaken the argument that any organization can be considered as having an overarching dominant culture of one particular type. Like a company, a nation is composed entirely of subgroups with their own cultural identity, but it is still meaningful to talk of national cultures, characteristics and cross-cultural differences.

What exactly is organizational culture?

The publication of the best selling book *In Search of Excellence* by Peters and Waterman in 1982 was influential for two reasons. Firstly, in providing explanations of organizational success which extended beyond the balance sheet, it highlighted to managers the role played by the 'people factors' in determining organizational outcomes. Secondly, it raised managerial consciousness to the concept and importance of organizational culture. Subsequent research has demonstrated a link between organizational culture and managerial style, market strategy and the quality of customer service (Harrison, 1987).

Organizational culture is a well used, but perhaps less well understood concept. There are many definitions of organizational culture within the management literature. All tend to reflect the essence of the classic sociological/anthropological definition of the concept as concerning the internalization of a set of values, feelings, attitudes and expectations, which provide meaning, order and stability to members' lives and influence their behaviour.

- 'Culture is taken to be the shared attitudes, values, belief and customs of members of a social unit or organization' (Martin, 1985).
- 'Organizational culture ... shared meanings – patterns of belief, symbols, rituals and myths that evolve across time and that function as social glue' (Smircich, 1985).
- '... fairly stable taken for granted (set of) assumptions ... meanings and values that form a kind of backdrop for action' (Smircich, 1985).
- 'A pattern of basic assumptions – invented, discovered or developed by a given group as it learns to cope with its problems of external adaptation and internal integration – that has worked well enough to be considered valid and, therefore, to be taught to new members as the correct way to perceive, think and feel in relation to those problems' (Schein, 1985).

While values are considered a sufficient basis for action, in that values are what we act to keep, the essence of organizational culture is more deeply rooted. Culture is not merely a set of shared values, but a set of basic assumptions and beliefs which operate in an often unconscious 'taken for granted' fashion, as a powerful determinant of individual and group behaviour. Culture has visibility and 'feelability' of which one is often more conscious when moving from one culture to another, what is termed the 'culture shock'.

Put simply, organizational culture is 'the way in which things get done within an organization'. The cultural assumptions and beliefs of an organization are learnt by its members through socialization. To the newly recruited, 'learning the ropes' means more than learning how to apply the requisite task skills; it involves a wider socialization process of inculcating and subsequently accepting the culture.

The culture of an organization is reflected in many ways and influences not only structure and managerial style, but also the way in which an organization conducts its business in the widest sense. This includes the market strategy it adopts, the quality of customer service it offers, as well as creating a particular kind of psychological working environment for its employees.

Culture manifests itself in:

1 The way in which people interact, their terms of address and the language and technical jargon or argot they use. Also the way in which they dress, e.g. formal business suits versus smart casual wear, the importance attached to wearing the company tie or similar corporate symbols of identity.
2 The norms which govern the way in which work is organized and conducted, e.g. reporting arrangements, preference for written or verbal forms of communication.
3 The organization's self-image and the dominant values it espouses, both within and outside the organization, e.g. the importance it places on particular organizational functions, the extent to which it wishes to be recognized as a 'tough' or 'caring' and/or environmentally friendly organization.
4 The way in which it treats its employees and responds to its customers.
5 The rules for playing the organizational game, e.g. what it considers to be a 'good' employee or 'effective' manager.
6 The climate as conveyed by its physical layout and general atmosphere, e.g. whether it receives its visitors or customers with warm friendliness or cold efficiency, whether it maintains executive-only dining rooms and similar restricted facilities.

Tom Peters and Bob Waterman presented clear evidence linking organizational performance with a strong, dominant and coherent culture. Although the level of performance of several of the 'excellent' companies has declined in the years since their study, this does not weaken the argument that a fragmented, ambiguous or contradictory culture is unlikely to result in optimum organizational performance. The organizational performance of even 'excellent' companies is likely to decline if they are unable either to continue to maintain a cohesive culture or to recognize the need to change.

Organizational culture and the individual

Selecting individuals on the basis of their skills alone is no guarantee that they will subsequently become effective and committed employees. Work takes place in the presence of others, in a particular organizational setting. The individual worker has to fit in with other employees, with the organizational climate, style of work, organization, etc., which are manifestations of the underlying culture of the organization. The incongruity of poor person–work environment fit (PE-fit) has been shown to result in low job satisfaction and stress, which affect individual outcomes (i.e. physical, psychological and mental well-being) as well as organizational outcomes. If two organizations come together, and their cultures are incompatible to the extent that many employees no longer 'fit' into the environment, the resultant effects are likely to have a substantial and large-scale impact.

In the normal everyday functioning of an organization, culture operates in a 'taken for granted' fashion, and only assumes salience in people's minds when it is disturbed or threatened. Mergers and acquisitions are the greatest disturbers of the cultural peace, and frequently result in 'culture collisions'. Minor issues and differences assume major proportions. In that this creates ambiguous working environments, conflict, employee incongruity and stress, it will adversely affect organizational performance and the quality of work life. The effects of combining different cultural types as it influences managerial style and behaviours, both prior to and during the integration period, and the extent to which a single coherent culture emerges, has important consequences for both organizational and human merger outcomes.

Mergers and acquisitions have therefore to be understood as simultaneously impacting at the macro (organizational) and micro (individual) levels. The cultural dynamics, and their outcome in terms of what happens to the culture of the acquired or merged organization, cannot be separated from their impact upon and outcome for the individual.

Types of organizational culture

While the widespread success of *In Search of Excellence* can be considered to have raised corporate culture to popular consciousness in highlighting various cultural attributes or properties associated with excellent companies, academic debate still continues as to the most appropriate way to study the concept and its usefulness in the comparative analysis of organizations (Denison, 1990). Researchers who have sought to draw tangible distinctions and comparison between organizations in terms of their culture have either favoured a dimensional (Hofstede *et al.*, 1990) or a type approach (Harrison, 1972). The first 'true' introduction of the concept into the literature would seem to date from an article published in the *Harvard Business Review*, ten years earlier, in 1972. The paper, by Roger Harrison, a psychologist and management consultant, was entitled *How to Describe Your Organization*. Prior to this, earlier work of the 1960s had tended to draw distinctions between organizations at the structural, rather than the cultural, level.

Harrison has suggested that there are four main types of organizational culture, these being *power, role, task/achievement* and *person/support*. Alternative typologies have been proposed by other writers. Deal and Kennedy (1982) propose four generic cultures as being determined exclusively by one aspect of organizational behaviour, i.e. the degree of risk and the spread of feedback on whether decisions or strategies are successful. These they describe as:

1 *The tough guy macho culture* – an organization of individualists who regularly take high risks and receive rapid feedback on their actions; an entrepreneurial culture.
2 *The work hard/play hard culture* – a dynamic culture where employees are encouraged to maintain a high level of relatively low risk-taking activity.
3 *The bet your company culture* – described as a high risk but slow feedback environment.
4 *The process culture* – a bureaucracy where employees receive little or no direct feedback on the consequences of their actions.

More recently, Hofstede *et al.* (1990) have conducted a study of the culture of twenty organizations in Denmark and the Netherlands. From this, they concluded that it was more meaningful to account for differences between organizations in terms of their practices (i.e. conventions, customs, habits and moves) on the following dimensions:

(a) Process oriented versus results oriented.
(b) Employee oriented versus job oriented.

(c) Parochial versus professional – dependent upon whether employees derive their identity from the organization (parochial) or from the type of job they perform (professional).
(d) Open versus closed systems of communication.
(e) Loose versus tight control – dependent on the degree of formal internal structure.
(f) Normative versus pragmatic – dependent upon whether customer orientation is market driven (pragmatic) or the organization perceives their task towards the outside world as the implementation of inviolable rules (normative).

With the exception of (b) and (d), which are considered to be related to the philosophy of cultural founders and leaders, an organization's relative position on these dimensions is considered to be the outcome of the type of business activity in which it is involved. Deal and Kennedy's typology similarly equates culture as solely the outcome of type of business activity.

Trompenaars (1993) emphasizes three aspects of organizational structure as important in determining corporate culture:

1 The general relationship between employees and their organizations.
2 The vertical or hierarchical system of authority defining superiors and subordinates.
3 The general views of employees about the organization's destiny, purpose and goals and their place in this.

According to Trompenaars, this contributes to create four possible culture types, described as:

1 *The family.* A highly personal but hierarchical and power-oriented culture. It displays a highly paternalistic attitude towards its employees and their welfare and gives a low priority to efficiency (doing things right) but a high priority to effectiveness (doing the right things).
2 *The Eiffel Tower culture.* A highly structured culture with a bureaucratic division of labour and roles. The logic of subordination is clearly rational and coordinative and is manifested in rules.
3 *The guided missile culture.* This culture differs from the previous two in that it is egalitarian. It is also impersonal and highly task oriented. Its members tend to be intrinsically motivated by their enthusiasm for the task.
4 *The incubator culture.* The basis of this culture is its minimal structure. Its belief being that, if organizations are to be tolerated at all, they should exist as incubators for self-expression and self-fulfilment.

In seeking to explain how different horizontal combinations result in different cultural dynamics and, hence, different outcomes, we found it useful to draw and elaborate upon Harrison's typologies, primarily because this framework can accommodate intra-industry differences, but also because experience has demonstrated that in practice the four types are easily recognized, have high face validity and are considered meaningful by both managers and their employees. These are, therefore, now outlined in some detail.

Power cultures

The centralization of power is the most important feature of this type of culture. It is found in organizations where power rests with a single individual, usually the founder, or a small nucleus of key individuals. Power cultures are generally considered more typical of small organizations, because they are often impossible to sustain as the organization grows larger, necessitating the diffusion of power, or when key individuals leave. Therefore, although more frequently encountered in small entrepreneurial organizations or traditional family businesses, certain large organizations which have continued to maintain a highly identifiable and often charismatic leader (e.g. Anita Roddick's Body Shop empire) are recognized to have strong power cultures.

Because, in this type of culture, the emphasis is on individual rather than group decision making, power cultures have the advantage of being able to move and react swiftly should they so choose. Decisions tend to be based as much on intuition and past successes as on logical reasoning.

Individual members are motivated by a sense of personal loyalty to their boss or the owner, frequently one and the same, or out of a fear of punishment. Power cultures are associated with inequitable reward systems, in that salary and other benefits are often awarded on the basis of personal preference in return for demonstrated loyalty, perceived favours or long service as much as on ability. As the culture is essentially autocratic and suppressive of challenge, low morale and feelings of powerlessness amongst the workforce are frequent features.

Long-established power cultures tend to be overladen with tradition. Offices and reception areas tend to display mementos and pictures commemorating past achievements and former leaders. As they tend to retain a distinctly formal managerial style, outsiders frequently experience long-standing power cultures as being 'old fashioned' or conservative.

Power cultures can be further differentiated in terms of the type and perceived legitimacy of the power exercised into *patriarchal* as opposed to purely *autocratic* power cultures.

Patriarchal power cultures

Power derives from the ownership of the means of production or at least some financial or recognized personal stake or commitment to the continuing future of the business. The nucleus of power rests with an individual or group of individuals who are perceived by the rest of the workforce to be its 'champions' or 'protectors'.

Such cultures may be experienced as oppressive, but the exercise of power is considered legitimate, often benevolent, and, therefore, understood. Patriarchal power cultures can be experienced as exercising a high degree of concern towards their employees.

The psychological contract which patriarchal power cultures create between the organization and the vast majority of its members is similar to that between parent and child. As employer, it assumes parental authority to direct and instruct its employees how to act, and involves them minimally in 'grown up' organizational matters. Characteristically, employees of power cultures are ill-informed of the overall performance of the organization and its long-term strategic goals and plans. At the same time, while such organizations retain a parental prerogative to scold or reward, they often adopt an extremely responsible and protective attitude towards the workforce.

Organizations such as the Morgan Car Company, featured in the Sir John Harvey-Jones *Troubleshooter* television series, presented a good example of a patriarchal power culture. Other much larger organizations with deeply rooted Quaker backgrounds, particularly in the food and confectionery industry, are also still recognized as having maintained a patriarchal power culture. (A good example of a power culture in action is illustrated by Greenside Motors, one of the case studies included in Appendix 1.)

Autocratic cultures

In contrast, purely autocratic cultures are those in which power is justified as being legitimate by those who exercise it, as derived from their leadership status or position in the organization, rather than any links of ownership or personal involvement or self-sacrifice. Unlike patriarchal power cultures, those in authority are not considered to be genuinely interested in the continuing future of the organization *per se*, because they are likely soon to 'move on' to other opportunities. Such cultures are likely to be frequently experienced as more oppressive and dissatisfying than patriarchal cultures, because power is resented. Worker alienation, poor industrial relations and high staff turnover are common features.

People remain within autocratic cultures because they consider themselves to be well paid, feel a strong sense of commitment towards their fellow workers or subordinates, or derive considerable intrinsic satisfaction from the actual job they do, rather from than any great sense of commitment to the organization and its leader(s). (Again, for those interested, one of the case studies in Appendix 2, the acquisition of Fill-it Packaging, presents a good example of an autocratic power culture.)

The quality of service offered by power cultures is often tiered to reflect the status and prestige of the individual customer. This is akin to a situation frequently experienced in restaurants and hotels, where the 'best' tables or rooms are held back by the head waiter or manager for allocation to those considered most deserving.

Role cultures

The role culture epitomizes the Weberian concept of a bureaucracy, as its guiding principles are logic, rationality and the achievement of maximum efficiency. The organization's view of itself is as a collection of roles to be undertaken rather than a collection of people/personalities. It is frequently encountered in large organizations with highly specialized dimensions of labour, in both the private and public sector. Because commercial organizations with role cultures tend to be exclusively results orientated, finance and accounting are often recognized as being the most important organizational functions.

In a role culture, things get done according to the 'corporate bible' – usually in triplicate. Role requirements, boundaries of authority and reporting arrangements are clearly defined. Consequently, formal procedures and regulations concerning the way in which work is to be conducted are a central feature of this type of culture. A good employee is one who recognizes protocol and always sticks to the rules.

Power tends to be hierarchical and is derived from one's role or position in the organization. Role cultures tend to be extremely status conscious, and often breed competition between departments or divisions. One gets to know how important an executive is in the organization by reference to indicators such as the size of their expense account, the type of car he or she drives and the dimensions and quality of furnishings of his or her office. Moving up the organization frequently means becoming less accessible to employees. This often also has physical implications in terms of one's position in the organization. Hence, a further indicator of status may be the physical distance between an executive's office and the front reception area or general office/production area.

Role cultures function well in stable conditions, but their high degree of formalization makes them slow to change. Once they have found a winning formula, they tend to stick with it. They offer security and predictability to the individual, but often constrain innovative and risk-taking behaviour. They are frequently experienced as impersonal and frustrating. Also, employees of such cultures tend very much to feel they are small cogs in a large organizational wheel.

Role cultures can also differ in terms of the openness of their communication systems and managerial style, and the degree to which they are people oriented. Organizations which depend upon mass volume sales and standardized product quality, such as MacDonalds, reflect the scripted type of customer service associated with role cultures.

Task/achievement cultures

The salient feature of a task culture is the emphasis which it places on accomplishing the task, and the energy which it directs toward securing the necessary task-related resources and skills. Task cultures tend to exist within organizations, e.g. in specific departments such as research and development, rather than as organizations, although the culture is often found in new start-up organizations, particularly in high technology. A task culture is a team culture, in that commitment to the specific task bonds and energizes the individuals. It is the specificity of the task requirements which dictates the way in which work is organized rather than individuals or formal rules and regulations – *what* is achieved is more important than *how* it is achieved. Consequently, relevant task expertise is highly valued, and frequently more powerful than personal or positional power.

Task cultures are characterized by their flexibility and high levels of worker autonomy, making them potentially creative and satisfying environments in which to work. The lack of formal authority means that control is problematic to task cultures. Also, in times of crisis (e.g. scarcity of resources), they tend to change into role cultures.

Task cultures seek to offer their customers tailored products, and this type of culture is often encountered in high technology and service industries such as advertising and public relations. While task cultures tend to evoke strong commitment and passion, members often become 'burnt out' or disillusioned over time. When task cultures go wrong, everybody blames everybody else.

Roger Harrison (1972) describes a task culture as 'marching to its own drum', in that the service it gives to its customers is that which it feels is right rather than the service the customer may demand. Apple Computers under Steve Jobs is a classic example of a task culture which ultimately brought about its own destruction. Employees at Apple were so concerned with changing the world and constantly being innovative in product design, that they lost sight of customer needs altogether. Models quickly became obsolete and customers experienced difficulties in obtaining parts or adapting earlier models to suit current needs. John Sculley had then to impose a role culture on the organization to ensure its continued survival. The more recent experience of Acorn has similar parallels.

The person/support culture

The main characteristic of the person/support culture is egalitarianism. In person/support cultures, structure is minimal; the culture exists and functions solely to nurture the personal growth and development of its individual members. Information, influence and decision making are shared collectively. The organization is subordinate to the individual for its existence.

Not surprisingly, in its purest form, it is more often found operating in communities or cooperatives, e.g. the Kibbutz, rather than in profit-making enterprises, although it may be encountered in certain professional partnerships, where this is a common agreement to share facilities such as office space, secretarial services, etc. (as an example, see the case study of the Princess Garage in Appendix 1).

However, as discussed, commercial organizations may differ in the degree to which they and their individual members are person oriented. They are also likely to differ in terms of the time-scale in which they expect to see a profitable return on their investments.

Assessing organizational culture

To understand a culture, one has to be able to make sense of the many ways in which it manifests itself. It is generally considered (Lundberg, 1985; Schein, 1985; Denison, 1990) that culture operates at four levels:

1 *Artefacts or symbols*, i.e. the visible products of a culture.
2 *Patterns of behaviour* – the socially shared rules and norms/concrete actions.
3 *Values and beliefs*, which underlie these actions.

4 *Basic assumptions* about the world ... and how it is, which uncon-
  sciously underpin the other three levels.

Artifacts and behavioural patterns may be a more amenable level at which
to compare and even measure organizational differences. However, in
order to retain the usefulness of the concept and not risk reducing it to
simply a series of multiple attitudinal and behavioural dimensions, it is
important to probe and understand its more abstract elements, i.e. basic
assumptions and guiding values.

One can be said to have understood or learnt the culture of an
organization when one is no longer surprised by its actions, and can
even predict the likely response of its members to most situations.
Assessing an organization's culture is rather like completing a jigsaw,
in that a clear and coherent picture only emerges when one has
collected and accurately put together all the pieces. In the same way
that occasionally the picture assembled bears little or no resemblance
to that on the box lid, sometimes the managerial or 'espoused culture'
has little correspondence with the 'culture in use', i.e. that practised by
those on the shopfloor or within certain individual departments or
units.

Previous studies into organizational culture (Peters and Waterman,
1982; Deal and Kennedy, 1982; Schein, 1985) have followed the
anthropological tradition or 'botanizing' approach in producing qual-
itatively rich idiographic, 'fly on the wall' descriptive accounts of the
culture of individual organizations. These are typically based on
observation and interviews with organizational members. In particular,
such studies have stressed the importance of a number of observable
cultural 'artefacts', such as:

1 Physical setting and layout.
2 Product and company literature.
3 Press releases.
4 Company slogans and rituals.
5 'In-house' journal and manuals.
6 The presence/absence of organizational charts, etc.
7 Stories, myths and other critical incidents which have become part of
  organizational folklore.

While there is a strong argument that culture can only be accurately
described and assessed from the impartial, objective and external
viewpoint of someone outside the organization, there are several
techniques which can be employed to uncover and increase self-
awareness of organizational culture.

The main and more useful techniques are:

(a) Think of your organization and how you might describe it in terms of an animal, which perhaps could be appropriately used as a company logo. In North America, it has become the practice for large corporations to adopt and sponsor a zoo animal. What kind of animal would be appropriate for your organization to adopt? Which would be in keeping with its image and culture? For example, is it agile and aggressive like a tiger, or slow and ponderous like a tortoise? Would other members think of the organization in the same animal imagery? Test it out by asking them – their answers may be surprising! Take it a stage further by asking yourself and others why you/they chose a particular animal. Such projective techniques are useful; not only do they have a novelty value, which inevitably motivates people to respond, but they circumvent the difficulties which many people experience in consciously 'talking about culture' in a more direct and specific way.

(b) Imagine you are a member of the 'All Too Honest' Advertising Agency. Think of a realistic slogan or jingle which expresses the culture of your organization. For example, 'Always stick to the rules', might be an appropriate slogan for a role culture.

Alternatively, draft a brief job advertisement informing the would-be applicant what it is *really* important to know if he or she joins the company. For example, consider what kind of people 'get on' in the organization. Is it:

1 *The political*, i.e. the party liners, those who know how to work the system and the people in power in that system.
2 *The competitive*, i.e. those who achieve objectives at all costs.
3 *The competent or qualified*, i.e. those who are quick and clever at their jobs or who have the 'right' qualifications.
4 *The committed*, i.e. the 24-hour organization man or woman?

This is an activity which is likely to benefit from the participation and shared discussion with others in the organization.

For the more conventional or less creative, we have included this short culture questionnaire, based on an instrument designed by Roger Harrison and Herb Stokes (1990). We would emphasize that because this abridged questionnaire contains only a small sample of items, it is not intended to be diagnostic, but rather to give you some general feeling for the culture of your organization.

Consider the following items, and choose the *one* response which most applies to your organization:

1 In this organization, individuals are expected to give first priority to:
  (a) Meeting the challenges of the individual task in which they are involved.
  (b) Cooperating with and attending to the needs of their fellow workers.
  (c) Following the instructions of their superiors.
  (d) Acting within the parameters of their job description.

2 The organization responds to its members as if they are:
  (a) Associates or colleagues.
  (b) Family or friends.
  (c) Hired help.
  (d) Contracted employees.

3 In this organization, people are motivated and influenced most by:
  (a) Their own commitment to the task.
  (b) The respect and commitment which they have for their co-workers.
  (c) The prospect of rewards or fear of punishment.
  (d) The company 'bible' or rule book.

4 A 'good' employee is considered to be one who:
  (a) Is self-motivated and willing to take risks and be innovative if the task demands it.
  (b) Gets along well with others and is interested in their self-development.
  (c) Always does what his/her boss tells him/her to do without question.
  (d) Can be relied upon to stick to the company rules.

5 Relationships between work units or inter-departmentally are generally:
  (a) Cooperative.
  (b) Friendly.
  (c) Competitive.
  (d) Indifferent.

6 In this organization, decisions tend to be:
  (a) Made by the people on the spot who are close to the problem and have the appropriate task expertise.

(b) Made after considerable discussion and with the consensus of all those involved regardless of their position in the organizational hierarchy.

(c) Referred up the line to the person who has the most formal authority.

(d) Made by resort to established precedents.

7 It is most important for a new member of this organization to learn:

(a) To use his/her initiative to get the task completed.

(b) How to get on with his/her fellow workers.

(c) Who really counts in this organization and be aware of the political coalitions.

(d) The formal rules and regulations.

8 The dominant managerial style of this organization is:

(a) Democratic and open.

(b) Supportive and responsive to individual needs and idiosyncrasies.

(c) Authoritarian.

(d) Impersonal and remote.

If you scored mostly (a)s, the dominant culture of your organization as you perceive it is 'task/achievement'; mostly (b)s – is likely to be 'person/support'; mostly (c)s – 'power'; and mostly (d)s – 'role'.

Although organizational cultures predominantly fall into one of the four main types outlined, in reality there are likely to be few pure or 'ideal' types. Therefore, it is possible that your answers to the questionnaire were fairly evenly distributed between two categories, suggesting that your culture is perhaps a combination of types, e.g. 'role/task' in that you scored four (a)s and four (d)s, or if it is 'patriarchal power' culture, one would expect the scoring pattern to be fairly evenly balanced with an approximately equal number of (c)s and (d)s.

In this chapter we have described in detail the four main types of culture, and hence given an indication of the possible permutations for organizational combinations or marriages. We will return to the question of recognizing and assessing the culture of a potential acquisition or merger partner later in the book. In the next chapter, we consider which culture types are likely to mesh well together.

References

Bhagat, R. S., Kedia, B. L., Crawford, S. E. and Kaplan, M. R. (1990). Cross cultural issues in organizational psychology: Emergent trends and directions for research in the 1990s. In *International Review of Industrial and Organizational Psychology* (C. L. Cooper and I. T. Robertson, eds), Chichester: John Wiley & Sons.

Cartwright, S., Cooper, C. L. and Jordan, J. (in press). Managerial preferences in merger and acquisition partners. *Journal of strategic Change*.

Davis, R.B. (1968). Compatibility in corporate marriages. *Harvard Business Review*, **46**, 86–93.

Deal, T. and Kennedy, A. (1982). *Corporate Culture: The Rites and Rituals of Corporate Life*. London: Penguin Business.

Denison, D.R. (1990). *Corporate Culture and Organizational Effectiveness*. New York: John Wiley & Son.

Harrison, R. (1972). How to describe your organization's culture. *Harvard Business Review*, May/June, 5/1, 119–128.

Harrison, R. (1987). *Organizational Culture and Quality of Service*. London: Association for Management Education and Development.

Harrison, R. and Stokes, H. (1990). *Diagnosing Your Organization's Culture*. Berkeley, California: Harrison & Associates Inc.

Hofstede, G., Neuijen, B., Daval-Ohayr, D. and Sanders, G. (1990). Measuring organizational cultures: A qualitative and quantitative study across twenty cases. *Administrative Science Quarterly*, **35**, 286–316.

Jemison, D. and Sitkin, S. B. (1986). Corporate acquisitions: A process perspective. *Academy of Management Review*, **11**(1), 145–163.

Lundberg, C. (1985). On the feasibility of cultural intervention in organizations. In *Organizational Culture* (P.J. Frost, L. Moore, M. Louis, C. Lundberg and J. Martin, eds), Beverly Hills, California: Sage Publications.

Martin, J. (1985). Culture collisions in mergers and acquisitions. In *Organizational Culture* (P.J. Frost, L. Moore, M. Louis, C. Lundberg and J. Martin, eds), Beverly Hills, California: Sage Publications.

Morgan, G. (1986). *Images of Organizations*. London: Sage Publications.

Peters, T.J. and Waterman, R.H., Jr (1982). *In Search of Excellence*. New York: Harper & Row.

Schein, E.H. (1985). *Organizational Culture and Leadership*. San Francisco: Jossey-Bass.

Smircich, L. (1985). Is the concept of culture a paradigm for understanding organizations and ourselves. In *Organizational Culture* (P.J. Frost, L. Moore, M. Louis, C. Lundberg and J. Martin, eds), Beverly Hills, California: Sage Publications.

Trompenaars, F. (1993). *Riding the Waves of Culture: Understanding Cultural Diversity in Business*. London: Nicholas Brealey Publishing.

6

The implications of culture type for inter-organizational combinations

Following a review of almost thirty major studies on the benefits and gains from mergers, Hall and Norburn (1987) suggested two possible hypotheses relating to the culture match between partnering organizations. These were:

Hypothesis 1. The extent to which there exists a fit between the culture of the acquiring organization and the acquired organization will be directly correlated to the success of the acquisition.
Hypothesis 2. Where a lack of fit in organizational culture exists, the success of the acquisition is determined by the amount of post-acquisition autonomy granted to the acquired organization.

In attempting to establish criteria by which cultural compatibility or culture match could be assessed, we considered the relationship between organizational performance and the effects of combining similar/dissimilar culture types in the context of a number of recent joint ventures and related mergers and acquisitions. A variety of sources, such as public information, financial press reports, and the like, as well as approaches to business advisers active in the field, were used to identify potential subjects for the study. Two of the case studies, reported in Appendices 2 and 4, effectively 'volunteered' themselves in that they contacted us directly because they were either anticipating or already experiencing post-merger problems.

The problem of gaining research access to potential acquisition or merger targets, prior to any formal legal announcement, will be well appreciated. While, as academics, we would ideally like to have been able to assess the cultures of both the combining organizations prior to their legal combination, we recognized this to be impractical. Therefore, we selected our sample on the basis that access was at least possible within days of the announcement and/or before any major changes had been introduced. Furthermore, while retrospection generally has recognized weaknesses, it is regarded as presenting less of a problem to merger research (Louis, 1985). Because of the taken-for-granted fashion in which culture operates, it tends only to assume salience in people's minds, and so perhaps is more easy to discern, when threatened or disturbed.

The research comprised assessing the culture type of both partnering organizations prior to integration, and then reassessing the culture of the new appendix or merged organization approximately twelve months post integration. In addition to collecting data by the traditional methods of observation and interview, employees completed a culture questionnaire on organizational behaviour and practices, e.g. managerial and decision-making style, communication patterns, problem-solving behaviours, etc., which could be related to and interpreted in terms of the four main culture types. This was completed by employees both before and after integration, so that we could then objectively measure any subsequent culture change in respect of key dimensions of organizational behaviour. In order to assess the extent to which employees are affected by culture collisions or changes in culture, interviews and questionnaires were also used throughout the merger/acquisition process, to monitor levels of organizational commitment, job satisfaction, employee stress and mental well-being.

In this chapter we discuss the implications of this research and the role played by culture type in determining organizational outcomes. As well as discussing which cultures are likely to mesh well together, we present models developed and tested during the course of our research which will enable managers to understand the merger process more fully.

Cultural compatibility

Prima facie, cultural compatibility between combining organizations would seem to imply cultural similarity. In which case, making a successful merger or acquisition hinges on the ability of decision makers to identify a potential merger partner or acquisition target which represents both a good strategic and cultural match, i.e. that its values and organizational practices are approximately similar in type.

Although strong on common-sense appeal, the assumption that organizations with similar types of culture automatically or exclusively make ideal and unproblematic marriages has not been verified by any previous empirical evidence. Furthermore, as, in practice, financial and strategic considerations are always likely to outweigh any selection criteria based on cultural similarity, combinations between organizations of different culture type are inevitable. It is perhaps more appropriate often to ask whether the combination of dissimilar cultures such as a 'role culture' with a 'power culture' has more chance of success than a 'role culture' with a 'task culture'.

More importantly, is the concern necessarily that of how well will the two cultures integrate, or of how easily will one of the cultures be displaced? When a chief executive attributes merger success to the compatibility of the combining parties, does he or she always mean that the two cultures fused or blended well together, or that there was cultural acquiescence on the part of the smaller or less powerful merger partner? In other words, shareholders can be thankful that the union proved to be an 'old-fashioned' marriage with accepted subjugation rights, and one partner converted to the culture of the other without putting up too much of a fight!

The issue of cultural compatibility is therefore related to the type, and implicit terms of the organizational 'marriage' contract or partnership agreement. When an organization acquires or merges with another, there are three possible forms such a contract may take, dependent upon the motive, objective and power dynamics of the combination.

The open marriage

This occurs when the acquirer or dominant partner is satisfied with the present performance of the acquired organization, and has confidence in its existing management and their ability to realize its future growth potential. In such circumstances, the acquisition is usually considered to represent a purely strategic extension of the acquiring organization's business activities. In an open marriage, the acquirer sees its own role primarily as supporting its acquisition and further facilitating its development and growth, perhaps by providing increased investment. The essence of the open marriage is that of non-interference, whereby the acquirer is quite happy to allow the acquired organization to operate as an autonomous business unit and maintain its existing culture. In which case, change is likely to be minimal. However, it is usual for the acquirer to act to introduce controls on the 'household budget' by integrating reporting systems and procedures. Provided that the acquisition continues to produce the expected financial results, the acquirer is prepared to tolerate any cultural differences and will not move to introduce any managerial or wider scale sociocultural integration.

Provided an acquisition or merger partner fulfils these two conditions – a healthy prognosis for future growth and a competent management team – a policy of non-interference is the most appropriate strategy. Although open marriages tend to occur more often in unrelated acquisitions, they can also work well for related acquisitions. Many promising acquisitions turn sour because the acquirer cannot resist the temptation to change things for their own sake; alternatively, they are so sure of their own cultural superiority, as being 'the one best way of doing things', they are not prepared to tolerate any multiculturalism amongst their appendix organizations. The W.H. Smith Group, which has grown as a result of a number of related (e.g. the booksellers, Sherratt & Hughes) and unrelated (e.g. the Do It All DIY chain) acquisitions has a clear tolerance for multiculturalism and a preference for 'open marriages'. In a statement in its company report (1990), the management stresses: 'the culture is and will continue to be different from those of the other W.H. Smith high street stores and it exemplifies the group's commitment to foster the virtues of its specialist chains and to add value to all its acquisitions.'

Open marriages start to falter if financial results decline, or the existing management changes, and the acquirer begins to lose trust and confidence in the union. At which time, it is likely that the acquirer will decide to terminate the contract, either by 'selling on' the acquisition or reverting to a more traditional form of relationship.

The traditional marriage

This occurs when the acquirer or dominant partner is dissatisfied with the present performance of the acquired organization and/or its existing management. In such circumstances, the acquisition may have been made for strategic and/or financial reasons. In a traditional marriage, the acquirer sees its own role as primarily being to redesign the acquired organization. The essence of the traditional marriage is that of radical and wide-scale change, whereby the acquired or 'the other' merger partner totally adopts the practices, procedures, philosophy and culture of the acquirer.

The success of the traditional marriage depends upon the willingness of the combining partner to adopt and assimilate into the culture of the acquiring organization. 'Traditional marriages' develop difficulties when the partner who is expected to conform, resists or seeks to renegotiate the terms. When this happens, the acquirer or dominant partner usually responds with a 'heavy hand', and starts to fire people.

The modern or collaborative marriage

This occurs when there is a high degree of respect between the parties, and a genuine recognition that the integration of operations or exchange of technology or expertise will ultimately be of mutual benefit. In such circumstances, it is not the case of the 'successful' organization taking over the 'unsuccessful', but a combination of different but com-plementary forces, wherein both parties have a contribution to make.

The case study of the Gable–Apex Building Society merger, presented in Appendix 4, is an example of a genuinely collaborative exchange merger. While there were major differences in size, both parties had something to offer and could learn from each other. In this particular case, Apex provided the infrastructure and established branch network system, whereas Gable had a higher degree of expertise, being arguably more 'streetwise' in a rapidly changing and competitive market environment.

The essence of the collaborative marriage is shared learning. In contrast to traditional marriages which centre around destroying and displacing one culture in favour of another, collaborative marriages seek positively to build on and integrate the two to create a 'best of both worlds' culture.

As the case study demonstrates, collaborative marriages are not without their problems. In particular, because they are so rare, or perceived to be, the vast majority of organizational members are often slow to recognize a collaborative marriage, and automatically assume and respond as if it is of a traditional type. Successful integration then becomes dependent upon the ability and speed with which senior management act to diffuse any feelings of threat which exist between the two merging workforces, and move to facilitate meaningful cooperation between the two.

It is obvious that if an 'open marriage' exists between the combining parties, culture type matters little, provided that they both remain successful and the marriage continues on the same terms. The issue of culture type only assumes importance, as we shall now reveal, in traditional or collaborative marriages, which represent the bulk of M & A activity today.

The relationship between culture types

If there are four basic culture types, there are, therefore, ten possible permutations or forms that a combination might take:

1 Power with power
2 Power with role
3 Power with task
4 Power with support

  5 Task with support
  6 Role with role
  7 Role with task
  8 Role with support
  9 Task with task
10 Support with support

Only four of the ten possible permutations outlined above relate to combinations between similar types. One of which, support with support, is extremely unlikely in practice to occur with any frequency.

There is therefore a greater probability that a merger or acquisition will result in a combination of organizations with dissimilar cultures, rather than similar cultures. Traditional marriages almost always lead to such combinations because the acquired company is usually smaller and/or less successful than its acquirer. Size, structure and attitude to the market play a major role in shaping organizational culture type and vulnerability to takeover activity.

Having identified the culture type of the combining organizations, one must then consider the degree of similarity/dissimilarity between them. As we discussed in the previous chapter, in practice, there are likely to be few pure or 'ideal' types; it is, therefore, more appropriate and useful to regard the types not as being mutually exclusive, but rather ranging on a continuum in terms of the degree of constraint they place on individuals. (See Figure 6.1.)

Although some organizations maintain cultural rigidity throughout their business life, often at great cost, others are able to accommodate a certain degree of flexibility. This enables them to oscillate their position on the continuum within certain parameters, dependent on their current circumstances.

In times of organizational crisis, such as rapid growth, changing market conditions or change in priority from a long-term to short-term orientation, most organizations will to some extent 'close' their communication systems and move to tighten control by increasing the degree of

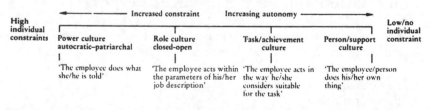

Figure 6.1   The relationship between cultural types in terms of the degree of restraint they place on individuals

constraint they place on individuals. Characteristically, decision making becomes more centralized, and 'head office' moves to play a more interventionary and directive role in the day-to-day running of the organization. For example, individual units might suddenly find that they can no longer employ staff 'as and when' they need them, but are now required to obtain head office approval. When the situation stabilizes, such constraints may be loosened, and communications become less restrictive and more open. Because reorganization plans are invariably formulated in an *ad hoc* or piecemeal fashion post merger, mergers and acquisitions are or very soon develop into organizational crises. At a time when demand for information is often at its highest, mergers and acquisitions are frequently characterized by 'closed-door' decision making, even within combinations involving organizations which would normally regard themselves as placing a high priority on their openness. Therefore, employees of the acquired organization or other merger partner are likely to perceive the culture of their acquirer or merger partner as being more constraining than perhaps it is.

By plotting the relative position of both parties to any combination on the continuum at the outset, one can assess the degree of similarity/ dissimilarity of the initial cultural relationship between the two.

Because the objectives of 'traditional marriages' and 'collaborative marriages' are different, the 'suitors' require different characteristics in their partners. For the traditional marriage, success depends on the ability of the acquirer to *change* the culture of the acquired, whereas in the collaborative marriage success depends on the degree to which the cultures can work together and *integrate*. The initial cultural relationship between the organizations therefore has different implications.

In circumstances of acquisition or pseudo merger (really an acquisition or redesign merger, but presented under the semantic guise of merger), the relationship will take the form of a traditional marriage. The acquirer or dominant partner will intend to maintain its own culture and position on the continuum throughout the integration period. It will act to move its acquisition to adopt the same culture/position on the continuum.

To illustrate, consider the example of one of our case studies, Fast Car (reported in detail in Appendix 1). Fast Car, with a role/task culture, made two acquisitions in the same year. The first, Greenside Motors, was a patriarchal power culture and the second, Princess Garage, was a person/support culture. The initial cultural relationship, and the direction of culture change can be seen in Figure 6.2. The outcome of these acquisitions was that one of the acquisitions proved successful, and the other was unsuccessful.

As we shall discuss in more detail, it is not so much the distance between the two parties that was important, but the direction in which

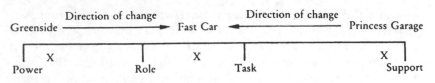

Figure 6.2 Directional of cultural change

the other culture has to move, i.e. whether members of acquired organizations experience the culture which they are expected to adopt as imposing more or less constraint on them as individuals. At this stage, we will leave you to draw your own conclusion as to which of the two acquisitions proved successful! Cultural similarity is therefore not a prerequisite to the success of the traditional marriage.

In circumstances of a genuine merger, when the relationship takes the form of a collaborative marriage, integration requires compromise. The distance/degree of dissimilarity between the two culture types is important in determining the degree of change each partner will have to accommodate, to achieve the middle ground and create a new 'best of both worlds' culture. It is, therefore, important to the success of the merger that the partners, if not exactly matched in culture type, are of adjacent types, e.g. 'open' role with 'task', and not at diametrically opposite ends of the continuum. (See Figures 6.3 and 6.4.)

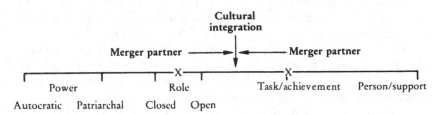

Figure 6.3 Potentially successful merger – 'role' with 'task' culture

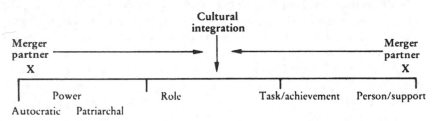

Figure 6.4 Potentially unsuccessful merger – 'power' with 'person/support' culture

The cultural dynamics of organizational combinations

In order to be able to predict whether the combination is likely to be a good 'culture' match, one has also to consider the likely wider response of the employees of the acquired organization or other merger partner (i.e. those outside the decision-making circle). Having identified your own culture type, made your own assessment of the culture of the 'other' culture and plotted their relative and desired future position on the suggested continuum, you must then consider whether the vast majority of members of 'the other' organization would represent the relationship similarly! For, although 'the other' party may not be drawing any formal diagrammatic representation of the kind we suggested, they will certainly be engaged in some similar form of mental activity. Many acquisitions and mergers fail or develop serious problems because one of the partners does not recognize or accept the marriage terms and/or holds very different perceptions of the culture of the other.

When two organizations combine, the resultant contact invariably produces some form of culture shock, particularly if one has not chosen to make that contact. The effects may be mildly unpleasant or extremely disturbing, depending upon how the individuals evaluate the attractiveness of the other culture in comparison with their own. The more dissimilar the cultures, the greater the culture shock. If the individual considers the culture of the other is likely to impinge upon his or her own, the more extensive and usually the more critical the evaluation. Altendorf (1986), in his study of the Getty–Texaco combination, concluded that the first thing organizational members do in a merger situation is to make assessments and draw conclusions about 'the other culture'. In our own research, in which we examined the experiences of a number of joint ventures and acquisitions as well as both pseudo and genuine mergers, our conclusions were similar.

Irrespective of the terms of the so-called 'marriage contract', which for many were unclear from the outset, from the time the merger or acquisition became known or was rumoured to be imminent, the culture of 'the other' came under close scrutiny. Because comparative evaluation is by definition an activity which tends to focus on the differences between the two cultures rather than the similarities, even when the two cultures are approximately similar in type, this is not usually immediately recognized by the vast majority of employees. In making an assessment of the cultures of 'the other' employees will take into account two factors:

1 The extent to which they value their existing culture and consider it worth preserving. Obviously, employees are likely to be willing to

Managing Mergers, Acquisitions and Strategic Alliances

Willingness of employees to abandon
their old culture

Very attractive	Very willing		Not at all willing
	Assimilation ↓		**Integration** ↓
Perception of the attractiveness of 'the other' culture	Potentially smooth transition	Culture v collision	Satisfactory integration/ fusion
Not at all attractive	**Deculturation** ↓		**Separation** ↓
	Alienation	Culture v collision	Satisfactory tolerance of multi-culturalism

Figure 6.5   Modes of organizational and individual acculturation in
mergers and acquisitions, and their potential outcomes
Source: Adapted from Nahavandi and Malekzadeh (1988), *Academy of
Management Review,* 13, No. 1

abandon their own culture if they consider it to be unsuccessful or
oppressive.
2 The extent to which members perceive the culture of 'the other' to be
attractive.

The implications of this process of cultural evaluation in terms of
potential outcomes for the organization are represented in Figure 6.5.
  On the basis of this evaluation, an individual is likely to decide:

(a) That he or she prefers the culture of 'the other' to his or her present
    culture and therefore is willing to relinquish it and adopt and be
    absorbed into the culture of the other. If the majority of employees of
    one of the combining parties make this evaluation, the combination
    will not result in any wide-scale culture collision, and there will be
    assimilation.
(b) That he or she finds certain aspects of 'the other' culture attractive and
    would like to incorporate these aspects into his or her culture. At the
    same time, he or she considers that there are aspects of his or her
    present culture which he or she values and would wish to retain. If
    this evaluation is shared by the vast majority of employees of both
    organizations, there is potential for successful cultural *integration.*
    However, as successful integration requires change and ultimate
    balance between the two cultural groups, which rarely seems to occur

in practice, this situation represents considerable potential for cultural collisions and fragmentation.
(c) That he or she prefers his or her present culture and would not wish to change it. If 'the other' partner is not prepared to respect this wish and is intolerant of multiculturalism, then any attempt to change that culture will meet with considerable resistance. If the vast majority of employees make this evaluation and decide to maintain their existing culture, *separation* will occur. If this separation is unsanctioned by the other party, there will inevitably be culture collisions.
(d) That he or she is indifferent to both, in that he or she is dissatisfied and does not value his or her present culture and perceives 'the other' culture as being equally dissatisfying or valueless. When an individual feels dismembered from his or her existing culture, contact with the other and potentially alternative culture, if evaluated as being equally 'as bad', serves only to heighten feelings of alienation. If the response of the vast majority of organizational members of one or both of the combining organizations is similar, the combination will result in wide-scale alienation or deculturation.

In all the mergers, acquisitions and joint ventures we investigated, deculturation, unsanctioned separation and unsatisfactory integration resulting in culture collisions and fragmentation had an adverse impact on organizational and human outcomes. For example, the case study of the takeover of Princess Garage (see Appendix 1), an acquisition of a person/support culture by a role/task culture, led to wide-scale and unsanctioned separation. As a result, at the end of the first financial year, despite drastic action on the part of the acquirer, Princess Garage recorded a greater financial loss than it had ever experienced before.

When members of one organization are expected totally to adopt the culture of another, successful assimilation depends not only upon the type and perceived acceptability and attractiveness of the new culture, but also on the willingness of employees to abandon their old culture. Willingness to abandon a culture will be determined by the extent to which that culture is valued and considered worth preserving. Employees may choose to abandon their old culture, perhaps because it is considered to be unsuccessful, oppressive or dissatisfying. Unless both factors are present, the outcome will be deculturation, unsanctioned separation or unsatisfactory integration, all of which are likely to have an adverse impact on organizational and human merger outcomes.

Applying the cultural dynamics model to traditional marriages

The success of the traditional marriage relies upon the willingness of the acquired organization or the other merger partner to abandon their existing culture, and totally adopt the culture of the acquirer/dominant merger partner. The possibility of learning from and perhaps retaining some aspects of its existing culture (integration), or allowing the acquired organization to continue as an autonomous business (sanctioned separation), assuming this is practical, is never considered. The typical cultural interaction is as shown in Figure 6.6.

Effective assimilation depends upon shared perceptions between both the acquirer/dominant merger partner and the acquired/other merger partner regarding the unsatisfactory/unsuccessful nature of their existing culture, and the attractiveness/superiority of the acquirer/dominant partner's culture. The greater the number of employees who share this perception, the easier it will be to change/displace the existing culture.

On the basis of our research into mergers and acquisitions, and that previously undertaken in the context of joint ventures, certain types of culture are generally experienced as being more satisfying and invoke a deeper level of organizational commitment from their members (Cartwright and Cooper, 1989). Consequently, certain types are less immutable and more amenable to change than others, and so make potentially 'better' traditional marriages (Figure 6.7).

Power cultures

Because in power cultures, employees are expected to accept that 'the boss knows best', they impose a high level of constraint on the individual. They tend therefore to invoke a superficial compliance-based level of organizational commitment from their members. In power cultures, many employees tend to 'attend' the organization out of financial necessity, rather than any deeper feelings of attachment arising from any sense of active involvement or deeper organizational attachment. In patriarchal power cultures, there may be a high degree of personal loyalty to certain individuals, but not any wider commitment and identification with the 'organization' as a whole. When such individuals leave or are replaced, as is invariably the case following merger or acquisition, employees are likely to feel detached from 'the organization' causing them to seek to 're-attach' themselves to another powerful individual or be willing to accept a more satisfying new culture which invokes a deeper

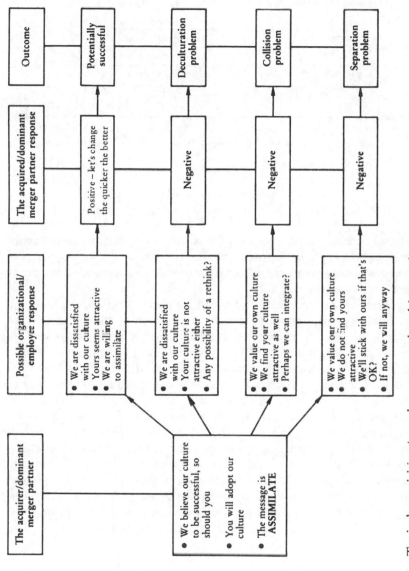

Figure 6.6 Typical acquisition/pseudo-merger cultural interaction

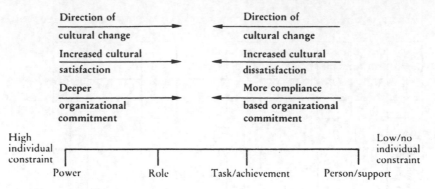

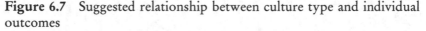

Figure 6.7 Suggested relationship between culture type and individual outcomes

sense of commitment. Power cultures are potentially more easily displaced than any other culture type, and are likely to be willing partners to any traditional marriage with an acquiring/dominant merger partner of another culture type.

If both the acquirer and the acquired are power cultures, the marriage may not necessarily prove successful, particularly if the culture of the acquiring organization is autocratic and that of the acquired more patriarchal. For, although such combinations result in minimal cultural change in that the emphasis on control is maintained, there is a likelihood of deculturation and/or that the substitution of one authority figure or power group for another will not be necessarily accepted by the vast majority of employees. The success of power cultures often depends upon the charismatic quality of their leader. Therefore, when the leader is removed, they often fall apart as members begin to doubt their success, or question the legitimacy of any new leader (e.g. the Next Corporation following the demise of George Davis). The success of a traditional marriage between two power cultures depends upon the accepted removal or successful integration of those who currently exercise power, and the willingness of the acquired employees to accept the new authority figure.

Role cultures

As role cultures impose less constraint on the individual than power cultures, they are generally experienced as being more satisfying and are less likely to be relinquished. If a traditional marriage involves the acquisition of a role culture by a power culture, the acquirer/dominant partner is likely to encounter considerable resistance to change. Conversely, role cultures are likely to be willing partners to any traditional marriage with an acquirer or dominant merger partner with a less constraining task or person/support culture.

If both the acquirer and the acquired are role cultures, the marriage is likely to prove successful, as effectively it only involves rewriting or presenting a new 'rule book' or company bible.

Task/achievement cultures

Because task cultures are generally experienced by their members to be highly satisfying and invoke a high degree of commitment, they do not make 'ideal' or acquiescent partners to traditional marriages involving power or role cultures. If the culture of the acquired organization is of the task/achievement type, it is likely to mesh well with a partner with a similar culture type or a person/support culture.

Person/support cultures

Because person/support cultures offer the individual the opportunity for self-actualization, their members are likely to resist any culture change. Person/support cultures are more difficult to displace than any other culture type, and are likely to be unwilling partners to any traditional marriage with an acquiring/dominant merger partner of another culture type.

Table 6.1 shows the constraints placed on individuals by traditional marriages of different cultural types.

Applying the cultural dynamics model to collaborative marriages

The success of the collaborative marriage relies upon the ability to integrate two cultures to create a coherent and unitary culture which combines elements of both cultures. Successful integration depends upon the shared perception of both partnering organizations that the aspects of the other culture are attractive and worth preserving. For this to occur, members of both organizations:

1 Have to recognize that the intended mode of acculturation by decision makers from both partners is *integration* and that the merger represents a 'win/win' rather than a 'win/lose' situation.

Table 6.1 *The traditional marriage: the suitability of the culture match*

Culture of the acquirer/dominant merger partner	Potentially 'good' marriage partners	Potentially 'problematic' marriage partners	Potentially 'disastrous' marriage partners
Power	–	Power	Role Task Person/support
Role	Power Role	Task	Person/support
Task	Power Role Task	Person/support	–
Person/support	All culture types	–	–

N.B. While any culture type would potentially 'marry well' with the person/support culture, most acquisitions and pseudo-mergers are between organizations in which the dominant partner has a power, role or task culture.

2 Have to perceive aspects of 'the other' culture to be attractive.

Until members of both partnering organizations realize that the merger is not intended to become a battle for 'cultural supremacy', they are unlikely to evaluate the culture of 'the other' positively. As we have already discussed, because employees intuitively treat a merger as a 'win/lose' game and assume the power dynamics to be that of a traditional marriage, all 'collaborative marriages' are potentially problematic. However, the greater the dissimilarity between the culture types, the more problematic 'the honeymoon period', and the longer it will take to achieve sociocultural integration.

The basic ingredients for a successful organizational marriage

In this chapter, we hope we have demonstrated that successful organizational marriages are not 'made in heaven' or purely a matter of chance, but are the outcome of the cultural dynamics of the combination, and therefore potentially predictable. The culture type of both organizations before integration plays a crucial role in determining whether an acquired culture will change or integrate as it influences the cultural dynamics and the likely response of the employees concerned. There are two basic ingredients to a successful marriage.

A good culture match

In circumstances of an acquisition or redesign pseudo merger, cultural similarity is not necessarily a precondition for satisfactory assimilation. Provided that the intended direction of culture change is perceived as increasing employee participation and autonomy, traditional marriages are likely to be successful. Considering the way in which most mergers and acquisitions are currently managed, most marriages are of the traditional type. Consequently, the possibility of a meaningful cultural integration by the formation of a collaborative marriage is only likely to occur in genuine exchange mergers. In such circumstances, where there is a recognized potential for creating a 'best of both worlds' culture, a reasonable degree of cultural similarity would seem desirable if integration is to be achieved in a relatively short time.

Mutual agreement by members of both combining organizations as to the terms of the marriage contract

For a merger or acquisition to be successful, members of the acquired organization/other merger partner must recognize and accept the terms of the marriage contract. In acquisitions, because the power dynamics are more clear cut, acquired employees are more likely to recognize that they will be expected to assimilate and adopt the culture of their acquirer. In mergers, because the power dynamics are likely to be more ambiguous, the terms of the marriage have often to be negotiated and clearly communicated, as well as accepted by those involved.

References

Altendorf, D.M. (1986). *When cultures clash: A case study of the Texaco takeover of Getty Oil and the impact of acculturation on the acquired firm* (Dissertation). Faculty of Graduate School, University of Southern California, August.

Cartwright, S. and Cooper, C.L. (1989). Predicting success in joint venture organisations in information technology – A cultural perspective. *Journal of General Management*, **15**, 39–52.

Hall, P.D. and Norburn, D. (1987). The management factor in acquisition performance. *Leadership and Organizational Development Journal*, **8**(3), 23–30.

Louis, M.R. (1985). An investigator's guide to workplace culture. In *Organizational Culture* (P.J. Frost, L. Moore, M. Louis, C. Lundberg and J. Martin, eds), Beverly Hills, California: Sage Publications.

Nahavandi, A. and Malekzadeh, A.R. (1988). Acculturation in mergers and acquisitions. *Academy of Management Review*, **13**(1) 79–90.

7

Cross-border M & As and international alliances

'What the US does best is understand itself, what it does worst is understand others – if only we could see ourselves as others see us.'

(Carlos Fuentes)

So far, we have tended to focus on similarities and differences in corporate cultures and their relevance to inter-organizational combinations. When mergers, acquisitions and other forms of strategic alliance are performed at an international level, then the dynamics are complicated by differences in national cultures and associated managerial styles.

National or societal culture is a pervasive influence on the behaviour of societal members. National ideologies are reflected in the relationship between business and government, the shape and orientation of the economy, financial institutions and trade union influence. The national culture in which an organization operates will to some extent influence the type of culture and style of work organization companies will adopt. However, as discussed in Chapter 5, within the same national economy, research has demonstrated the potential diversity and plurality of corporate cultures which operate across different business sectors and industries, although admittedly, in the main, this research has tended to focus more on organizations operating in the US and Western European economies. It is suggested that this potential plurality of corporate cultures is more likely to be appreciated in the context of domestic rather than international mergers and alliances. Whereas in domestic M & As the compatibility of corporate cultures will be the most salient issue in partner selection and may serve as a potential barrier to integration, in international combinations, the attention of those involved is more likely to focus on the perceived compatibility of national cultures.

It has been consistently observed that the first thing organizational members do in a merger situation is to make assessments and draw conclusions about the 'other culture'. Comparisons of similarities and differences can be based on direct experience, rumour, second-hand

reporting and implicit theories, and involve inference. As the Age–
Nouvelle case study illustrates (see Appendix 3), when the partnering
organization is also foreign, assessment of the 'other culture' is likely to
involve reference to national cultural stereotypes and ideologies.

Olie (1990) has noted that the perceived threat of concentration and
nationalism is a potential barrier to international M & A. One of the
characteristics of culture is that it creates a form of ethnocentrism in
which one tends to regard activities that do not conform to one's own
view of doing business as abnormal and deviant. However, the
globalization of trade is increasing the need and demand for cross-border
collaboration, particularly within Europe, as numerous small nations
attempt to consolidate into a trading block large enough to compete in a
world market. Cultural awareness and sensitivity towards different
'realities' and views of the world are an important facet of cross-border
collaboration.

Cross-cultural differences towards business activity

One of the most influential studies on national differences in a cultural
context was undertaken by Hofstede (1980), who conducted an attitude
questionnaire survey of 117,000 employees of IBM in over forty different
countries. Since IBM had a strong corporate culture, Hofstede assumed
that corporate culture was a constant factor for all respondents, thus any
differences reflected national cultural differences. On the basis of his
findings, Hofstede suggested that it was meaningful to compare cultures
on four key dimensions:

1 *Individualism/collectivism.* Individualism pertains to societies in which
 ties between individuals are loose and where everyone is expected to
 look after his- or herself and their own immediate family. Collectivism,
 on the other hand, pertains to societies in which individuals from birth
 onwards are integrated into strong cohesive in groups which, throughout their lives, continue to protect them in exchange for loyalty.
 Countries such as the USA and the UK are characterized by strong
 individualistic tendencies, whereas countries like Japan and Spain
 display strong collectivist tendencies. In a business context, this
 translates into very different employer–employee contracts. In the US
 and UK, this contractual relationship is based on supposed mutual
 advantage whereas in Japan the relationship is more like a family
 relationship, with a heavier moral foundation.

Such differences in orientation will be reflected in collaborative negotiations between cultures which differ considerably on this dimension. While US companies will emphasize and rely more upon the judgement of experienced senior executives to convince the other party of the mutual strategic advantage of a partnership, Japanese companies will adopt a wider consultative approach by involving more middle managers in identifying opportunities and in collecting cultures; the pronoun 'we' will dominate over the expression 'I'. Negotiations are likely to be more protracted and focus on 'people' as much as 'task' issues – after all, highly collectivist cultures like Japan are committing 'their family' to the venture.

Peter Vicars, president and chief executive of the American company Tekelec Inc. (Vicars, 1992), reporting on the partnership established between Tekelec and the Japanese NTT, confirms the importance placed by their partners on demonstrating trust and commitment in cementing personal relationships. According to Vicars, the negotiations spanned several years before any specific projects were discussed and required considerable patience; not a characteristic routinely associated with Anglo-American negotiators.

2 *Power distance*. This dimension refers to the equality of power distribution between boss and subordinate and the extent to which any inequality of power is expected and accepted. Cultures like France and many South East Asian countries are characterized by high power distance in that bosses have much more power than their subordinates. In contrast, German and British cultures prefer low power distance. Individuals in low power distance cultures are therefore more likely to need or expect a greater degree of individual autonomy and be more challenging of authority and status.

3 *Masculinity/femininity*. Cultures which are masculine in their orienta-tion possess the following attributes: ambition, assertiveness, decisive-ness and the desire to achieve recognition by doing a good job and increasing earnings. Masculine cultures are paternalistic in preferring the quantity of things to the quality of life. On the other hand, femininity is characterized by consensus seeking and is more concerned with interpersonal relationships, the environment and a sense of service.

Scandinavian and French cultures were identified by Hofstede as displaying femininity whereas Japanese and, to a lesser extent, Italian cultures were found to be strongly masculine.

It has been suggested (Schneider, 1989) that the Swedish concern for quality of worklife issues, employee health and safety and product quality means that they are often seen by more masculine cultures as not being sufficiently task-oriented, in that these issues may be awarded priority over profit and efficiency.

4 *Uncertainty avoidance.* Uncertainty avoidance refers to the extent to which members feel threatened by ambiguous situations and have created beliefs and institutions that try to avoid these. Therefore, high uncertainty avoidance indicates that the culture likes to control the future. According to Hofstede, this is associated with dogmatism, authoritarianism, traditionalism and superstition. Cultures which score high on this dimension are Japan, France, Italy and Austria. In contrast, cultures like the UK, Canada and the USA are rated low on uncertainty avoidance suggesting that they are less cautious and more tolerant of uncertainty and ambiguity.

Differences between national cultures on this dimension are likely to influence attitudes towards long-range planning and time pressures. Cultures which are more bound by tradition are more likely to place an emphasis on past historical precedents and require considerably more detailed information before making a decision than cultures which are more tolerant of uncertainty and more inclined to take risk.

Schneider (1989) also suggests that cultures differ in the preference and importance placed on different types of information. She suggests that the French, Japanese and Asian cultures are more intuitive and philosophical in their reasoning than Anglo-American cultures which are perceived to oversimplify reality. Consequently, Japanese organizations make greater use of qualitative information than US–UK organizations which place more emphasis on quantitative information – empirical evidence, hard facts and linear deductive reasoning models.

Differences in national cultures have clear implications, not only for the negotiation of alliance in terms of understanding how issues are perceived by the other party and the presentation of the type and sources of information that are more congruent with their culture, but also for the joint formulation of future business strategies.

Similar themes have emerged from the later work of Bhagat *et al.* (1990) who suggest the following major dimensions of culture variations:

● Emphasis on people, ideas and action.
● Emphasis on abstractive versus associative modes of information processing.

In cultures where people are emphasized, the quality of interpersonal relationships is significant, e.g. in some Mediterranean cultures what one does is less important than whether one is a friend; on the other hand, in India or in communist countries, the ideology is more important – it does not matter who the person is as long as they believe in the same thing; in cultures such as the USA, action is significant – what the individual does is far more important than who they are or what they say.

In cultures that emphasize associative modes of information processing, the processing is dependent on the context and it occurs amongst individuals who share a great deal of common information and common ways of thinking. According to Bhagat, this reflects an affective–intuitive approach common in Japan, China, Greece and Spain. In abstractive cultures, such as Germany, UK and USA, information processing adopts a factual inductive approach which is context independent. The main point which would seem to emerge is that different cultures hold different assumptions about the nature of 'truth and reality' and the way it is determined.

More recently, Charles Hampden-Turner and Fons Trompenaars (1993) conducted a questionnaire survey of 15,000 international managers. As a result, they have suggested that there are seven elements of national culture that determine the manner in which business is oriented:

1 Individualism versus communitarianism/collectivism (the individual versus the group).
2 Universalism versus particularism (rules versus relationships).
3 Analysing versus integrating.
4 Inner directed versus outer directed.
5 Time as sequence versus time as synchronous.
6 Achieved status versus ascribed status.
7 Equality versus hierarchy.

Their concept of individualism–communitarianism closely parallels that of Hofstede which has been discussed previously. Similarly, Hampden-Turner and Trompenaars consider the cultures of North America to be highly individualist. While their findings also confirm that Japan is much less individualistic than North America, the results of their study suggest that Japan is less collectivist than many other nations such as France, Thailand and Singapore. This may reflect social and economic changes in Japan which have occurred in the years since Hofstede's original work.

In a report for the Department of Trade and Industry, Coopers and Lybrand (1989) analysed the structural and technical barriers to M & As in the European Community. Once more, this report highlighted the salience of the individualism–collectivism concept which consistently features in the taxonomic classifications discussed. The high individualism inherent in the UK culture comparative to other European cultures is alluded to in the following passage, as a factor affecting cross-border M & A activity:

The raison d'être of a company in the UK, is generally understood to be the goal of maximising shareholder value ... This concept is by no means held to be valid, let alone practised, throughout all the EC countries ... where there is an explicit view that management's duty lies to the business as a whole (employees, creditors and shareholders) ... Furthermore, the business culture and ethics of accountability and of free disclosure prevalent in the UK are generally seen as being extreme. (p. 46)

Managerial attitudes towards international partnerships

There has been surprisingly little research conducted in the area of international M & As. A recent survey of almost 500 international managers (reported in more detail in Cartwright, Cooper and Jordan, in press) provides some interesting insights into current managerial attitudes towards cross-border M & A activity. The findings of the study are based on questionnaires collected from managers representing seventeen different nationalities. The majority were Northern European; over half were British and worked for large organizations employing over 10,000 employees. In terms of function, the sample were split 50/50 between strategists and operational/non-strategists. The respondents were representative of organizations which were highly active in international collaborations. In the period 1989–1994, 52 per cent had made an acquisition, 30 per cent had been party to a joint venture and 30 per cent had made some other form of strategic alliance. Approximately one in six of the organizations represented had merged in the same period.

The managers sampled expected their organizations would continue their involvement in this type of activity during the next three years at a similar or slightly increased level. Fifty per cent thought it highly likely that they would make further acquisitions, 40 per cent predicted that they would become involved in more joint ventures/strategic alliances, while 10 per cent expected to merge. Only 5 per cent considered the possibility of becoming a takeover victim themselves. This latter finding may be indicative of the size and perhaps even the financial health of the organizations represented in the survey. Alternatively, it could indicate a developing preference for joint ventures and strategic alliances.

The study found that the mainly Northern European sample expressed strong preferences for business partnerships with other North European and American organizations. The preferences of the main national groupings and the reasons for their choice are presented in Table 7.1

Table 7.1 *Most preferred merger partner or acquirer*

Nationality	No. of cases	First preference	Rationale
British	262	American	Positive attitude
French	34	French	Know where you stand
German	58	German	Market access
American	19	British	Professional approach
Dutch	17	German/ American	Professional approach/market access
Swedish	34	American	Professional approach
Danish	18	British	Positive attitude

Source: Cartwright, S., Cooper, C.L. and Jordan, J. (1995) Managerial preferences in international mergers and acquisitions, *Journal of Strategic Change*

While both the French and German managers chose themselves, this was actually found to be legitimate in terms of the question wording, in that the managers sampled worked for foreign (i.e. non Franco-German) organizations.

There was a high correlation between managerial preferences and perceptions of compatibility in terms of managerial style, as shown in Table 7.2.

Table 7.2 *Most compatible managerial style*

Nationality	Most compatible	Rationale
British	American	'Makes it happen' style
French	American	Clear style, decision makers
German	American	'Makes it happen' style
American	British	Can do business
Dutch	German	Clear decision makers
Swedish	German	Clear decision makers
Danish	British	Compatible language

Table 7.3   *Least preferred merger partner or acquirer*

Nationality	No. of cases	Least preferred	Rationale
British	262	Japanese	Incompatible language
French	34	Japanese	Incompatible understanding
German	58	Japanese	Incompatible understanding
American	19	Japanese	Incompatible language
Dutch	17	Spanish	Incompatible understanding
Swedish	34	Italian	Never know where you stand
Danish	18	Italian	Incompatible language

The attractiveness of doing business with the USA is attributed to a positive attitude and a 'make it happen' style of management, which is consistent with a culture characterized by a 'low uncertainty avoidance' and a propensity to tolerate uncertainty and take risks.

The nationalities that were ranked as the least preferred partner were Japan and the Southern European organizations of Italy and Spain, as illustrated by Table 7.3.

Understandably, language is a barrier to international collaboration. As English is the mother tongue of 350 million people, and the population of countries in which it is an official language is 1400 million (Jordan, 1994), this places UK and USA businesses in a position of distinct advantage. Yet language, in itself, would appear to be an insufficient explanation for the choices expressed.

'Incompatible understanding' has rather deeper connotations and was a term used by managers to indicate a gap in the way individuals interpret the world around them, i.e. 'not being on the same wavelength'. Peter Vicars' (Vicars, 1992) experience of Japanese partnerships highlights the difference between shared language and shared understanding in his comments: 'An American businessman with no French or Italian still operates within a common cultural context in either country. But fluency in Japanese, while a distinct advantage, is no safeguard against misunderstanding.' Different cultures have different rules for social engagement. This is particularly evident in Japan. For example, in Japan, business cards are regarded as extensions of the person carrying them. Writing on the back of them, an acceptable practice in the USA, is responded to by the Japanese as a sign of disrespect.

This divide is evident in the results of our study. All of the managers included in the analysis considered that the Japanese managerial style was the least compatible with their own. The main reasons given for this were 'a desire to dominate', 'protectionist attitude', 'arrogance' and 'bureaucratic'. However, it is interesting that 23 per cent of the total managerial population stated that Japan was the country they most admired in terms of the way in which it conducts its business activities. This was only 3 per cent lower than the most admired country, Germany, chosen by 26 per cent of the sample, with America ranking second at 25 per cent.

It is interesting that, once again, the individualism–collectivism dimension appears to be an important factor in influencing managerial perceptions. The Northern European countries and the USA tend to cluster in terms of their orientation towards 'individualism', as opposed to 'collectivism' which is highly characteristic of both Japan and Spain.

Furthermore, it could be speculated that Japanese organizations invoke the admiration of their Northern European competitors for the very reasons that make them the least attractive merger or joint venture partners. Traditionally, the Anglo-American model of M & A tends to require the other partner or acquired organization to assimilate and adopt the culture of the dominant partner or acquirer. The 'desire to dominate', which is perceived to be characteristic of the Japanese management style, suggests an inherent cultural resistance to accept the type of cultural imposition usual in such organizational combinations.

Patterns of activity

On the basis of the available evidence, the managerial preferences expressed in this reported survey are in part reflected in the current patterns of actual M & A activity (Table 7.4).

Traditionally, the USA has been a major player in the international M & A arena, with a highly concentrated level of activity within the UK. There is a certain reciprocity between these two countries as the UK remains a large foreign investor in US business. The preferences and perceptions of compatibility expressed by the French, German, Dutch and Danish managers appear to be borne out by the 1993 figures.

Table 7.4 *Number of deals*

Acquirer	UK	France	Spain	Germany	Italy
USA	135	47	14	56	24
UK	–	34	8	32	10
France	13	–	5	17	5
Germany	14	11	3	–	4
Sweden	4	4	2	7	4
Netherlands	13	12	3	16	0
Denmark	9	2	1	0	1

Source: Mergers and Acquisitions International, January 1994, p. 8

Implications for international alliances

In the two previous chapters, we stressed the importance of under-standing the corporate cultures of the partnering organizations. This is also important in the context of international combinations. However, if alliances between organizations based in different national cultures are to prove successful – or even get off the ground – both parties need first to appreciate and understand the different views and interpretations each other may have on the world. Without this awareness, they cannot even begin to understand more specific behaviours within a corporate context. Comparing differences in management style, reward and decision-making processes may tell us 'how' things are different but without a wider contextual understanding of national ideologies and mores, this does not explain 'why' they are different. Consequently, negative cultural ster-eotypes are more likely to be reinforced rather than addressed. As Fons Trompenaars (1993) observes, people tend automatically to equate something different with something wrong: 'their way is clearly different from ours, so it cannot be right'.

Some form of intercultural training and research is an important way of facilitating and extending that understanding and has been adopted by many successful international collaborators such as Honeywell. Such training is useful for preparing negotiators and managers who have to liaise and work closely on a day-to-day basis with the venture partners once an alliance has been formed.

In developing their programme (Dotlich, 1982), Honeywell inter-viewed and surveyed over 400 of their employees who regularly worked abroad. Typical cross-cultural problems centred around misunderstanding of the rules of social engagement, communication and differing attitudes towards time. As the comments of one of Honeywell's managers illustrate, within US–UK cultures, time is not generally appreciated to be a cultural value until encountered in another culture: 'It took me six months to accept the fact that my staff meetings wouldn't begin on time and more often would start 30 minutes late and nobody would be bothered but me.'

As well as providing information about other cultures, the Honeywell training programme also provides what it terms 'self-specific information'. This concerns identifying one's own cultural paradigm including the values, assumptions and beliefs which shape perceptions about others. It becomes clear that cultural awareness and language skills are important aspects in negotiating and working within international partnerships and alliances. However, there are also important personal qualities required, such as patience, interpersonal tact and empathy and a low need to control people, situations and outcomes. Therefore, careful consideration has to be given to the selection of personnel who are assigned to negotiate and manage international collaborative activities.

References

Bhagat, R.S., Kedia, B.L., Crawford, S.E. and Kaplan, M.R. (1990). Cross cultural issues in organizational psychology: Emergent trends and directions for research in the 1990s. In *International Review of Industrial and Organizational Psychology: 1990* (C.L. Cooper and I.T. Robertson, eds), London: John Wiley & Sons.

Cartwright, S., Cooper, C.L. and Jordan, J. (in press). Managerial preferences in international merger and acquisition partners. *Journal of Strategic Change.*

Coopers and Lybrand (1989). *Barriers to Takeovers in the European Community.* London: HMSO.

Dotlich, D.L. (1982). International and intracultural management development. *Training and Development Journal*, October, 26–31.

Hampden-Turner, C. and Trompenaars, F. (1993). *The Seven Cultures of Capitalism.* New York: Doubleday.

Hofstede, G. (1980). *Cultures Consequences.* Beverly Hills, California: Sage Publications.

Jordan, J. (1994). *Managerial preferences in international merger and acquisition partners* (Unpublished dissertation). Manchester, UMIST.

Olie, R. (1990). Culture and integration problems in international mergers and acquisitions. *European Management Journal*, **8**(2), 206–215.

Schneider, S. (1989). Strategy formulation: The impact of national culture. *Organization Studies*, **10**(2), 149–168.

Trompenaars, F. (1993). *Riding the Waves of Culture: Understanding Cultural Diversity in Business*. London: Nicholas Brealey Publishing.

Vicars, P. (1992). Japanese–American partners: Patience makes perfect. *Data Communications*, **21**(5), 21 March, 114.

Part Three

Stages of Merger and Acquisition

8

The pre-combination or courtship stage

Better and more proactive management of the human aspects of mergers and acquisitions begins at the decision-making stage, by making the best use of available pre-acquisition information. It marks the first step towards the formulation of an informed human merger/acquisition plan.

In a recent UK study, John Hunt (1988) examined the relationship between the interpersonal impressions of the buying and selling teams, and their subsequent assessment of post-acquisition success approximately three years after the bid was accepted. The study emphasized that acquisition was a process, conceptualized as an information-gathering or 'getting to know' or 'dating process' between the buying and selling teams. It suggested that the ultimate success of an acquisition was dependent on the following factors:

1 The health of the seller – how potentially attractive it was to the buyer.
2 The expectations of the parties – what the terms of the marriage contract were likely to be and how they would affect the future management of the organization.
3 The degree of friendliness and secrecy.
4 The length of time over which negotiations are conducted.

The evidence of the study suggested that the more successful acquisitions are made by acquirers who are better informed about the organization they are acquiring, and have effectively 'dated' longer. The US experience has been similar. Indeed, it has increasingly become the practice for many large US corporations to extend merger or acquisition negotiations to a social level, by providing an opportunity for executives and their spouses from both the buying and selling teams to mix informally, perhaps by having dinner together.

Admittedly, because acquisition and merger negotiations usually centre on price bargaining and take place off site, any information other than that of a financial nature is likely to be limited. However, many of the acquirers whom we interviewed acknowledged retrospectively that they could have been better informed about what they were buying. While this may not have necessarily altered their decision to go ahead with the purchase, it would have enabled them to make more informed decisions as to how to plan the integration and evaluate the likelihood of their proposed marriage contract being accepted.

The pre-combination or courtship stage should be used, therefore, not only to assess the suitability of the financial or strategic fit, but also to make an initial assessment of the culture of 'the other' and the suitability of the culture fit. Negotiating organizations should therefore approach this opening stage of the merger acquisition, or collaboration in the following ways, almost as an extension of due diligence.

Information gathering – company research

By first 'doing their homework' and becoming acquainted with the company's history, background and corporate philosophy, acquirers/ partners can establish what the organization and its members are likely to value as important. Behavioural change may precede attitudinal change but unless underlying values and assumptions which reinforce previous learnt behaviour are challenged and modified, change will not be sustained. As discussed, in international negotiations, this involves developing an awareness and knowledge of inter-societal cultural differences in attitudes towards the environment, relationships with people, emphasis placed on different types and sources of information, etc. Public information, product literature, organizational charts, in-house publications, employee manuals, as well as the physical layout and style of work organizations, are useful source material.

While, it is becoming more popular for organizations to conduct some form of competitor research (Rankine, 1991), this does not extend to customer research. In horizontal combinations, it is likely that the negotiating parties will share common customers and data can be discreetly gathered from such sources. For example, attitudes and impressions on service quality, ability to meet deadlines, negotiation and decision-making style.

It is more useful to regard this stage in the process as if one is preparing to visit, rather than invade, a foreign country, in that the more one is informed as to the idiosyncrasies and habits of the indigenous population, the more likely it is one will be able to cope with the culture shock; alternatively, the more one is likely to decide that it is better not to undertake the venture in the first place, and to consider another possibility.

Style of negotiations

The style in which negotiations are conducted is indicative of a company's managerial style and culture, i.e. the degree of formality, the extent to which information is volunteered, the relationship between co-negotiators, etc. Negotiations with a power culture, for instance, are characteristically experienced as being distinctly formal by organizations of a different culture type. Task or support cultures are generally more likely to volunteer information than power or role cultures, because their managerial style is characteristically more open. Similarly in negotiations with power cultures, the buying team are more likely to feel that they are dealing with one particular individual, rather than a team or group of individuals. Although there is a tendency of debatable wisdom to immediately dispense with the incumbent senior management post acquisition, their personal managerial style is important as it will have influenced the way in which organizational members behave and conduct their business, particularly if they have helped to found or shape the culture of the company. If the culture of the target organization is an 'autocratic power culture', any pre-acquisition commitment to removing the entire top tier of management may mean the loss of creative talent which may have been stifled by the previous managerial style of one or two individuals.

Personnel functions

Consult with the personnel function of both organizations, if possible, in the negotiation and consultative process, because they have 'real' knowledge of the respective workforces. When an organization acquires or joins forces with another, it is acquiring people as well as physical assets, such as plant and machinery, and so their 'health' or 'value' should also be audited.

Rates of labour turnover, absenteeism and demographic information are legitimately available prior to acquisition, and can provide a useful indication of the current level of cultural satisfaction/dissatisfaction. If the company has enjoyed a consistently favourable rate of labour turnover/absenteeism, they must be doing something right! Therefore, it is reasonable to assume that organizational members are currently satisfied with their existing culture, and are likely to value and wish to retain at least certain aspects of it.

High staff turnover/absenteeism rates should not be automatically dismissed as historically irrelevant, and bound to improve with 'better' management. They should be investigated and treated as 'cultural data'. High turnover/absenteeism rates may be indicative of fragmented or changing cultures – perhaps because the organization is still reeling from the shock of an earlier takeover, or has recently undergone major restructuring or change following the introduction of new technology.

As demonstrated in the case study of Fill-it Packaging (see Appendix 2), high absenteeism and labour turnover rates were found to be indicative of wide-scale organizational distrust and worker alienation, characteristic of autocratic power cultures. In the case of Fill-it Packaging, this had become so widespread and acute that the acquiring management faced an extremely difficult uphill battle in introducing their 'new' culture, even though the new culture they initially wished to impose was considerably less constraining than the existing culture.

If it is not possible to include the personnel director/manager in any face-to-face negotiations, ask him or her to draw up an agenda of points or questions he or she would like to raise. It is usual for existing training programmes to be suspended post acquisition, pending their evaluation or integration with the practices of the acquiring organization. If current training arrangements are known in advance, then the acquiring organization is in a better position to assess present competencies and future training needs. As communication is considered a major influence on combination success, a knowledge of existing communication structures and channels is also important.

The personnel director/manager of the to-be-acquired, merged or collaborating organization may also be able to give some indication of the likely reaction of the workforce – particularly if rumours are already circulating. In our experience of mergers and acquisitions, the personnel manager frequently becomes the first contact point for employees requiring information and reassurance. Unfortunately, because the personnel function is usually little or no better informed, their credibility and relationship with the workforce often suffers as a result.

Clarifying the marriage contract

Discuss the terms of the proposed marriage contract to assess the likelihood of its acceptance and/or the extent to which it is open to renegotiation. If the terms of the proposed marriage are incorrectly inferred or misunderstood by the acquired management or other merger partner, they are likely to be miscommunicated to the rest of the workforce.

A traditional marriage between merger partners misrepresented as a collaborative marriage, arguably only serves to cause anguish to both sides. Conversely, an intended collaborative marriage misread as a traditional marriage is likely to result in wide-scale cultural retrenchment, which will make future cooperation and integration more difficult, particularly, if it is likely that the organizations will continue to operate separately for some months before there is any attempt to integrate the two operations. Later in this book (Chapter 11), we will report on the success of a planned assimilation programme which effectively originated pre-acquisition, and was the outcome of negotiation discussions between the buyers and sellers concerning their culture differences.

'What if' scenarios

The use of situational interviews has been shown to have a proven value in the area of personnel selection and assessment. Situational interviews involve presenting the candidate with a brief scenario which they might typically or critically encounter in the course of the future job or role. Candidates are invited to describe how they would respond. Scores are then usually allocated on the basis of responses to a variety of situations presented and evaluated comparative to other candidates. As the appropriateness of the response is influenced by both the situational and cultural context, the problems of social desirability are minimized. The use of such techniques in an M & A situation have potential benefit in understanding managerial style or thinking.

Re-examining M & A decisions

Finally, honestly question the wisdom of the initial decision to acquire or merge – both generally and as it applies to this particular target or potential merger partner. While certain types of culture are less immutable than others, change is a difficult and long-term process, not to be undertaken by the faint hearted, the inflexible or those with short-term organizational vision. If the culture types of the combining organizations suggest a potentially problematic or disastrous marriage (Chapter 6), are there other potential marriage partners worth considering? Alternatively, how feasible would it be to set up a brand new outlet on a greenfield site? Is it possible to achieve the desired financial or strategic objectives through a less permanent and less dramatic form of alliance?

Prior to undertaking a more specific study of mergers and acquisitions, we examined the variance in performance of a number of recently formed joint venture organizations in information technology, with a common parent. The study is reported in detail elsewhere (Cartwright and Cooper, 1989), but its findings highlighted the differences between creating new cultures as opposed to changing or integrating stable existing cultures.

In this particular study, the relationship between culture coherence and performance was inconclusive in the short term. Those ventures which established new, coherent and unitary cultures, different from those of the parenting partners, did not out-perform those with fragmented or ambiguous cultures. However, they were more 'healthy' and could be considered to have a better prognosis for future growth. Their managers and employees were significantly more job satisfied and committed to the organizations than their counterparts in ventures in which the culture was fragmented or ambiguous. Their mental health was also significantly better.

The salient point which emerged from this study was that creating a brand new culture from scratch is easier than changing or integrating two established cultures. It was found that cultural transitions were more problematic for employees who had not selected themselves for change, i.e. those who were 'drafted' into the ventures by the parenting organizations rather than volunteered. The ventures which were able to establish coherent and unitary cultures within twelve months of formation were those in which the greater proportion of their employees had volunteered to join the venture and selected themselves for change. Compared with the 'self-selectors', such employees were more likely to find themselves incongruent with the new culture, and reported lower levels of organizational commitment and job satisfaction. Employees who experienced the change in cultures as increasing individual constraint were significantly more clinically anxious and depressed than employees who experienced a culture change in the opposite direction.

Employees who are recruited for new ventures are clearly more willing to accept a new culture because by their own volition they have made a conscious decision to relinquish their old culture and participate in the creation of that new culture. In electing to leave their old organization and join a new venture, they have selected themselves for change and effectively left behind their old 'cultural baggage'. As we consistently found during our research into M & As, it was not necessarily the accommodation of change which adversely affected individuals, but the feeling of powerlessness and loss of control which accompanied the change event.

Development on a greenfield site may therefore be a more expedient alternative to acquisition, and is perhaps a lesson to be learned from the Japanese. As we have already discussed (Chapter 2), acquisition is considered by the Japanese to be a strategy of last resort, when all other alternatives are considered inappropriate. When the Japanese do decide to take over an organization, usually they will have already had some previous experience of working with that company on a joint venture or project, e.g. the Fijutsu–ICL combination and the Sony–CBS partnership. In other words, they will have already learned its culture, and are more informed as to the suitability of the 'culture fit'.

Furthermore, inter-organizational trust will have already been established between the parties. In contrast to the approach of British and American companies to takeover and other forms of inter-organizational negotiation, the Japanese rely and place great importance on unwritten or implicit contracts ('annoku no ryokai'), and the establishment of mutual expectations regarding the future. Whereas British and American negotiating teams are likely to consist of or be heavily dependent on legal advisers and consultants, Japanese decision makers are more likely to be influenced by the opinions and judgements of operational managers. Kester (1991) makes the interesting observation that although the USA has roughly twice the population of Japan, and 1.4 times as many corporations, it has 30 times as many licensed lawyers. Rather than immediately jumping into bed with a little known merger partner, organizations may be well advised to exercise some caution. A high rate of joint venture failure may perhaps be preferable to a high rate of merger and acquisition failure, if such ventures are used as an experimental vehicle to assess future merger compatibility.

It is therefore important for the acquirer or dominant merger partner to consider, at the decision-making stage, which aspects of the organization it is likely to want to change, and how easy it will be to effect such changes. If there is nothing about an organization to recommend it – in other words everything needs changing – then why acquire it in the first place? If there are redeeming features, perhaps an effective research and development department, then acknowledge it, be prepared to learn from it and avoid introducing change for its own sake at the risk of alienating good workers. If the organization is currently performing well and appears to be well managed, does it need to change other than perhaps minimally? This is a particularly important issue to consider in the context of foreign acquisitions.

The often inherent and mistaken belief on the part of the acquiring organization or dominant merger partner that only it 'knows' how to run a business successfully means that the issue of when the culture will change is likely to obliterate other important questions that need to be asked; questions such as how, if and to what extent the culture should change. As a result of social change in the last thirty years or so, we, as a society, have come to accept that 'traditional' civil marriages are not necessarily the only or the most satisfying and enduring type of relationship which can exist between two individuals. Collaborative organizational marriages, like 'modern' civil marriages, while they are initially more problematic and need working at by both parties, are nevertheless potentially more mutually satisfying, lasting and fulfilling relationships.

It is important to establish and remember why you are acquiring this particular company. In a recent 'friendly', and now widely recognized disastrous merger between two large multinational insurance brokers, one of the partners held a market reputation of 'being able to do business in the boardroom' while the other was good at 'doing business in the wine bar'. Both were successful, and the aim of the merger was to accrue the benefit of combining the two different but equally successful business styles. However, soon after the merger, the larger partner lost sight of the reason why they had courted this particular marriage, and within a matter of months they acted to change the way in which the smaller partner conducted its business, by moving it 'out of the wine bar' and 'into the boardroom', with the result, that many members were uncomfortable and less successful in this more formal setting, and within twelve months the rate of staff turnover reached an astronomical level, reportedly as high as 60 per cent in some areas.

In our research we found that one of the major problems faced by UK organizations who wish to expand by merger or acquisition policy is the external pressure exerted on them by financial institutions to achieve impressive short-term monetary returns. This is not usually such an acute problem for Japanese and most other European-based organizations, especially Germany. In contrast to the UK, the financial institutions of these countries are often notably more content to accept a longer term return on their investment. This is probably because, having provided the capital to facilitate expansion, they are more likely to adopt a more active and continuing advisory role in organizational matters. It is not uncommon for a bank appointee to occupy a seat on the board. Consequently, lenders tend to have greater confidence and trust in management, and a deeper and more genuine understanding of the organization.

In the UK, however, the relationship between financial institutions in the City of London and managers of commercial organizations tends to be more remote and impersonal. This may be the outcome of the long-established British social class and education system which tends to rate lawyers and bankers higher than managers. Whether this is the likely explanation or not, the result is that there is often less trust between the two groups and so, if an organization hits a bad patch, the financial sector in the City is likely to panic!

Another difference to most of mainland Western Europe is the British political system of 'first past the post', which, prior to 1979, regularly produced every four or five years a government with a completely opposite ideology to that of its predecessor. This historical tendency has arguably had the effect of destabilizing the long-term confidence of financial borrowing institutions, and contributed to their character-istically 'short-term' attitude towards British industry.

The decision to acquire or merge is arguably one of the most important and expensive decisions an organization ever makes. The most effective way of avoiding the culture collision is by not entering into an unsuitable and potentially disastrous organizational marriage in the first place, as recently reflected in the 'brave' merger-withdrawal decision made by the Leeds Permanent and National Provincial Building Societies last year. There would appear to be a need for an almost formal pre-nuptial agreement or foundation document between partnering organizations which sets out the basis and terms of the agreement and the expectations each has of the other. This kind of approach has been adopted by ICL in the formulation of their Memorandum of Understanding, which is regarded as a key acquisi-tion document. It is also increasingly becoming the practice for signatories to joint venture agreements formally to include 'exit' conditions and terms from the outset.

In this chapter, we have outlined ways in which selection decisions and post-integration planning and management can be improved. These are summarized in the following checklist.

1 Preplanning

- Know your own culture fully.
- Research the target company.
- Consult the personnel functions.
- Arrive with an agenda of people issues and areas for discussion which will test out your implicit or pre-formed theories about its culture.

2 Aims

- To make an initial assessment of the culture of the acquisition target or potential merger partner.
- To outline the terms of the proposed marriage contract.
- To establish the likelihood of its acceptance and so ascertain a realistic time-scale for integration.

3 Objectives

● To re-evaluate the suitability of the intended marriage partner in terms of its culture type and/or the terms of the marriage contract.

4 Outcome

● Acceptance or rejection of target company.
● If the acquisition or merger is to go ahead, start planning for what happens next, beginning with the acquisition/merger announcement.

References

Cartwright, S. and Cooper, C.L. (1989). Predicting success in joint venture organizations in information technology – a cultural perspective. *Journal of General Management*, 15, 39–52.

Hunt, J. (1988). Managing the successful acquisition: A people question. *London Business School Journal*, Summer, 2–15.

Kester, W.C. (1991). *Japanese Takeovers: The Global Contest for Corporate Control*. Boston, Massachusetts: Harvard Business School Press.

Rankine, D. (1991). Britain's buys dig deeper. *Acquisitions Monthly*, December, 51–52.

9

The legal announcement of the marriage

' "Would you tell me, please, which way I ought to go from here?"
"That depends on where you want to get to", said the Cat.'

(Lewis Carroll)

The acquisition or merger announcement is the legal endorsement of the new organizational combination or marriage. It also marks the termination of the existing psychological contract between the individual and his or her organization – whereby each party has certain expectations of the other. It is the beginning of a period of self-appraisal and critical risk analysis. Because we consider the acquisition or merger announcement to be an important and frequently overlooked stage in the merger or acquisition integration process, we have chosen to devote an entire chapter to the topic – like Berne (1972), we think that it is important to consider 'what you say after you've said "hello".'

It has been argued (Barrett, 1973) that the ultimate success of a merger or acquisition is determined by the way in which the transition is managed in the early months. Certainly, it represents a crucial period in which employees will assess the culture of 'the other' and evaluate its attractiveness in comparison with their own, as well as draw their own conclusions as to the terms of the marriage contract. Brian McGowan, chief executive of the extremely acquisitive UK conglomerate, Williams Holdings (*Financial Times*, November 1990), argues that the period in which an acquirer has to stamp its mark on a newly purchased target is very short – in his estimation, 'less than a week'. The response of his company is to make a 45-minute presentation of Williams and its culture to all its newly acquired employees within a matter of hours or days of the acquisition.

The handling of the acquisition or merger announcement is the first major task faced by those responsible for making the acquisition or merger a success. The announcement and the way it is handled is important as it is the primary source of 'official' information that the acquired or merged workforce will have about their future and about the culture of the organization they will be expected to integrate with or adopt. It is important both in terms of its content and the manner in which it is communicated, not only in paving the way for change, but also in providing the opportunity to allay fears, dispel rumours and introduce the acquirer or other merger partner to its new employees.

There is a sufficiently well-established body of research evidence (e.g. Asch, 1946; Luchins, 1957) which has repeatedly demonstrated that first impressions are important and powerfully shape attitudes and future behaviour. Furthermore, once formed, attitudes and behaviour are potentially resistant to change, particularly in a merger, when there is likely to be a lengthy time gap before employees confront any actual behavioural evidence which may be inconsistent with their initial impressions and expectations.

Yet, despite the widely accepted significance of first impressions in the formation of attitudes, most acquisition announcements are characterized by minimal information, insensitive handling and poor timing. Consequently, it is not uncommon for the cleaner to know the news before, say, the area sales manager. Or, as in another of our case studies, 11 per cent of middle managers first heard the news through a telephone call from a manager of the other merger partner.

Most people over the age of forty remember where they were and what they were doing when they heard of the assassination of John F. Kennedy. The shock and disbelief, the sense that things would never be the same again, were so profound that the event became indelibly etched on people's memories to the extent that they have total recall of the event more than three decades later. This phenomenon, known as 'flashbulb memory', is thought to be reserved for highly emotional and surprising events which are perceived to be of great importance.

In the course of our research, we frequently encountered the 'flashbulb memory' phenomenon when employees recounted their initial response to the news that their organization had been acquired. For example, the response of employees at Greenside Motors, described in some detail in Appendix 1.

Furthermore, that memory of the merger or acquisition event then influences the way in which subsequent information is assimilated. The area sales manager will always remember that he or she first heard the news of the company's takeover from the cleaner. This is hardly a good introduction to an era of change, and unlikely to convey the impression that the acquiring organization values or has any positive regard for its new employees.

An 'acquisition announcement' symbolizes the death of an organization as its members knew it. It is a time for reflection and reassessment. This analogy is usually rejected or unappreciated by the acquiring management, because it does not share the same view of the event. To the acquiring organization, the announcement is a celebratory event marking the end of a long period of negotiation and anxiety that goes with it. It is hardly surprising that the social gatherings between the two managerial groups which tend to accompany such announcements are so often characteristically uncomfortable, with one group treating the event as something of a birthday party and breaking open the champagne, and the other participating more in the spirit of a wake and taking solace in a few stiff drinks.

Following the acquisition or merger, a new psychological contract between the individual and the organization has to be established. The acquisition announcement is an important first stage in setting the scene for the renegotiation of that contract. Acquiring management should respond by approaching the announcement as an invitation to acquired employees to join the new organization. The objective of the acquisition announcement should be to achieve a balance between presenting an optimistic view of the future without appearing over critical of past endeavours. It should clearly prepare employees for change, but at the same time demonstrate sensitivity and an awareness of their concerns. If the acquisition announcement is unconvincing, poorly handled or fails to meet these objectives, there is a danger that it will be interpreted as a declaration of war rather than an invitation to cooperate and work together.

Matters of style and content

The medium of communication

Shocking information is better communicated face to face rather than by notices or standard letters. In acquisitions, the acquiring organization is likely to present more of an unknown quantity than in mergers which involve the combination of larger organizations 'known' to each other, at least by reputation. Because acquisitions generally affect less people than mergers, acquisition announcements do have the advantage of being potentially less faceless, and presenting a greater opportunity for reducing immediate uncertainty and creating a clear first impression.

Face-to-face communication by way of a group announcement or presentation wherever possible is preferable to the written word. Such announcements are better made on site if facilities allow than at some outside location such as a local hotel or conference centre, because employees are likely to feel more comfortable on home ground.

If the logistics of the situation make such verbal announcements impractical, every attempt should be made to reduce the impersonality of any announcement communicated in writing. Rather than sending out a standard letter headed 'Dear Employee', address each individual employee personally by name. Any such communication should be jointly signed by representatives of both merger partners, and presented on a letter head which displays the corporate logos of both organizations.

Synchronization

Wherever possible, aim to inform all employees at the same time, concurrently or in advance of any press release or radio announcement. If the acquired organization operates a shift system, plan to repeat the announcement procedure at the start of each shift.

This is important, as information that filters through the organization is more likely to be distorted in the retelling. Provide all managers and supervisors with some form of briefing document, perhaps reiterating the contents of any verbal group announcement, so that they relay consistent information to their subordinates.

Incorporate a feedback mechanism

Provide employees with the opportunity to ask questions so as to reveal any 'hidden agendas' which may become a future obstacle to integration. The success of any acquisition or merger depends upon the shared perceptions of members of both organizations as to the form of marriage contract, and the intended or desired mode of acculturation. Allocate time at the end of the acquisition announcement to deal with employees' questions. As employees may be reluctant to speak out directly at such forums, at the beginning of the session provide employees with pencil and paper so that they can prepare and anonymously submit any questions or issues they might wish to be raised. Acknowledge any issues raised concerning aspects of the combination which have not yet been considered, rather than making rash or uninformed promises, which may create false expectations.

When Fast Car announced its takeover of Greenside Motors (see Appendix 1), it intimated in its introductory briefing that the hourly pay rate for technicians in their established dealerships was considerably higher than those currently prevailing at Greenside. As a result, Greenside technicians inferred that a pay rise was inevitable. Although rate of pay was not a source of dissatisfaction at that time, when the expected pay rise did not materialize, technicians became increasingly convinced that Fast Car was not an organization to be trusted! By their own admission, technicians acknowledged that if the expectations of higher pay had not been created at the time of the announcement, it would never have developed into such an issue.

If it has not been possible to arrange a group announcement, provide some similar means by which feedback can be collected. One way might be to place 'question boxes' in common areas, or arrange for managers to conduct feedback sessions with members of their immediate work group. Having ascertained the areas of employee concern, give appropriate reassurances and directly communicate any planned action.

Avoid the 'critical parent' mode

Be prepared to allow a decent period of mourning for employees to come to terms with the shock. When outlining plans for the future, do not totally ignore the organization's past and its culture. Even though the existing culture may be of a type which is relatively easy to displace, acquisition announcements result in 'collective remembering' and a shared sense of loss, which have an immediate, if only temporary, cohesive effect on organizational members.

At this stage in the merger or acquisition process, it should be remembered that the culture of the acquirer or other merger partner is relatively unknown and, therefore, employees are not usually in any informed position to evaluate its attractiveness in comparison with their own. Avoid using expressions such as 'You *must* adopt ...' or 'You *ought* to recognize ...', which convey the tone of a 'critical parent', and preface intentions with expressions such as 'We are considering ...' or 'We will assess the feasibility of ...'. Merely telling people that the company (and hence its members) were unsuccessful, and 'debunking the past', is not a good way of rebuilding commitment. Employees are more likely to positively respond to change if they consider they will be afforded the opportunity to participate in that change. Demonstrating an intention to consult, and just getting to know the acquired organization, are effective ways of reducing negative emotions and diffusing feelings of threat and loss of control.

Choose the messengers carefully

The choice of personnel initially appointed to represent the acquirer is crucial. To the acquired employees, the acquisition manager or evaluating team *becomes* 'the organization', and comes under close scrutiny. For example, if the representatives of the acquiring organization are all male and under thirty-five, acquired employees are likely to conclude that the organization is a 'young man's company', in which women or older men have no important role to play. The person appointed to manage the acquisition may be the only member of the acquiring organization to occupy an active role in the new organization. If the intention is to assimilate the acquired organization into the culture of the acquirer, the choice of role occupant is important. He or she should have charismatic and strong leadership qualities, and be already fully socialized into the culture he or she is required to impose on the acquisition. Many of the problems of poor culture match experienced by Fast Car in their unsuccessful acquisition of Princess Garage (see Appendix 1) were exacerbated by their limited and unfortunate choice of acquisition manager(s). It is better to appoint a committed and ambitious individual from within the organization, who initially may be considered under-weight for the job, but nevertheless will rise to the challenge, than make an external appointment.

To emphasize the 'friendly' or cooperative nature of the combination, of especial importance in collaborative marriages, senior members of the acquired organization or other merger partner should also attend the announcement and appropriately affect the initial introductions. Their presence is likely to facilitate any response from employees, and is a visible endorsement of the marriage.

If the organization or members of the acquiring team have themselves been on the receiving end of an acquisition announcement, communicate this empathy to employees.

Overcommunicate

Avoid ambiguous language and jargon specific to your own organization. This is important both at the time of the announcement and throughout the integration period in order to dispel rumours, reduce uncertainty and overcome the 'fear-the-worst' syndrome. Employees in acquisitions and mergers have a tendency to attend to information which reinforces their worst fears regardless of the validity of the source. Clearly communicate the terms of the marriage contract, and the extent to which these are open to negotiations, by creating a climate conducive to shared learning. Assign a specific individual or group of individuals to handle acquisition- or merger-related communication to ensure it provides consistent and reliable information. Large organizations might consider setting up a merger press office. Communicate on a regular basis, even if the content of the message is only to reaffirm that at the current time, there is little or no information to communicate. It is important that all communications are reinforced by written statements, again to avoid confusion or distortion.

In the course of our research, it was consistently found that, particularly in merger situations, employees respond more to their expectations of the likelihood and direction of future change rather than any actual change itself. In the case of the Age–Nouvelle merger (see Appendix 3) 23 per cent of the senior/middle managers from Age, questioned six months after the merger, had left the organization some eight months later, although there had still not been any changes introduced, even at this level, and the organization was still continuing to operate very much as it had pre-merger.

The period between a merger announcement and any sociocultural integration is critical, in that the competence value of those who choose to leave in that period is unknown to at least one of the merger partners. The importance of clear and consistent communication during this period cannot therefore be overemphasized.

Effectively presenting one's own culture

The extent to which acquired or merged employees are prepared to abandon or change in part their existing culture depends not only on their satisfaction with that culture but also the extent to which they perceive 'the other culture' to be attractive. It is therefore most important that they are given the opportunity to form a clear, consistent and realistic understanding of that culture as early as possible. It is difficult for employees to evaluate how or if they are likely to 'fit into' a culture if they are ignorant, uncertain or ambivalent about its nature.

This process can begin at the time of the acquisition announcement by presenting employees with the kind of information one might provide to candidates at a recruitment interview. A brief account of the history, development, structure, aims and values of the organization is likely to provide a realistic preview of the organization and its culture. This may be supplemented by a short video presentation or a specifically designed booklet for employees.

Do not avoid referring to areas where there are clear culture differences – these should be outlined but not comparatively evaluated or overtly criticized. Employees are well able to make – will already be making – such an evaluation. In contrast, emphasis should be placed on focusing employee attention to areas of similarity and common ground.

Acquisition announcements are proud moments for acquirers. They may feel 'winners' on the day, but if the venture is ultimately to prove successful they must 'win over' their acquired employees. The acquisition announcement is an important step in that process and requires considerable planning and forethought.

A checklist of the points discussed in this chapter follows:

1 Preplanning

- Decide the when, where, how and who of the acquisition/merger announcement.
- Prepare and consult with the acquiring management or other merger partner on the broad content and style of presentation in advance.
- If possible, rehearse the presenters of any proposed group announcement to ensure consistency, and critically evaluate the content and style of the performance.
- Decide on the appropriate feedback mechanism.

2 Aims

- To introduce employees to the new organization that they have now become a part of.
- To set the scene for future change and integration.
- To identify potential obstacles to integration and sources of concern, and learn more of the culture of the acquired or other merger partner.

3 Objectives

- To diffuse negative feelings and reduce uncertainty.
- To win the trust and cooperation of the acquired workforce as far as possible.

4 Outcome

- A favourable first impression.

References

Asch, S.E. (1946). Forming impressions of personality. *Journal of Abnormal and Social Psychology*, **4**, 258–290.

Barrett, P.F. (1973). *The Human Implications of Mergers and Takeovers.* London: Institute of Personnel Management.

Berne, E. (1972). *What Do You Say After You Say Hello?* London: Corgi.

Luchins, A.S. (1957). Primacy–recency in impression formation. In *The Order of Presentation in Persuasion* (C.I. Hovland *et al.*), New Haven: Yale University Press.

10

The honeymoon period – making the marriage work

Changing the cultures

Sir James Blyth, Chief Executive Officer of Boots plc, describing his own achievements as a change maker (British Academy of Management Conference, 1989), emphasized the importance of working 'with the grain' of the existing culture. He also attested to the value of identifying, learning from and developing the confidence of key cultural informants. Such informants are likely to be respected individuals, perhaps with personnel experience, who have been with the organization for some time and are close to its people. Such individuals are often important in providing feedback on actions, and are arguably an invaluable ally to any newly appointed acquisition manager, particularly if he or she is without the support of familiar colleagues.

While the culture match between the two organizations may be promising, any decision radically to change, integrate or maintain the existing culture requires an understanding of the cultural and subcultural values and beliefs throughout the acquired or merged organization. We have already discussed the importance of comparing any 'espoused' or managerial culture with the wider 'culture in use' (Chapter 5). While an initial assessment of the culture of the acquired organization or other merger partner should have been made at the pre-combination stage, the accuracy of that assessment should be addressed early in the post-acquisition period.

This is necessary if employee response patterns are to be accurately predicted, and should become the foundation of any well-planned merger or acquisition integration programme. This necessity has been well exemplified by reports of expensive and unsuccessful programmes of cultural change at AT & T, which have appeared in the management literature (Buchowicz, 1990), and is consistent with the comments made by Sir James Blyth.

The early weeks

The post-acquisition phase, in the case of merger the period between the time the legal announcement is made and any physical or sociocultural integration, should be spent getting to know the organization and its culture. In Chapter 5 we discussed several ways in which culture can be learnt. These can be applied to the merger or acquisition situation as follows.

Informal discussion and observation

Having made the initial announcement, those responsible for the management of the acquisition or merger should maintain high visibility. Rumour becomes endemic when employees feel that they have entered a period of 'suspended organizational limbo', i.e. they know that things are no longer as they were before, but are uncertain as to the way things should or will be in the future.

Regularly touring the organization and talking informally with managers and employees at all levels accomplishes two objectives. Firstly, by observing and discussing with employees the rationale behind the way in which they conduct their day-to-day activities, it facilitates cultural understanding. It is easier to change systems and procedures when one has knowledge and appreciates the logic of such practices, and so can generate rational counter arguments against their continuance. Informal discussion and observation of current practices also identifies any local and specific barriers or considerations which may affect the smooth introduction of new systems and procedures in the future. Secondly, it reduces the 'facelessness' of any threat employees may be experiencing, and is a first step towards re-establishing organizational trust. Jones (1983) makes the following observation on paving the way for cultural change:

> When people believe that they will be treated fairly and that if they are honest, they will have time to learn a new paradigm, they seem quite willing to experiment with new ideas. On the other hand, when the paradigm doesn't change they seem quite resistant.

Maintaining high visibility is an effective way of maintaining the change momentum. All too often, having made the announcement, the acquiring or merger management retreat behind closed doors in some distant and remote head office, and spend weeks or months drawing up 'merger plans'. An expectancy of change has been created, so if nothing happens or is seen to be happening within the acquired or merging organizations, the likelihood of any large-scale integration or cultural change in the immediate future becomes increasingly more abstract and remote. Consequently, employees become more firmly entrenched in their existing or old cultural habits and customs, making any future change more difficult to introduce. The case studies of the Age–Nouvelle merger and the acquisition of Princess Garage (see Appendices 1 and 3) demonstrate this point well.

Touring the organization in the early days, putting faces to names, perhaps by requesting those involved to wear name badges, is an effective way of getting to know the acquired organization and its people. Becoming acquainted with organizational rituals and unfamiliar but valued practices is likely to highlight important areas of employee concern which are often overlooked and may lead to confrontation. For example, it may be the tradition within the acquired organization to pay token Christmas bonuses or allow staff a half-day holiday for Christmas shopping. If known, there may be no reason why such practices should not be continued, at least temporarily, in the interest of maintaining good industrial relations. If such perks are discontinued through ignorance, this may result in unnecessary and unintentional bad feeling.

The establishment of joint working parties and inter-organizational team-building initiatives

The initiation of any culture change or integration will emanate from the top of the organization. In our experience, acquiring or merging organizations act to impose cultural change or integration at the senior managerial level, and rely on the 'trickle down effect' for its wider acceptance and implementation by the rest of the organization at grass roots level. The disadvantage of this approach is that culture change is slow. At least two different cultures are often in effect operating at the same time, for example, in acquisitions, 'the new' and 'the old', or in the case of mergers, it may be 'the new', 'theirs' and 'ours'. The result is that multiple culture collisions occur at all levels of the organization. Any misunderstanding of the terms of the marriage contract serves to exacerbate the problem further. In circumstances of both merger and acquisition, the establishment of joint working parties and inter-organizational team-building initiatives at all levels is likely to facilitate future merger integration, accelerate any process of culture change and help employees feel part of the new organization.

The introduction of focus groups or quality-circle type initiatives, within the early weeks post acquisition, should be used to ascertain existing behavioural practices within the acquired organization, as well as employee expectations and concerns. They should also be used as a forum in which to present a realistic understanding of the culture of the acquirer. Similar initiatives should be introduced early in the merger process, prior to any physical integration, and involve employee groups composed of members of both merger partners. If the merger is a collaborative marriage, then this should be emphasized by allocating an equal number of individuals from each merger partner to any group.

It is important that such groups operate in a non-threatening and participative environment, conducive to shared learning. For example, a joint working party or group could be convened to discuss a specific but typical organizational problem or aspect of organizational process. Members of one of the merger partners could present their existing practice or approach, which then could be compared and discussed in light of that of the other merger partner. Acquired or merged employees are more likely to respond and be more committed to any cultural change or integration, if they feel that they have participated and understood the logic or rationale behind that change. Managers report that the formation of such 'best of' or 'best practices' groups are successful in getting employees to work together *provided that* they consider that their recommendations are likely to receive a fair hearing from senior management. One member of such a group reported the disappointment and disillusionment felt by her working party when they presented their suggestions to senior management:

The group had really worked hard in formulating an integrated policy on career development. Unfortunately, the situation at the top was still very political. Certain individuals took the recommendations as personal criticism and our ideas were subsequently shelved.

Mergers and acquisitions are experienced as important events affecting everybody in the organization. Any successful programme of wide-scale organizational change should therefore also be experienced as widely participative, involving as many people as possible. As illustrated in both the merger case studies presented in Appendices 3 and 4, the managers who reported experiencing more merger-related change in their working lives were more positive in their attitude towards the combination than those who had experienced little or minimal change. It would seem therefore that if the merger is experienced as affecting you personally, this is taken as a positive indication that you have a part to play in the new merged organization. Perhaps, not surprisingly, what people object to more than change is the feeling that they are being ignored!

Changing the culture means more than changing overt behaviour. It requires the acceptance and internalization of a set of shared beliefs, values and feelings to the extent that they become or are the basis for action. Merely telling employees that they will now do things in a certain way is no guarantee that they will actually do so.

Developing cooperation between two or more previously discrete small groups of employees within a single organization, or inter-organizationally in the context of the project environment, has been well researched (Deutsch, 1949; Sherif, Harvey, White, Hood and Sherif, 1961; Cartwright and Zander, 1968; Davis, 1969). Such research has stressed that group cohesiveness and cooperation develop through the establishment of high levels of trust and communication, the creation of unifying 'superordinate' goals and experience and reformulation of group norms. All of which can be extrapolated and be considered crucial to merger success. In the Sperry–Burroughs combination, employees from both organizations were offered an incentive to participate in creating the new company name (UNISYS) and corporate identification programme.

Conducting a formal employee survey

Inviting acquired employees or members of both merger partners to participate in a questionnaire survey specifically designed to assess current attitudes and to establish a pre-integration culture measure has several advantages. Firstly, it provides a more objective means by which similarities and differences in culture can be compared and discussed between the two parties. It also provides a baseline whereby the success or progress of any programme of cultural change or integration can be assessed or monitored, by readministration of the measure at a later date. Because questionnaires can be relatively easily administered throughout the entire organization, they can be useful in identifying regional or departmental attitudinal or cultural differences or sub-cultures. Finally, employee participation can be anonymous and hence non-threatening.

Questionnaire response rates in themselves can be revealing. As we found (see case study of Fill-it Packaging in Appendix 2), they can be an indicative measure of current levels of organizational trust, apathy and commitment. The development, administration and analysis of any questionnaire-type survey is likely to be more reliable and achieve greater credibility and response from employees if it is conducted by some independent third party, particularly if this appointment or commission is made with the agreement of both combining organizations.

When ascertaining employee attitudes, whether in the context of interviews, focus groups or questionnaire surveys, ask non-threatening questions such as 'How do your subordinates or members of your work group feel about ...?' If everybody describes everybody else as being angry or upset, then one can assume the entire organization is angry or upset. In our research, we found that when asked to rate how they personally felt about the merger or acquisition managers tended to ascribe more negative feelings to both their subordinates and their co-managers than they would ascribe to themselves.

Questionnaires can also be usefully extended to consider issues such as job satisfaction and/or employee stress, and provide ongoing feedback on change events. Employee concerns tend to change throughout the M & A process. In the early stages, immediate concerns centre around *quality of life issues*, e.g. job security, communication and information and employee benefits, etc. Typically, employees focus not surprisingly on the 'me' issues and the continued maintenance of their existing lifestyle – 'Will I have a job?', 'Will I have to relocate?', 'What personal rewards or benefits may be taken from me?'

When organizational members anticipate change, a great attachment develops towards existing cultural *symbols and values*. Consequently, issues of corporate name and logo, loss of identity and cultural differences also become a focus of concern and anxiety. Experience suggests that these issues assume a greater importance to those at lower levels within the organization. Once restructuring plans have been unveiled and survival issues resolved, employees' concerns are then more focused towards *work organization issues* – 'How is my job going to change?', 'Will I be able to meet requirements?', etc.

Approaches to culture change

It has been suggested (Bate, 1990) that there are four broad approaches to culture change.

The aggressive approach

This is the most commonly adopted approach by acquirers who take over an organization considerably smaller and/or less successful than themselves. This approach was typified by Fast Car (see Appendix 1), and has been described as 'leadership with a machine gun' (Brissey, 1989).

Acquirers adopting this approach characteristically respond to acquisitions with militarist tactics as if they were invading a foreign and hostile country. The aim of the aggressive approach is to wipe out and tear down the old 'cultural regime' overnight. Acquirers will frequently talk of 'bringing in the big guns' or 'stamping their authority'. The aim of the approach is to change the culture by whatever means necessary to accomplish that objective, no matter how unpopular. This usually means getting rid of people, or at least threatening to do so. The aggressive approach is in many ways a form of cultural vandalism, and is characterized by its time urgency and lack of respect for organizational past. It seeks to achieve cultural change by creating disruption and fear amongst the workforce. Employees are expected to accept the new culture because 'they have to'. This approach is effective in delivering some kind of shock to the system, and triggering the process of culture change. However, while it may 'unfreeze' the old culture, the insensitivity of the approach frequently has an alienating effect.

The conciliative approach

The aim of the conciliative approach is to respond to people as rational beings, on whom external coercion is unnecessary. If the new culture presented is sensible, it is assumed that employees will eventually come round to accepting it. Such an approach is effective in avoiding conflict, and gradually introducing the rationale of the new culture. However, the 'soft sell' of the approach may be so soft that employees may not recognize that their old culture and its practices have become obsolescent and so they do not feel compelled to respond.

This approach was typified initially by the management team of Fill-it Packaging (see Appendix 2), but then appeared to be abandoned in favour of the more expedient aggressive approach.

The corrosive approach

This is essentially a political approach which depends on its success by gaining the participation of various alliances and coalitions within the acquired organization, and then skilfully manipulating these to achieve one's end. Whereas the aggressive approach depends on its overt power and might, the corrosive approach employs a more sophisticated 'intelligence' strategy. It is not the visible organization chart and its reporting lines which are all important, but the invisible covert and informal power network.

Such an approach can be effective in that by directing the process of cultural change at specific powerful individuals or groups, change throughout the rest of the organization will automatically follow. However, key individuals or groups are equally as likely to sabotage or resist cultural change as accept and endorse its wider implementation.

The indoctrinative or educative approach

The aim of this approach is to 'teach' the new culture to its new members through planned learning and training programmes. Such an approach is effective in communicating the 'contents' of the new culture to its members at a deep structural level. However, such indoctrination or cultural conditioning programmes, if they remain essentially passive experiences for the employees involved, may be responded to as merely being 'propaganda' and result in resentment and cultural resistance.

There is no 'one best way' or approach to culture change. Any single approach is likely to be ineffective and needs to be complemented by at least one other. If you consider a fairly recent wide-scale and important example of successful attitudinal and behavioural change, i.e. getting people to start wearing car seat belts, this change was brought about by initiatives operating from the premise of all four approaches:

- Legal action was introduced to punish non seat-belt wearers (*the aggressive approach*).
- Rational appeals were made to people's common sense through posters and other advertising media (*the conciliative approach*).
- Influential and popular media personalities were incorporated into the campaign (*the corrosive approach*).
- Information was widely disseminated, giving such details as the number of lives saved/lost as a result of wearing or not wearing a seat belt (*the indoctrinative or educative approach*).

Any effective programme for culture change or integration should therefore ideally incorporate the following elements:

1 *An understanding of both cultures.*
2 *Unfreezing of the existing culture(s).* A clear assertion that a degree of cultural change or integration will be necessary. Such a message should be communicated with assertion and sensitivity rather than with aggression and insensitivity – instead of applying a blow torch to thaw 'the culture', a sprinkling of salt is less dramatic but equally as effective.

3 *The presentation of a positive and realistic view of the future.* An approach to culture change which focuses on 'rational' justification for change rather than reliance on subjective evaluations as to what is 'good' or 'bad' by emphasizing that the objective of the combination is to create a new organization which is greater than the sum of its individual parts.

4 *The wide-scale involvement of organizational members.* This includes an identification and recognition of influential and widely respected members within the acquired organization, as well as the introduction of appropriate training programmes and forums at all levels of the organization founded on learning rather than teaching principles.

5 *A realistic time-scale for change or integration.*

6 *A process for monitoring the progress of any culture change or integration, to identify problems before they escalate.*

Change models, such as those proposed by Pettigrew (1990), emphasize that before change can successfully occur organizations have to be clear as to the context (the *why*), the content (the *what*) and the process (the *how*) of any action they intend to take.

Accelerating the process of change

The process of cultural change or acculturation occurs at the individual and group levels, and is considered to involve three stages of contact, conflict and adaptation (Berry, 1980). As any new culture is learnt through contact and socialization, communication and feedback are crucially important.

At the personal level, individuals may choose to avoid the acculturation process by leaving the organization. At the organizational level, the acquirer may avoid the process by replacing a substantial number of employees.

Mergers and acquisitions are associated with high levels of staff turnover (see Chapter 4). Several US studies report a managerial quitting rate as high as 75 per cent. In our research, we found that the 'decision to quit' was a widespread and common response to an acquisition, even among work groups whose jobs were never under threat. In some cases, the overall number of unplanned personnel losses were over 40 per cent, far exceeding the number of redundancies.

At present, most acquisition managers appear to accept this 'post-acquisition drift' as inevitable, unproblematic and at times even desirable on the basis that:

(a) The organization is secure in its belief that suitable replacements can be easily recruited.
(b) The company has chosen to reduce overstaffing by adopting a policy of natural wastage as a less expensive alternative to redundancy.
(c) It is seen as presenting an expedient way of displacing the old organizational culture.

Such a *laissez faire*, almost a 'people are cheap', approach has obvious shortcomings. Competitors tend to poach valuable staff when an organization is in a state of flux. When a valuable member of the organization leaves, they often take with them the competent members of their work group and, particularly in the financial services sector, their clients or customers too.

If the labour turnover rate reaches a level whereby an organization finds itself replacing a substantial proportion of the workforce, then there may have been little point in acquiring an existing business in the first place. Abnormally high rates of labour turnover attract attention in the wider community and potential labour market, and adversely affect future recruitment.

People will leave acquired or merged organizations. However, it is important that those who make that decision do so because they correctly recognize that they are unwilling or unable to fit into the culture of the new organization, or because they are aware that they will not be able or are not prepared to meet the required performance, even if the appropriate training is available.

'Resistant to change' seems to be a widely used label to justify unpopular actions such as removing people. Employees may be wrongly labelled as 'resistant', because they are unsure of the culture, or the organizational climate in which the learning or socialization process is to take place is unsatisfactory, time urgent or insufficiently supportive. If acquired employees in a traditional marriage know the terms of the marriage and the culture which they are expected to adopt from the outset, they are quite capable of making their own decision as to whether they will 'fit into' the new organization. It is preferable for both the organization and its employees that it is the individual who makes that decision rather than the organization, for then the organization does not have to bear the cost and ill-feeling associated with redundancy. The individual is able to leave the company with dignity and without the psychological scar concomitant with such dismissals. If the intended mode of acculturation from the outset of the acquisition is assimilation, the acquirer should move to communicate this with speed, and coherently present their culture. Dependent upon the culture type of the acquirer and acquired, this may not necessarily increase the attractiveness and acceptability of the new culture, but will dispel uncertainty and enable employees to make a more informed and realistic cognitive appraisal earlier, and so avoid many of the problems incurred by Fast Car in their acquisition of Princess Garage (see Appendix 1).

Changing aspects of the physical environment are also likely to facilitate culture change. Moving to new premises, resiting departments in different parts of the building or changing the physical layout, furnishings and internal decorations, etc., are most effective ways of breaking old habits and cultural norms and destroying existing cliques. In the past, organizations recognized to have strong unitary cultures, such as IBM, adopted a practice whereby employees changed job/department every two years, creating a more flexible workforce and reducing the development of counter-productive sub-cultures.

Many acquirers like to stage some 'welcoming' or celebratory event to mark their new acquisition. Such social events have a legitimate role to play in developing cooperation and laying a foundation for the future. However, rather than coupling such events with the shock of the acquisition announcement, it is psychologically more appropriate to delay the celebrations for some weeks post acquisition, when refurbishment has been completed. Then the gathering has the more positive air of a relaunch than the finality and funereal atmosphere of a takeover.

Culture change is also facilitated by the influx of 'new blood' into the organization, and the introduction of more identifiable and accessible role models not, as is usual in acquisitions, solely at the level of senior management. Of equal importance, as already discussed, is the creation of an appropriate psychological environment in which employees are able to experiment and test out the new culture without fear.

Assessing employee competencies and culture fit

As discussed in Chapter 4, mergers and acquisitions invariably involve job losses and redeployment as a result of rationalization and role duplicity. The evidence suggests that such decisions are often based exclusively on a need 'to reduce numbers'. Consequently, they tend to be made indiscriminately, on inferred past precedents – as in the 'well, everybody starts by getting rid of the top tier of management' approach – or are based on intuitive assessments made in the early weeks post acquisition. While acquiring managers are likely to attempt to come up with some plausible rational reason to back up such decisions, they are nevertheless driven by subjective assessments, such as who appears really to understand the new management priorities, rather than on any objective evaluation of competence or technical proficiency. The basis on which retention or merger reselection decisions were made was a common concern of employees who for the most part recognized the need for rationalization, but were unhappy about the quality and sensitivity with which such decisions are made.

Individuals initially respond to a merger or acquisition as presenting a personal threat or an opportunity. Until such time as they have decided whether or not they wish to remain with the new organization, survival becomes an obsession. In the 'sizing up' period which follows an acquisition or merger announcement, this obsession to survive – the need to hold on and remain with the organization so that ultimately they can regain control, plan and make their own decisions – often produces uncharacteristic behaviour. As McManus and Hergert (1988) neatly describe it, in the early days or weeks post acquisition, 'followship' becomes the tactic of the majority of individuals. In our research, we consistently found that:

1 Those employees who had previously felt oppressed or under-appreciated by the organization perceived the merger or acquisition as an opportunity to redress the situation.
2 The obsession to survive produced a marked tendency among individuals to exhibit or exaggerate extrovert behaviour, presumably because they were keen to present themselves as enthusiastic and 'fit' for the challenges of the new organization.

Subjective assessments of individuals, made on the basis of their overt behaviour in the first few days or weeks post acquisition, are likely to be an even less reliable indicator of future behaviour than in normal circumstances.

Mergers and acquisitions constitute a new contract between the organization and its members, and this point was well recognized by employees. 'Why don't they sack us all and let us reapply for our old jobs?' was a frequent comment made by acquired and merged employees alike. The introduction of formal more objective assessments of compe-tence, e.g. a reselection or merger appraisal system, would be considered fairer and less political by employees. Many acquiring or merging organizations already have sophisticated selection systems available to them, but do not use these in the merger or acquisition situation. Apart from guiding staffing decisions, such a process would also provide the acquirer/new organization with the opportunity to uncover any pre-viously hidden talents and assess future training needs. Employees are likely to welcome a change in culture which is perceived as increasing individual autonomy, but they may lack the necessary skills or training which would enable them to assume wider responsibilities. For example, employees of power cultures may be keen to play a more participative role in organizational matters, but may need encouragement and perhaps interpersonal skills training to develop their confidence to speak out in group situations.

The problem of role duplicity is a major issue in mergers. Rather than leaving such decisions up to the discretion of a single individual, who will inevitably be adjudged as having 'backed his or her own favourites', panel interviews with representatives of both merger partners are likely to be considered more balanced. Again, they would also reinforce, to those involved, that the merger is a cooperative venture.

Selecting an appropriate acquisition target or merger partner is one important decision, but usually in the post-acquisition integration period there will be over 200 important changes and an estimated 10,000 major non-routine decisions to be made (Wallace, 1966). Many of these will concern staffing arrangements. Recent US evidence suggests that employee turnover can cost as much as £2,000 to £13,000 per individual, depending on the job (Karasek and Theorell, 1990). The Xerox Corporation estimates that it costs $1 million to $1.5 million to replace a top executive (Elkin and Rosch, 1990).

In terms of culture fit, as we discussed in the previous section, employees are able to make their own decisions provided they are given sufficient information. However, it may be useful to include some measure of preferred culture or cultural compatibility in any assessment or reselection system.

If it is necessary to make a substantial number of people redundant, the provision of 'outplacement' facilities or agencies is also likely to be useful in maintaining the goodwill of past, present and future employees. Such a service could also be extended to provide financial advice and planning concerning severance pay.

Dealing with other aspects and employee concerns

If the acquiring organization has incorporated appropriate feedback mechanisms, it will generate its own agenda of employee issues and concerns. These are likely to include the following:

(a) Pay, pension arrangements and other employee benefits.
(b) The introduction of new systems and procedures.
(c) Job security.

Pay, pension arrangements and other employee benefits

Differences in culture in areas such as reward and evaluation systems have not been found to be direct predictors of subsequent M & A performance (Datta, 1991). However, they are key areas of potential conflict.

If employees are unaware of the current level of pay throughout the organization, you may be certain that they will be well informed within days or weeks of the announcement. This is likely to be a particular problem in power cultures, which, because they tend to lack formalized reward policies, are generally associated with inequitable salary structures.

It will be appreciated that consultations between the two personnel managers at the negotiation or pre-combination stage will place the acquiring or merging management in a position whereby such issues can be proactively handled. In any event, a suitable working party, or external agency in the case of mergers, should be appointed to integrate the two systems. Pay becomes an important issue in mergers and acquisitions because one cannot expect renewed organizational commitment to develop overnight, and so the attachment between the individual is likely initially to revert to an exclusively financial arrangement. Mergers and acquisitions result in increased workload and so employees tend to consider that if they are expected to do more, they should be paid more. There is also the tendency among employees who survive a merger or acquisition to consider that their economic worth has not only been proven and recognized by the acquirer, but has substantially increased.

While it is not always a good or enduring practice to attempt to 'buy' commitment, in that it has been repeatedly demonstrated that the majority of employees expect more from their work than financial remuneration, in certain circumstances it may be an appropriate short-term strategy, particularly if one wants to retain key employees. In a recent successful acquisition integration programme, outlined in detail in Chapter 11, the acquiring management was keen to retain, at least in the short term, as many of its acquired employees as possible, because it was operating in a potentially difficult recruitment market. On this basis it did not want to lose any employees before it had the opportunity to assess their talent more fully, and the extent to which they would fit into the radically different new organizational culture it hoped to create. It was therefore decided to introduce a form of commitment or 'loyalty bonus', which employees received if they remained with the new organization for the first six months. The scheme proved effective in that employees felt more secure about their job future, and were committed to undergoing a six-month socialization process in which to learn the new culture and make more informed decisions as to their future with the new organization. The amount of such payments was related to previous length of service with the acquired organization. The average length of service employees had with the acquired organization was seventeen years, and this recognition played an important role in developing trust and a sense of continuity by demonstrating that loyalty was not a devalued currency.

The scheme was successful in that the inevitable 'post-acquisition drift' did not occur even when the six-month period had elapsed. Only one employee out of the 150-strong workforce left the organization within the first six months. This parting was entirely amicable, and the individual involved volunteered to remain with the acquired organization for an agreed 'handing over' period to familiarize his replacement with the job. There was no evidence that this six-month 'trial' period adversely affected motivation. Instead, productivity rates exceeded pre-acquisition levels. Absenteeism rates also fell in the same period from 15 per cent pre-acquisition to around 7 per cent.

The introduction of new systems and procedures

Employees who 'know' their way through an organization's systems and procedures consider themselves, and are considered by others, to be 'experts'. When such systems are replaced and everybody has to learn from the same starting point, such expertise immediately becomes obsolete. It is therefore not surprising that the introduction of new accounting systems and centralized reporting procedures is considered by many to be a major threat, and may even result in sabotage attempts.

When new systems and procedures are introduced, it is important to involve the cooperation of these 'experts'. Because they know the capacity and capabilities of the existing systems, they will be able to spot any shortcomings or oversights in the new system. Promoting coopera-tion rather than conflict is likely to be achieved if acquired personnel are reassured that existing skills are transferable, and that any further training which might be necessary will be provided.

Rather than sending in a team from head office to set up new systems and procedures as quickly as possible, and then immediately return from whence it came, it is important to provide on-site support for several weeks post introduction to handle and advise on the inevitable teething problems. The formation of specific acquisition task forces, who temporarily base themselves within the acquired organization, relieve the pressure on the acquisition manager and increase employee exposure to the new culture at an operational level.

Job security

Mergers and acquisitions make everybody uneasy about their job security, often unnecessarily. Successful assimilation or integration is achieved through the development of trust, rather than prolonged anxiety and fear for the future. Open communication and consultative discussion of future acquisition or merger plans can reduce that anxiety and fear. If it is necessary to reduce staffing levels, rather than playing a numbers game, discuss the need and provide opportunities for employees to generate their own solutions, e.g. job sharing or part-time working, rather than feeling decisions are made 'behind their backs' and that they have little control over what happens.

In Chapter 8 we emphasized the importance of getting to know the other negotiating team and the organization they represent. In this chapter we have emphasized the importance of the 'honeymoon period' in getting to know and dealing with the concerns of those unconsulted but most directly affected by the arranged marriage, and on whom its success critically depends. The aim of the honeymoon period should be to pave the way for the successful assimilation or integration of the two cultures by establishing the appropriate preconditions to facilitate the change event.

We conclude the chapter with a checklist for the initial stages of the change/integration process:

1 Aims

- To create the appropriate psychological environment for change or integration by moving from a 'win/lose' to a 'win/win' situation.
- To conduct a human audit of the indigenous talent and capabilities.

2 Preconditions for change/integration

- A sensitive appreciation and understanding of the cultural and sub-cultural values and beliefs prevailing throughout the acquired or merging organizations.
- An understanding of employee attitudes, expectations and concerns.
- A shared perception of the terms of the marriage contract and the direction of any future culture change.

3 Facilitating factors for change/integration

- Continued visible top management support and endorsement of the marriage contract.

- Changes in the physical environment.
- Consultation with and participation of employees at all levels.
- A multi-approach to culture change which incorporates a clear and consistent articulation of the values of the new/integrated culture, reinforced and supplemented by rational justification, example and training which supports such values.
- A progress-monitoring mechanism.

References

Bate, S.P. (1990). *A description, evaluation and integration of four approaches to the management of cultural change in organizations.* Paper presented to the 4th British Academy of Management Conference, Glasgow.

Berry, J.W. (1980). Social and cultural change. In *Handbook of Cross Cultural Psychology, Vol. 5* (H.C. Triandis and R.W. Brislin, eds) pp. 211–299, Boston: Allyn & Bacon.

Brissey, J.F. (1989). Leadership in the courtroom: A Belgian experiment. In *Responsive Law*, Paper presented at the 4th International SCOS Conference on Organizational Symbolism and Corporate Culture, INSEAD, Fountainebleau, France, June 28–30.

Buchowicz, B.S. (1990). Cultural transition and attitude change. *Journal of General Management*, 15(4), 45–55.

Cartwright, D. and Zander, A. (1968). *Group Dynamics: Theory and Research*, 3rd edn. London: Tavistock.

Datta, D.K. (1991). Organizational fit and acquisition performance: Effects of post acquisition integration. *Strategic Management Journal*, 12, 281–297.

Davis, J.H. (1969). *Group Performance*. Reading, Massachusetts: Addison-Wesley.

Deutsch, M. (1949). An experimental study of the effects of cooperation and competition upon group processes. *Human Relations*, 2, 99–131.

Elkin, A. J. and Rosch, P. J. (1990). Promoting mental health at the workplace: The prevention side of stress management. *Occupational Medicine: State of the Art Review*, 5(4), 739–754.

Fulmer, R.M. and Crikley, R. (1988). Blending corporate families: Management and organization development in a post merger environment. *Academy of Management Executive*, 2(4), 275–283.

Jones, G.R. (1983). Transaction costs, property, rights and organizational culture: An exchange perspective. *Administrative Science Quarterly*, 28, 454–467.

Karasek, R. and Theorell, T. (1990). *Healthy Work: Stress, Productivity and the Reconstruction of Working Life.* New York: Basic Books.

Kester, W.C. (1991). *Japanese Takeovers: The Global Contest for Corporate Control.* Boston, Massachusetts: Harvard Business School Press.

McManus, M.L. and Hergert, M.L. (1988). *Surviving Merger and Acquisition.* Glenview, Illinois: Scott, Foresman & Co.

Pettigrew, A. (1990). Is corporate culture manageable? In *Managing Organizations* (D.C. Wilson and R.H. Rosenfeld, eds), London: McGraw-Hill.

Sherif, M., Harvey, O.J., White, B.J., Hood, W.R. and Sherif, C.W. (1961). *Intergroup Conflict and Cooperation: The Robert Caves Experiment.* Oklahoma: University of Oklahoma Press.

Wallace, F.D. (1966). Some principles of acquisitions. In *The Corporate Merger* (W. Alberts, ed.), Chicago: University of Chicago Press.

11

Establishing marital allegiance – monitoring the success of the marriage

'Marry in haste, regret at leisure'

(Anon)

There is a notable tendency amongst strategic decision makers and senior management, once the initial excitement has worn off, major decisions have been made and the mechanisms for change appear to have been introduced, to relax and assume the worst is over. While the formulation of a well-informed human merger plan, introduced in the early stages, will enhance the integration process, no matter how much pre-planning is done, post-merger/acquisition problems can never be completely alleviated.

According to Kurt Lewin's model (1947), change is a three stage process involving (a) the unfreezing of existing attitudes, (b) the introduction of change, and (c) the refreezing of new attitudes, development of new group norms and return to stability. A merger can only be considered to have stabilized when a clear, coherent and unitary culture has developed throughout the organization, and when everybody is clear as to the new organizational values and goals, shares and accepts these values and knows what is expected of them. It is impossible to estimate the exact time-scale within which post-merger stabilization will occur, but it is the point at which problems cease to be attributed as being 'merger-related', and once again become simply 'organizational' problems.

Post-merger stabilization, particularly if the organization relies on the traditional 'knock-on' or 'domino' approach to culture change or integration, is likely to take several years depending on the size of the organization. Indeed, in some circumstances, the merger may never achieve a satisfactory and fully stabilized state, in which case the marriage will ultimately be dissolved. The merged organization will either cease to exist and go out of business altogether, because its internal difficulties so adversely affect its external market performance, or it will be taken over or merged again and become the subject of another organizational marriage. It is more than likely that this will be of the 'shotgun' variety.

In this closing chapter, we consider the final stage in the merger process, that of monitoring the progress of the integration process and the longer term success of the organizational marriage.

Continuing to keep in touch

The findings of our study emphasized the need for acquiring or merger management to continue to remain in touch with the rest of the workforce, particularly its middle managers. The failure to link the negotiating team and the implementation team was found to be a major stumbling block to acquisition/merger integration, and is consistent with previous research (Hall and Norburn, 1987).

In all three of our acquisitions and the Gable–Apex merger (reported in Appendix 4), both the interview and the questionnaire data suggested that senior management were not experienced by their subordinates to be as accessible as they perceived themselves to be. Frequently, the perceptions of senior managers that the acquisition or merger was successfully working out were clearly not shared by those who were charged with actually implementing the integration at the operational level. Comments such as 'They'll [senior management] tell you the merger is a great success – but from where I stand it certainly doesn't seem like it', or 'When they [senior management] talk about the new merged organization, it's as if they are talking about a different organization', were typical of those made by middle managers six or seven months post merger. Such comments are illustrative of the gulf which characteristically develops between the ideas and attitudes generated from head office, or the 'dream factory' as one manager aptly described it, and the operational reality of the merger.

Increased organizational size in itself reduces feelings of pressure to participate. Because employees frequently feel as if they are even smaller cogs in an even larger wheel, they find it more difficult to identify with the organization. In the previous chapters, we have emphasized the importance of *communication* in the earlier M & A stages, in providing clear and consistent information which focuses on the positivity of the change and emanates from a credible source. In the early stages, the primary function of communication should be to inform. This means providing information in areas where the implications of the merger and acquisition are certain, rather than providing speculative comments on areas where no firm decisions have yet been made. Such speculation inevitably fuels rumour and breeds insecurity. The acquiring management then unwittingly becomes the architect of its own problems.

Once integration is underway, the primary function of communication should be to supplement initial information and, most importantly, give direction, in order that values and beliefs can be translated into clear behavioural practices. Problems develop after acquisition or merger if the culture becomes nebulous, intangible or inconsistent, e.g. if reporting arrangements are frequently changed or decision-making responsibility is unclear. While culture change amounts to more than changing overt behaviour, behavioural change may be a necessary antecedent or facilitator of attitudinal or value change. Behaviour consistent with the new cultural values should be reinforced and visibly encouraged.

The energy which is expended in introducing and integrating systems and procedures tends to stretch managerial resources almost to breaking point. Because systems tend to assume an overwhelming priority in the integration process, management usually react by subordinating all but their most immediate problems. 'People issues' typically get pushed to one side, and subsequently land on the desk of the personnel manager, characteristically at a time when the demands of his or her current work schedule are also approaching overload, leaving little available time for employee counselling.

In a recent study of the existing unit managers of an organization which had been involved in acquisition activity during the previous twelve months, we assessed the impact of acquisition on core businesses. All the managers questioned reported that they had experienced a notable reduction in the level of support they had received from head office personnel over the last year. Estimates as to the extent to which support had declined varied from 30 to 65 per cent. This reduction occurred at a time when the managers concerned were experiencing severe pressure to increase the profitability of their own units to maintain the forecasted profit/earnings ratio. Many managers reported feelings of discontent and jealousy concerning the special and wide-scale attention which was being directed to their new organizational colleagues. This jealousy manifested itself in the uncooperative attitude of existing managers towards those within the newly acquired organizations.

Dealing with people-related problems as a result of merger and acquisition is time consuming. As evidenced by the experience of one of the acquirers who participated in our study (see Appendix 1), making several acquisitions over a relatively short time period exacerbates the problem of resource and time allocation. It is therefore desirable from the outset to charge the responsibility of monitoring and facilitating human resource integration to a specific individual or team of individuals within the organization, or an outside third party/consultant with appropriate expertise.

This appointment should be seen as being reasonably long term and extending beyond the early weeks/months. The role of employee liaison officer or the task force should not be viewed as being an additional responsibility for those involved, but should remove them from their regular duties. If a transition team or task force is created, it should be composed of members of both organizations, irrespective of the terms of marriage contract. This point is echoed in a statement made by the CEO of Allied Signal Inc., speaking from experience of over 100 acquisitions, and reported in Fulmer and Gilkey (1988): 'If you are ever going to make the people part work out, you have to treat the deal as a merger even, maybe especially, if it is an acquisition.' This is not to imply that traditional marriages should be manipulatively presented as collaborative, but that acquirers should be more flexible in their approach and treat acquired employees with respect.

The utilization of outside expertise has the advantage of introducing objectivity into the integration process, and conveying a more credible sense of 'fair play'. Because M & As are such emotional and volatile events for all those involved, a more 'helicoptering' approach of a third party has obvious benefits. At the same time, drawing on past experience gained in the area avoids the necessity of duplicating the mistakes others have already made.

Integration can be monitored by the use of questionnaires or regular liaison meetings throughout the organization. Pre-integration culture measures could be compared with those twelve or eighteen months after integration, to assess the degree to which the organization has been successful in creating a new unitary and coherent culture, and identifying specific areas where ambiguity exists.

The importance of monitoring the integration cannot be over-emphasized. Feedback mechanisms introduced in the early stages should remain in place and operate for some time post merger/acquisition. A concentrated outflow of communication in the early stages should have the effect of diffusing the initial nightmare scenarios. However, reverting to restrictive communication and providing information solely on a 'need to know' basis, once the initial aftermath appears to be over, only serves to resurrect or fuel new and equally dysfunctional scenarios.

Recognizing the warning signs

Throughout the integration process it is important to continue proactively to manage the 'people factor'. Early identification of problems requires an awareness of potential indicators that the marriage is not working as well as expected. Lowered productivity, high rates of labour turnover, sickness and absenteeism are the most obvious indicators. While not intended to be extensive, others might include:

1 A rising incidence of customer complaints and poor quality output.
2 Increasing threat of industrial action and increased membership of trade unions.
3 Low level of employee participation in social events arranged by the organization, or participation confined to ex-employees of only one of the merger partners.
4 Poor take-up rate for employee training or management courses. Similarly, a predominance of candidates for training courses or internal promotions from only one of the merger partners.
5 Increasing incidence of professional or product liability claims.
6 Increasing rate of petty theft.
7 A deteriorating accident or safety record not only in relation to personal inquiries but also damage to or caused by company motor vehicles or third parties.
8 A rise in private health insurance premiums or increase in use of such facilities. According to an American psychologist, Michael Mercer (1988), mergers produce a whole range of psychosomatic health problems such as ulcers and liver problems as a result of nervousness and excessive drinking.

At a more local level:

9 Increasing frequency of short-term absence, e.g. dental/medical appointments – possibly to attend job interviews or as a result of a stress-related condition.
10 Unprecedented high level of interest in securing any circulating trade journals, previously only awarded a cursory glance – again presumably in order to study the job advertisements.
11 A general and previously uncharacteristic sluggishness in responding to communications and requests for help, e.g. working late to meet deadlines.
12 Poor time keeping.
13 Increasing incidence of 'personality clashes' between members of the same department, or inter-departmentally.
14 Negative feedback from locally based external recruitment agencies. If the organization utilizes specialized industry-based recruitment agencies, these are usually willing to give some indication as to the level of unrest within the workforce. They can also provide feedback on the general impressions and current reputation of the company in the

wider recruitment market, e.g. the reasons why applicants may have refused job offers.

Any of the above may be indicative of low levels of employee morale, commitment, motivation and job satisfaction. They are highly likely also to be manifestations of 'merger-related stress'.

Dealing with employee stress

Mergers and acquisitions are potentially stressful events for all those involved. Those who initiate the merger or acquisition decision, for example, may have staked their personal career or financial resources on the successful outcome of that decision. Those responsible for managing and implementing the change process face an exhausting and often time-urgent challenge to make the merger or acquisition work. For the vast majority of employees, the experience and uncertainty of a major change event which has often been suddenly and unexpectedly thrust upon them is also likely to be stressful. Furthermore, for most of those involved, merger or acquisition will be an unprecedented event in their lives, and they are unlikely, therefore, to have developed any effective way of coping with the stress of the experience.

In many respects, the role of the middle manager, in bridging the interface, is often the most stressful. For it is the middle manager who has the responsibility of putting often unpopular, ill-explained or poorly conceived top management policy decisions into practice. Effective implementation hinges on their ability to convince themselves and their subordinates of the wisdom of such actions. If the middle manager is perceived by his or her subordinates to lack trust or commitment to the new organization, this has a demotivating effect on the entire workgroup. When senior management issue the order to cut costs and 'trim the bottom line', it is the middle manager who usually has to make the decision as to how such cuts should be achieved. He or she usually decides whose services are to be dispensed with, and has the unenviable task of communicating these decisions.

Robertson and Cooper (1983) have highlighted that career development is a particularly common source of stress at middle age and hence usually middle management. Mergers and acquisitions only serve to exacerbate the problem in eroding status and heightening feelings that one may have reached one's 'career ceiling'.

The middle manager is likely to feel particularly trapped by the new organizational restructure, in that he or she feels too young to qualify for voluntary retirement and too old to find other or better opportunities elsewhere. Similarly, other studies (Kahn *et al.*, 1964; Kay, 1974) have identified that certain pressures are to be found more at middle than other management levels. In operating at an organizational boundary between senior decision makers and the main body of the workforce, they are often torn by divided loyalties. They implement major organizational decisions, but have limited influence and little real authority in changing or modifying such decisions.

The middle managers we talked to in the course of our research frequently felt torn between their commitment to the organization and their commitment to their subordinates. When presented with the opportunity to leave the acquired or merged organization, and possibly improve their future promotion prospects, many agonized over the decision, reluctant to be seen to be abandoning a 'sinking ship' and abdicating the deeply ingrained responsibility they felt towards their subordinates.

A common response to the problem of role duplicity created by the merger is to 'reshuffle the pack'. The possibility of relocation was found to be a real worry, and to have a particularly disruptive effect on the lives of middle managers, many of whom were in dual career families, with the added problem of teenage children at a critical stage in their schooling – as illustrated by the following comments made by one middle manager who relocated as a result of the Gable–Apex merger (Appendix 4):

> The person who has suffered most from the merger is my wife – and my family. My wife has had to cope with the problem of moving to a new house, leaving old friends and settling the children into new schools. She has also had to leave a job she enjoyed. I have been so busy settling into my new job, working long hours, etc., I have tended to leave everything else to her. She's also had to put up with listening to me for hours talking about the merger. It may have helped me cope with the stress, but it has effectively transferred my worries on to her.

There is a notable tendency for merger stress to spill over into home life. Discussing anxieties and worries with colleagues at work is not tended to be considered a good tactic, in that managers do not wish overtly to demonstrate any vulnerability which may suggest to others that they are not 'merger fit'. Our research suggested this to be more of a problem for female managers who, presumably because of their minority position within the organization, felt more vulnerable and isolated than the men.

The impact of stress on merger performance has not been directly quantified, primarily because its direct impact is not necessarily immediately felt. However, there is mounting evidence to demonstrate the cost of stress in the workplace more generally. A US report in the *Journal of Occupational Medicine* (Elkin and Rosch, 1990) claims that 60–80 per cent of accidents on the job are stress related. Overall, the total cost of stress to American business and industry assessed by absenteeism, compensation claims, diminished productivity, medical expenses and health insurance is estimated to be excess of $150 billion a year (Karasek and Theorell, 1990). For many years, it has been possible for US employees to sue their employers for 'cumulative trauma' or work-related stress. In the UK, we are beginning to see a similar trend developing, and a number of 'test' cases are being brought before the courts. One wonders how long it might be before an attempt will be made to sue an organization for 'merger-related stress'.

We consistently found mergers to be potentially more stressful than acquisitions, and to have a longer term adverse impact on the psychological and mental well-being of employees. Mergers also tend to be associated with a high incidence of long-term stress-related absence.

On the basis of our research, which compared the mental health of employee groups at various stages in the merger/acquisition process, it is more the 'expectancy of change' and 'fears of future survival' which trigger merger stress than the actual change process itself. In a study of over 150 middle managers involved in the Gable–Apex building society merger (see Appendix 4) only 24 per cent considered that the merger had caused them no stress whatsoever. This particular merger was initially perceived by managers at this level to be a traditional marriage. Consequently, for managers of the smaller building society, the merger became a significantly greater source of stress to them than their counterparts in the other larger society. Six months post integration, and over a year since the merger announcement, their mental health was significantly poorer than the managers of the larger partner. For example, 21 per cent of male managers self-reported mental anxiety levels similar to, and in some cases even higher than, psychoneurotic outpatients. Furthermore, 17 per cent reported abnormally high levels of depression and phobic anxiety, again comparable with psychoneurotic outpatients.

Cultural incompatibility and culture collisions were frequently cited as a source of stress. In addition, in all the mergers and acquisitions we studied there were five main universal stressors:

1 Work overload.
2 Rates of pay.
3 Lack of job security/unclear promotion prospects.
4 Lack of consultation and communication.
5 Work anxieties spilling over into home life.

For middle managers, relationships with senior management were a particular source of stress, as was the prospect of another merger in the future.

The experiences of the mergers and acquisitions we studied would suggest that continuation of the change momentum created by the announcement of the merger or acquisition is preferable to and less stressful than change which is suddenly introduced after a protracted period of uncertainty during which there has been no change. It was found that 'merger uncertainty' was frequently experienced by those who joined the new merged organization as long as twelve months post integration. New joiners reported that existing organizational members tended to assign new recruits to one or other of the 'camps' according to various criteria, e.g. according to the perceived allegiance of the person who recruited them, the area or department in which they worked, etc.

Other suggested methods of addressing the problem of merger stress include the provision of stress and/or career counsellors, the introduction of stress management training programmes and the use of 'attitude surveys' and 'stress audits' to monitor stress levels regularly throughout the organization. As we have already discussed, in the merger or acquisition situation, personal survival appears to be equated with the ability to play politics and become noticed. This causes individuals to affect or exaggerate extroversion and emphasize to others that they are 'merger fit'. The continued maintenance of such a pretence is likely to have detrimental and dysfunctional psychological and physiological consequences.

While stress can never be eradicated from life – according to Selye (1974) 'the only person without stress is a dead person' – individuals can be helped to cope with stress more positively. The efficacy of stress intervention programmes has been well demonstrated (Cooper, Reynold and Sadri, 1989; Sutherland, 1990), particularly in reducing absenteeism. The introduction of stress management workshops in the merger situation would provide a further opportunity for members of both merger partners to talk about the merger and share their experiences and anxieties, and so diffuse any feelings of threat or conflict between the two. As well as having therapeutic value for the individual, such events are also likely to increase organizational cohesiveness, through the sharing and discussing of merger-related problems.

However, it is important that both groups are composed of individuals at a comparable level in the organization. It is also important that participation is voluntary and not taken as a sign of weakness, and that individuals are assured that the organization does not receive any feedback on individual participants. The endorsement, and ideally the participation of those most senior in the organization, will greatly increase the beneficial effect of such workshops.

A successful acquisition integration programme

In this closing section, we present a brief outline of a recent acquisition programme which incorporates many of the elements we have discussed and is illustrative of proactive acquisition management. The Allied–Bendix merger in 1985 has been described as 'an almost text book case in successful mergers' (Fulmer, 1986). One of the main factors which contributed to its success is suggested to be the extensive management development programme which was introduced immediately post merger. This programme was founded on the following principles:

1 Selling the concept at all levels.
2 Involving line managers.
3 Checking recommendations for objectivity.
4 Utilizing outside expertise.

These principles are also well exemplified in the more recent programme we will now outline, which is based on one of the authors' case studies, with the corporate names modified to protect the organizations' anonymity.

The Smith Group, a large multinational, was a supplier of packaging material to the Jones Group. When the Jones Group decided to sell off their own small 'in-house' packaging division of 150 employees, the Smith Group were naturally an interested buyer. Both buyer and seller did have the advantage of some prior knowledge and experience of each other. The organizations had very different cultures. The sellers (the Jones Group) had a strong, deeply ingrained 'patriarchal power culture'. In contrast, production units within the Smith Group operated as autonomous profit centres, and tended to maintain predominantly 'task or team cultures'.

These differences in culture were recognized by both organizations and were a major point of discussion at the negotiation stage, which involved input from the personnel function on both sides. Because the Jones Group was a patriarchal power culture, it felt a high degree of responsibility to its employees in the packaging division, many of whom had long service records and had been with the organization since leaving school. There was deep and real concern about the impact of the culture shock which would result from the change of ownership. This concern was also shared by the Smith Group, which was planning to build a new factory in the area to accommodate their new acquisition. Consequently, in the period between the time the deal was agreed and the completion of the new factory, the acquirer, with the consent and full cooperation of the divesting organization, decided to initiate an 'acquisition integration programme'. This was implemented in a three-stage process.

Stage 1

At the outset of the programme, the acquirer made a clear statement to all employees communicating their recognition that the acquisition was a major event in the working lives of those involved, and that as a result they had decided to initiate an integration programme. The organization stressed that it would welcome the full participation of all organizational members, and to maintain objectivity had appointed an outside consultant. Employees were assured that any discussions between themselves and the consultant would remain confidential, and would not be attributed to any specific individual.

Stage 2

A detailed objective assessment of the two cultures and their compatibility prior to integration

This task was assigned to the external consultant and involved the assessment of the existing cultures and sub-cultures of both organizations. A systematic investigation was conducted to identify the prevailing values and current organizational practices and procedures of both organizations to identify the areas of divergence and potential problems to integration. As part of this assessment process, a series of in-depth individual and group interviews were conducted with a randomly selected sample of managers and employees at all levels throughout the acquired organization. These interviews involved approximately 30 per cent of the workforce, and members of the acquiring management were not present. On the basis of these interviews, a culture questionnaire was prepared and distributed to all employees. Employees were presented with a series of statements (e.g. 'Factory management are friendly and easy to approach', 'Employees are frequently told if they are doing a good job'), which they were asked to rate in terms of the degree to which they agreed/disagreed with the statement. The questionnaire received a response rate of over 80 per cent.

A similar exercise was conducted at the plant within the Smith Group which most closely matched the acquired organization and was an appropriate 'role model' for the acquiring management. Discussions were also held with the acquisition management team, to establish their ideas and plans for the new organization.

The technique described earlier of animal imagery was also used

(Chapter 5). The frequent projection of the Smith Group as a 'tiger' and the Jones Group as a 'donkey' provides a summative description of the culture differences between the two.

An identification of employee concerns and expectations

Employees' behaviour post acquisition or merger is determined by their expectations. As well as eliciting an understanding of the cultural values and norms of the acquired workforce, the interviews were used to ascertain current attitudes, concerns and expectations employees held toward the acquisition and the acquirers. For example, employees were asked what they thought it would be like working for the new management, i.e. did they expect that the new managerial style would be tougher? stricter? or similar to the existing style?, etc. Employees were also asked to choose which aspects of their present organization they would wish to retain, which aspects they would like to see changed, etc.

One of the interesting points which came out of the interviews concerned the question of company uniforms. Within the Jones Group, employees were supplied with uniforms with their names embroidered on the breast pocket. To those new to the organization, this seemed a useful practice and one the acquiring company intended to continue. However, it was discovered from the interviews that this practice was unpopular with the vast majority of the workforce. The presence of the name labels meant that factory management never bothered to take the trouble to learn the names of their employees, because they knew they could read them off the overalls. Employees felt that given the size of the workforce and its stability over time, it was not unreasonable for managers to commit the names of their employees to memory. As a direct result, the new overalls were supplied without names. The acquiring organization saved money and the workforce were very happy about the new arrangements.

Again, on the basis of the interviews, a list of concerns and expectations were drawn up and included in the questionnaire. Employees were asked to rate the extent to which they were concerned about the issues raised. They were also asked to consider what they expected to happen as a result of the sale, and to rate the likelihood of each event. A job satisfaction measure was also included. From an analysis of the questionnaire results, the acquiring organization was able to identify the areas, degree, level of concern and expectations throughout the organization, as well as any more specific departmental or localized issues, and then develop a detailed and informed integration plan.

Each employee received a letter giving detailed feedback on the interview and questionnaire data collected, together with the response of the new management to the points raised and the action they intended to take.

Maintaining the momentum for change

This was a particular problem with this acquisition. The takeover announcement was a great shock to employees, many of whom had no experience of working for any other employer, and had come to regard a job with the Jones Group as a job for life. Because there was a considerable period of time, about a year, between the announcement of the takeover and its actual implementation, the void created facilitated a long nostalgic and potentially unproductive and demotivating period of 'collective remembering', often of the 'rose-tinted spectacles' kind.

Positive steps were taken to focus employee attention on the future and maintain the momentum for change, involving a variety of actions. Acquiring management made a positive effort to maintain visibility during this period, by regularly touring the site. Employees were kept up to date on the progress of the acquisition and the new factory building programme via regular newsletters. Plans of the new factory and photographs of the work in progress were displayed on noticeboards and regularly updated. Employees were consulted about the purchase of new machinery, possible changes in working hours and work organization, etc.

It was decided in advance that once the factory was completed, in addition to having an 'official' opening event for local dignitaries and senior group management, a similar less formal event would be held specifically for employees and their families. This event and the preparations which surrounded it proved extremely effective in positively focusing employee attention on the future. It also led to an improvement in employee morale and created considerable goodwill between the new management and its workforce. This was reflected in many comments made directly to the new managing director by the employees. This was a change in itself, in that such an approach was entirely uncharacteristic of the previous culture. Delightedly, he recounted this particular comment made by the spouse of a machine operator:

This [the opening event] was a wonderful idea. My husband has worked for the Jones Group for over twenty years, and this is the very first time I have had an opportunity to see exactly where he works and what he spends most of his days doing.

The success of the event had other ancillary benefits. When the 'official' opening took place several days later, employees acted to respond to this goodwill by 'putting on a good show' for their important visitors. As the MD described it, 'They really did us proud! Visitors commented on the smiling faces, courteous response and eagerness with which employees explained various aspects of the work process.'

Stage 3

Monitoring the success of the integration

The acquisition of the packaging division of the Jones Group by the Smith Group proved to be less problematic than originally expected. Six months post acquisition, everything appeared to be going well, and all the signs seemed indicative that the acquisition would prove financially successful. However, as a confirmatory check, a further series of interviews were conducted, and a questionnaire prepared and distributed to all employees to establish the current culture of the organization, the present level of job satisfaction, motivation and commitment and to identify any continued areas of employee concern. All employees who had been previously interviewed were invited to participate in this re-evaluation, together with a number of randomly selected employees who had joined since the acquisition. Again, this initiative was well received by employees and achieved a good response; 85 per cent of the original sample volunteered to be re-interviewed.

This acquisition integration programme was particularly successful in helping the acquiring management to plan their integration strategy. It was most effective in re-establishing organizational trust and renewed organizational commitment in an extremely short period of time.

Stage 3 of the project proved to be critical. While acquiring management had devoted a considerable amount of time and energy to paving the way for the change, the level of communication had decreased since the transfer to the new factory. Employees reported a high level of satisfaction with the way in which the transfer had been handled but considered that, six months post acquisition, they were notably less well informed on organizational matters than they had been initially. Other organizational issues, particularly the setting up of new machinery and the pursuit of new markets, had tended to dominate managerial thinking and distract from continuing 'people' issues. The interview and follow-up questionnaires were effective in refocusing managerial attention and identifying areas in which the acquisition was not working out as well as expected.

The results of a study (Schweiger and DeNisi, 1991) carried out in the USA has provided further support of the efficacy of realistic merger previews and communication programmes. The research was conducted in two manufacturing plants belonging to one of two merging *Fortune* 500 companies. The study compared levels of employee uncertainty and job satisfaction between the two plants. Measures were taken four weeks before the announcement of the merger (Time 1), two weeks after the merger announcement (Time 3), ten days later (Time 5) and finally a further three months later (Time 6). Measures were also taken to assess employee perceptions of the company's trustworthiness, honesty and caring. Over seventy employees at each plant completed questionnaires at each time stage.

At one of the plants, the Control Plant, employees did not receive any formal communications concerning the merger other than the initial letter from the CEO. This provided minimal information and was typical of the approach adopted by the company in previous circumstances of organizational change.

Employees at the other plant, the Experimental Plant, received a similar letter but in addition were provided with a Realistic Merger Preview (RMP). This programme began one week after the second survey administration (Time 5). The RMP programme was designed to provide employees with specific information about how the merger would affect them, immediately that information became available:

1 Twice a month employees received a merger newsletter detailing the organizational changes that would result from the merger.
2 A telephone hotline was set up. This was answered by the personnel manager who dealt with general queries concerning the merger.
3 Weekly meetings/briefings were held between the plant manager, supervisors and employees to provide information and discuss implementation–integration plans.

The results demonstrate the effectiveness of such programmes in reducing the negative impact of merger, particularly in reducing employee uncertainty. (See Figures 11.1 to 11.3.)

Immediately following the merger announcement, a change for the worse occurred at both plants, but once the RMP programme was introduced the situation in the Experimental Plant began to stabilize. Over time, perceptions of the company's trustworthiness, honesty and caring, together with self-reported performance levels, almost returned to pre-merger levels.

The authors raise an interesting issue as to whether the actual content of the communication at this time is of lesser importance than the mere

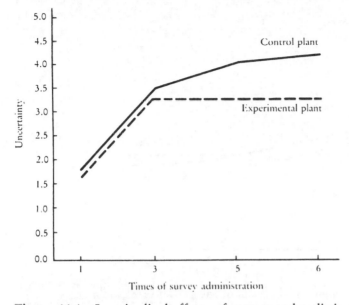

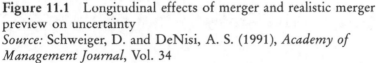

Figure 11.1 Longitudinal effects of merger and realistic merger preview on uncertainty
Source: Schweiger, D. and DeNisi, A. S. (1991), *Academy of Management Journal*, Vol. 34

process of communicating. In this particular study, the accuracy of the content of the communications could not be verified in that the company only communicated its *intended* future actions. It is suggested that employees in the Experimental Plant responded less negatively towards the merger primarily because they felt that the organization cared about them.

The way forward

Throughout this book we have focused on two important aspects of the merger/acquisition process:

1 The issue of culture and the role of culture type in influencing response to culture change.
2 The way in which the merger/acquisition integration process is managed.

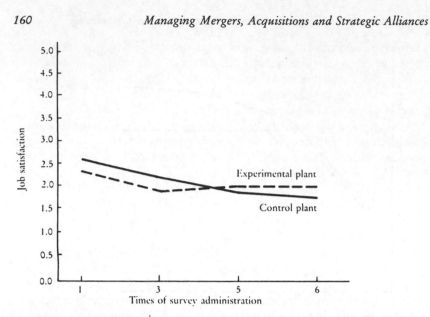

Figure 11.2 Longitudinal effects of merger and realistic merger preview on job satisfaction
Source: Schweiger and DeNisi (1991)

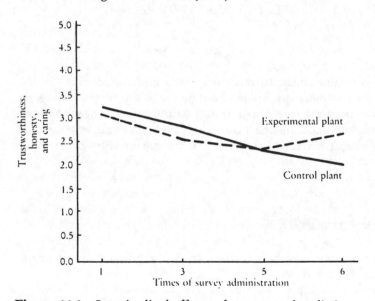

Figure 11.3 Longitudinal effects of merger and realistic merger preview on perceived trustworthiness, honesty and caring of the company
Source: Schweiger and DeNisi (1991)

We have conceptualized organizational marriages as falling into three types: the open marriage, the traditional marriage and the collaborative marriage. We have chosen to continue to draw upon the analogy between merger and marriage throughout this book, as we consider the analogy most fitting in communicating the perceived consequential importance, emotionality and difficulties which organizations face when they elect to combine forces with another. Furthermore, on the basis of the existing evidence, both civil and organizational marriages would seem to have about the same chance of long-term success.

In the same way as society is having to rethink its attitudes towards marriage, and move away from the concept of the traditional marriage, organizations would be well advised to re-examine their approach to merger and acquisition and other similar forms of strategic alliance. A successful organizational marriage, like a civil marriage, develops over time and requires give and take from both partners. Cultural evolution through collaboration and cooperation may be a more appropriate approach than that of cultural revolution, which is the dominant mode of most mergers and acquisitions at the present time. The concept of mergers and acquisitions as a 'win/lose' game, with one partner automatically achieving and exercising supremacy over the other, has had a powerful effect in shaping attitudes towards the activity.

The role of people in determining merger and acquisition outcomes is in reality not a soft, but a hard issue. Without the commitment of those who produce the goods and services, make decisions and conceive strategies, mergers and acquisitions will fail to achieve their synergizing potential as a wealth-creating strategy.

Whether the combination is technically a merger or an acquisition, it should be responded to as presenting an opportunity for shared learning and collaboration. It is the responsibility of those who initiate and implement merger decisions to create the appropriate psychological climate, which reduces the negative feelings associated with merger. Throughout the book we have emphasized the importance of recognizing and understanding the culture of the acquired organization or other merger partner and the formulation of an informed human-merger plan. In summary, if the rate of future merger failure is to be improved, organizations should be guided by the following six-point inventory to merger success:

- Make an informed choice of merger partner that takes into account culture fit as well as financial and strategic fit.
- Begin effective 'people' planning prior to the merger event.
- Recognize the importance of people and their concerns, and take action to address the latter.

- Get to know the acquired organization or other merger partner and the way it operates, particularly at grass-roots level.
- Establish effective communication networks and opportunities for employee involvement.
- Remain in touch with employees, and reassess and monitor the success of the integration process.

References

Cooper, C.L. Reynold, P. and Sadri, G. (1989). *Stress counselling in industry: The Post Office experience*. Paper presented at the Annual Conference of the British Psychological Society, St Andrews, Scotland, March.

Elkin, A.J. and Rosch, P.J. (1990). Promoting mental health at the workplace: The prevention side of stress management. *Occupational Medicine: State of the Art Reviews*, 5(4), October–December.

Fulmer, R. (1986). Meeting the merger integration challenge with management development. *Journal of Management Development*, 5(4), 7–16.

Fulmer, R.M. and Gilkey, R. (1988). Blending corporate families: Management and organization development, in a postmerger environment. *Academy of Management Executive*, 2(4), 275–283.

Hall, P.D. and Norburn, D. (1987). The management factor in acquisition performance. *Leadership and Organizational Development Journal*, 8(3), 23–30.

Kahn, R.L., Wolfe, D.M., Quinne, R.P., Snoek, J.D. and Rosenthal, R.A. (1964). *Organizational Stress*. New York: John Wiley & Sons.

Karasek, R. and Theorell, T. (1990). *Healthy Work: Stress, Productivity and the Reconstruction of Working Life*. New York: Basic Books.

Kay, E. (1974). Middle management. In *Work and the Quality of Work Life* (J. O'Toole, ed.), Cambridge, Massachusetts: MIT Press.

Lewin, K. (1947). Frontiers of group dynamics. *Human Relations*, 1, 5–41 and 143–153.

Mercer, M.W. (1988). The taken over: Crises, panic and a vanishing past. *Directors and Boards – Human Resources*, Spring, 12–15.

Robertson, I.T. and Cooper, C.L. (1983). *Human Behaviour in Organizations*. London: Pitman.

Selye, H. (1974). *Stress Without Distress*. Philadelphia: J.B. Lippincott.

Schweiger, D.M. and DeNisi, A.S. (1991). Communication with employees following a merger: A longitudinal field experiment. *Academy of Management Journal*, 34, 110–135.

Sutherland, V.J. (1990). Current developments. In *Health Psychology* (P. Bennett, J. Weinman and P. Spurgeon, eds), London: Harwood Academic Publishers.

Appendices

Appendix 1

Case Study 1: the Fast Car acquisitions – same acquirer, different outcomes

This case study concerns the acquisition of Greenside Motors (a power culture) and Princess Garage (a person/support culture) by Fast Car (a role/task culture). The case study serves to illustrate a number of points, in particular:

1 The problems of rapid growth caused by multiple and concurrent acquisitions.
2 The impact of the acquisition announcement.
3 The intuitive assessments of competence and ability to fit in that acquirers typically make in the initial days/weeks of the acquisition.
4 The role of culture type in determining employee response to culture change and its implications for organizational outcomes.

Background to the study

The Fast Car Company, a motor trader, had begun life almost eighty years ago as a small family concern. Having survived the difficulties of the Second World War, it became a public limited company under the management of the founding family. This tradition was still continuing in that two of its current directors were third generation family members. However, although the organization retained a sense of pride in its heritage, e.g. all employees who reached twenty-one years of service were admitted to a special in-house club, the organization had itself recently undergone a major structural and cultural transformation.

Five years ago, Fast Car had found itself in serious financial difficulties and as a result had appointed its first 'non-family' managing director, Mr Jones, who was recruited from outside the organization and already had a reputation within the industry as a 'high flier'. Since his appointment he had been successful in turning the company around from a loss-making situation to a turnover in excess of £150 million and an annual profit approaching £5 million. This feat, he was proud to point out, was achieved by displacing and changing the established patriarchal power culture while still essentially retaining the existing workforce, many of whom had been with the organization for a long time.

Fast Car operated as a multi-franchise dealer through a network of branches in the North of England, and at the time of the acquisitions employed approximately 800 employees. Each dealership functioned as an autonomous profit centre, and Fast Car was described by its managers as an organization in which managers were allowed to manage.

Because of franchise restrictions imposed by motor vehicle manu-facturers, Fast Car were unable to open any further new branches in the immediate area. Therefore, it had been decided to expand into neighbour-ing geographical regions, either by opening new dealerships in territories where franchises were still available or through the strategic acquisition of existing dealerships. The acquisition of Greenside Motors and Princess Garage, both in the same year, represented a major first stage in their strategic plan. The company had made acquisitions before but not for many years and not within the lifetime of the current senior management. The acquisitions' first-year performance was considered to be crucially important, as the high level of investment made the Fast Car Company itself, particularly given prevailing market conditions, vulnerable to takeover.

In common with most horizontal acquisitions, from the outset Fast Car was not prepared to adopt a 'hands-off' approach. Its objective was to impose its own culture on its newly acquired ventures as quickly as possible.

The culture of Fast Car

In the time we spent getting to know the culture of Fast Car before the acquisition negotiations were completed, it was apparent that the appointment of Mr Jones had resulted in a major change in the culture of Fast Car. Indeed, without any prompting, employees drew the distinction between the culture pre/post his arrival.

Pre-Jones, the culture of Fast Car had been essentially a patriarchal power culture. Employee loyalty was paramount, family members were referred to familiarly but respectfully as Mr William, Mr Arthur, etc. There were many unwritten rules, decisions were made by a small nucleus and, as a result, as the organization grew, the decision-making process was slow. Employees frequently recalled that if a problem arose and reference to a family member was not possible, employees tried to envisage 'what Mr William would want them to do'.

In contrast, Fast Car now had a high profile, aggressive market image and a large PR budget. Power was more diffuse, although there was still some hesitancy among managers to exercise that power. The organization had an energetic, highly visible open and informal managerial style. Competition between dealerships was positively encouraged, and there were regular well-published 'league tables' showing their comparative performance. Fast Car was an organization which expected its managers to work very long hours. There was a plethora of management meetings, many of which were held outside normal working hours. The physical open-plan layout of the refurbished headquarters reflected this open management style.

Fast Car took management and management training very seriously. It had an extensive training programme for all levels of staff, and both 'in-house' and external courses were held regularly. Since Jones' appointment, there had been an influx of professionally qualified managers. The importance Fast Car placed on professional management was reflected in the content of the reading material which littered the reception area at its head office, which included business school journals and other similar literature. They had introduced quality-circle type programmes and operated team-briefing procedures. Fast Car even ran an in-house training course specifically designed to socialize newcomers into the Fast Car culture.

Fast Car had become increasingly image conscious; it wanted all its branches to portray the same corporate image. Many of its branches occupied old premises and an extensive modernization programme was underway. This included the installation of coffee machines, children's play areas, televisions, soft furnishings, etc. to the customer service areas. The cost of any capital expenditure was charged to each individual unit. Although Fast Car operated from owned premises, dealerships were levied with the appropriate market rent. The present CEO was keen to improve communications and increase employee participation at all levels. A glossy in-house magazine had been introduced which, as well as providing company gossip, contained a considerable amount of information relating to company performance. The organization ran an 'Employee of the Month' award and photographs of the winning employee were prominently displayed. There were also plans to extend the 'clocking in/out' system to all levels of employees including managers, and an experimental scheme was already in place.

In recent years, a profit-sharing scheme had been introduced which extended to all employees and every employee was obliged to attend the Employees' Annual General Meeting. Employees seemed particularly impressed by this initiative, especially because of the CEO's demonstrated ability to greet each attending individual by name.

Fast Car wanted to be the MacDonalds or Marks & Spencer of the motor trade. It was unmistakably a profit-hungry company. If managers could not produce results they were replaced, and every employee knew and appeared to accept this.

Its size and type of business activity, which relied on mass volume sales and standardized customer service, dictated the adoption of a predominantly role culture in terms of its structure, formalization and regulation of working practices. There were detailed job descriptions, graded remuneration systems, and regular formal job-holder appraisals. The role function was as important, if not more important than the individual who filled it. Employees were expected to wear badges, ties, etc. displaying the company logo. Slogans were also frequently used to motivate and remind employees of organizational goals, e.g. 'Get it right first time', 'Second best is not good enough'. Each year a major campaign was launched to introduce a slogan which reflected the organization's theme for the current financial year. Consistent with a role culture, decisions and basis for action were supported by rational explanation and logic. While the culture of Fast Car was essentially role, it still retained the opportunity to function when required as a matrix organization. Therefore, it also displayed strong elements of a task culture in terms of its managerial style and the emphasis it placed on increasing employee participation.

During the time we spent within the Fast Car organization, observing its daily activities and talking both formally and informally with its members, we were impressed by the strength and coherence of its organizational culture, which we categorized as being an 'open role/task' culture. This assessment was further confirmed when we distributed the culture questionnaire to employees at all levels throughout the entire network of some twelve or more branches. Not only did the questionnaire achieve a high response rate of 77 per cent, but, irrespective of whether the respondents were managers, sales personnel, clerks or technicians, they expressed a consistent and commonly shared perception of the way in which things get done at Fast Car.

Summary

On the basis of the observational, interview and questionnaire data, the main characteristics of the Fast Car culture were:

1 A highly visible and approachable senior management.
2 Clear role definitions.
3 Highly formalized rules and regulations.
4 Strong team spirit.

5 An open and informative managerial style.
6 A deliberately promoted competitive environment.
7 Features consistency with an 'open role/task' culture.

Greenside Motors

The earlier history of Greenside Motors had in many ways paralleled that of Fast Car. Greenside had been established as a family business around the same time as Fast Car, but, while in the last five years Fast Car had been expanding, Greenside had substantially contracted its operations. Whereas at one time it had operated as many as ten branches, it now conducted its business from three locations, and had for three years only showed a modest profit.

In contrast with Fast Car, Greenside had remained a private limited company of whom all the shareholders were descendants of the original founding family. The managing director, Mr Charles, and the administrative director, Miss April, were family members, and together they ran the company.

Over the years, shareholders had been reluctant to make any additional funds available for modernization and the physical working conditions were generally poor, although not untypical of motor dealers. The present managing director, Mr Charles, in his late forties, was generally considered to live very much in the shadow of his predecessor, i.e. his father. One of the reasons that Greenside had been put up for sale was that there was no natural successor within the family to take over the business when Mr Charles retired.

At the time of the acquisition, Greenside Motors had 290 employees, many of whom had been with the company for over fifteen years. There were many similarities between the culture of Greenside Motors and that of Fast Car before the arrival of Fast Car's present MD. Greenside had a patriarchal power culture. Power was exercised by a small nucleus, referred to by employees as the 'inner sanctum' and decision making was centralized. The managerial style was distinctly formal, and Fast Car themselves had commented how surprised it was by the polite but formal manner in which negotiations had taken place. According to them, Greenside's managing director had 'played his cards very close to his chest' and was not particularly forthcoming with information even when pressed. To some extent this is to be expected in such circumstances, but Fast Car had already been involved in a number of previous unconsummated acquisition negotiations, and considered these to be markedly more formal than any previously experienced.

Employees at Greenside Motors were used to being told what to do. A 'good' employee was a 'loyal' employee. Discussion of organizational decisions was not encouraged and therefore rarely took place. While there were no formalized job descriptions, there were plenty of unwritten rules. Employees were little informed as to what was going on within the organization, and nobody below director level had any clear idea or factual information on the financial performance of the company. All communications were channelled through the managing director. Consequently, there was no direct interdepartmental liaison, and members of one department had little or no contact with their counterparts in another department. When all the employees were invited to an evening event Fast Car had arranged to introduce themselves the day after the acquisition announcement, they found that many of the Greensiders did not even know each other, and introductions had to be effected.

There was no formal salary structure or company car policy at Greenside. Salaries were reviewed at the discretion of the managing director, and so there were considerable anomalies. There was a general consensus among managers that salary increases were given in reward for personal loyalty rather than merit, or because an employee was bold enough to knock on the MD's closed door and broach the subject. Greenside Motors was an organization in which many employees were given the title of manager, but this only conferred an honorary status and carried little or no real power. In contrast with Fast Car, social activities outside working hours rarely if ever took place. A rather unprofessionally produced newsletter was circulated once a year.

Communications between superior and subordinate were consistent with a power culture, being essentially in the mode of 'parent to child'. The role assumed by Mr Charles was very reminiscent of that of headteacher. He knew all the employees by name and felt paternalistic towards them. While prepared frequently to tour the organization and exchange pleasantries, he remained remote and distant; employees would not voluntarily approach his office uninvited. Such a summons was therefore synonymous with 'bad news' and meant a scolding, in that employees only expected to receive feedback on negative aspects of their behaviour.

Summary

On the basis of the observational, interview and questionnaire data, the main characteristics of the Greenside Motors culture were:

1 Benevolent but formal managerial style.
2 Strong reliance on formal authority.

3 Poor communications – little/no organizational information to employees – poor feedback on performance.
4 No clear reward policy.
5 Centralized decision making – many managers/little power.
6 Lots of unwritten rules and regulations.
7 Features consistent with a patriarchal power culture.

Princess Garage

Fast Car acquired Princess Garage, another long-established business, within three weeks of acquiring Greenside Motors. Princess Garage was situated in a small prosperous spa town about twelve miles from Greenside. It formed a small unprofitable part of a family business, the primary activity of which was property ownership and development.

It had been originally formed to provide a garaging and servicing facility for the clientele of a local hotel owned by the family property business. It had then occupied premises adjacent to the hotel. Approximately thirteen years before, Princess Garage secured a franchise agreement to sell new cars and relocated to larger premises on the edge of town. At the time of its acquisition, it employed eighty-eight people.

According to organizational folklore, Princess Garage had been formed to satisfy the whim of one of the family members who fancied owning a garage. It had traditionally been regarded as something of a 'hobby' and had consistently failed to show a profit. When the 'hobby' eventually proved too expensive, reluctantly a decision to sell was made. Fast Car's MD confirmed the validity of this story when discussing the deal negotiations:

> Mr Hughes [the family member involved] had recognized for a long time that Princess was never going to make any money unless it changed – changed ownership or got rid of many of its people. But he didn't have the heart to impose that change himself so he allowed it to continue as it was – the people were happy there but they couldn't make money. That's how things were. It was OK for Princess Garage to lose money so long as it didn't lose too much. When that happened Mr Hughes had no alternative and he reluctantly put it up for sale.

The culture of Princess Garage

The present managing director, Mr Walters, a popular avuncular figure, had been with Princess Garage for over thirty years, in which time he acknowledged that he was never placed under any real pressure to improve financial performance. He also considered that he had very limited power over the affairs of Princess Garage other than, in his words, 'ensuring things ticked over and people were happy at their work'. Control and responsibility rested entirely with the individual family member, Mr Hughes, with whom he met on a monthly basis to refer and discuss matters relating to the business.

Mr Walters commented that if for some reason either party could not meet on the prearranged date, the meeting was then postponed for another month. This process of referral meant that decision making was sluggish and remote. One manager, who had been with Princess Garage three years, described Princess Garage and its employees as 'generally sluggish in their response to anything'. This comment was echoed many times throughout the course of the study, particularly by Fast Car in respect of their regular requests for monthly figures or other information from the organization.

We also found that one of the most remarkable features about Princess Garage was its marked lack of time urgency. Appointments to visit the premises were frequently cancelled or postponed, and deadlines for the return of questionnaires were ignored. The atmosphere was cosy and unhurried. The dominant mode of internal and external communication was by letter or memo, in contrast to Fast Car who preferred the expediency of the telephone and regarded car phones as a necessity rather than a luxury or perk.

Employees were referred to either by their forename or more formally addressed by their title and surname, whichever their personal preference. All were comfortable, and respected this mixture in form of address. The managerial style was soft, supportive and extremely tolerant towards the shortcomings and mistakes of employees. It operated from the premise that people are basically good. In contrast to Fast Car's slogan 'Second best is not good enough', Princess Garage's motto was more in the tolerant spirit of 'Do the best you can'.

While control and responsibility for business activities rested with one person external to the organization, the internal everyday culture of the organization closely approximated a person/support culture. Typical of such cultures, any critical evaluations about members' performance were avoided out of kindness. Also, there was a noticeable tendency for members to act towards each other in such a way that there was never any danger that they could be accused of interfering or treading on anybody's toes.

Harrison (1972) suggests that person/support cultures are a rarity in commercial organizations, but for over thirteen years, i.e. within the lifetime of most of its members, Princess Garage had indeed been a non-profit-making organization.

Summary

On the basis of the observational, interview and questionnaire data, the main characteristics of the Princess Garage were:

1 Soft approachable management with little real power – any control exercised from outside the organization.
2 Supportive, insular and unpressured climate.
3 Slow to respond to external environment.
4 Employee problems are organizational problems.
5 No clear reward policy, formalized rules, minimal structure.
6 Organization exists to serve its employees as much, if not more than, its customers.
7 Features consistent with external power culture and predominant internal person/support culture.

Initial cultural relationship between the combining organizations

At the time of the acquisition, the acquirer and the two acquired organizations each had a different type of organizational culture. Fast Car had a strong coherent open role/task culture; Greenside had a power culture; and the internal day-to-day culture of Princess Garage closely approximated a person/support culture.

While the cultures of both acquisitions were different in type from that of Fast Car, there were significantly more differences between Fast Car and Princess Garage than Fast Car and Greenside. In translating these differences to objectively measured organizational practices and behaviour, the culture questionnaire revealed statistically significant differences between Fast Car and Princess Garage in seven main areas. In contrast, the main differences between Fast Car and Greenside lay in two areas: openness of managerial style and the degree of competition inherent in the organizational climate. (See Figure App. 1.1.)

As discussed in the model outlined in Chapter 6, when two cultures come together there are four possible modes of acculturation: assimilation, integration, separation or deculturation. In common with most horizontal acquisitions, any possibility of allowing the acquired organization to maintain a separate and different culture from its acquirer was out of the question. The possibility of any integration of cultures was equally remote. Fast Car's strategic objective was to impose its own successfully proven culture, and it was not prepared to compromise with any forces

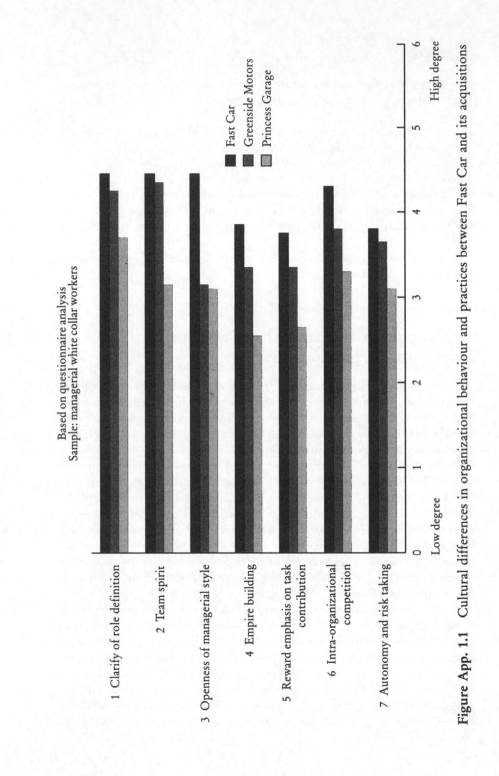

Figure App. 1.1 Cultural differences in organizational behaviour and practices between Fast Car and its acquisitions

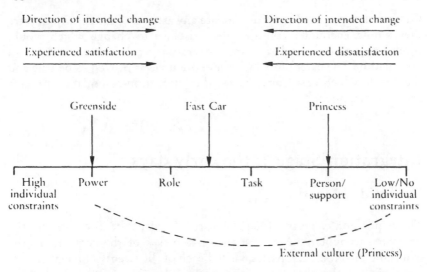

Figure App. 1.2 Initial cultural relations

acting upon it which emanated from the 'unsuccessful' cultures of its acquisitions. It was not a question of how well the cultures would combine, but more importantly, how quickly and easily they would be displaced and replaced by the Fast Car culture. Therefore, in the context of these and most acquisitions, successful outcomes for both the organization and its individual members were dependent upon the acquisitions becoming completely assimilated into the dominant culture of Fast Car. The model in Figure App. 1.2 illustrates the initial relationship between the cultures and the proposed direction of culture change.

The results of the earlier joint venture study had suggested that movement from a highly constraining culture was experienced by individuals as more satisfying than a move in the opposite direction, and is consistent with acculturation theory. Organizational members are likely to be more willing to abandon power or role cultures, because they are experienced as oppressive or dissatisfying, in favour of task or support cultures which are likely to be perceived as more attractive.

Given the cultural dynamics, it was predicted that Fast Car were more likely to achieve an effective and successful culture change at Greenside Motors than at Princess Garage, because there would be a greater willingness to assimilate. It seemed likely that employees at Princess would be unwilling totally to abandon a long-established and deeply ingrained person/support culture. Therefore, it was expected that if Fast

Car were not prepared to accommodate any aspects of the existing culture they would encounter considerable resistance to change which would result in growing insularity and separation at Princess rather than assimilation. The extent to which these predictions proved to be true and the way in which Fast Car managed the integration/assimilation process are now examined.

Integration Stage 1: the early days

Greenside Motors

The acquisition came as a total shock to all except the directors and the company accountant. At 11.00 am on the day of the acquisition, the managing director, Mr Charles, visited each of the twenty-three managers and told them that they were to be at a local hotel by midday. No reason was given for this unusual summoning and, as a further illustration of Greenside's culture, nobody asked for any explanation.

Nobody entertained the possibility that a takeover had precipitated such a mysterious event. The consensus of opinion was that the most likely explanation was that a 'surprise' party was being staged for Miss April's forthcoming retirement. And so, as one manager described it, 'they went like lambs to the slaughter'.

Fast Car as an organization was not well known in the Midlands, and it was anxious to impress its size and importance on its new members. To this end, it had commissioned an outside public relations company to prepare and stage a video presentation describing the organization, its goals and past achievements. Almost all of the senior executives of Fast Car attended the event and delivered a series of set pieces attesting to the strength and success of the organization. In the celebratory tradition of a birthday or christening party, all those who attended received gifts – a copy of a book published to commemorate Fast Car's recent 75th anniversary, and the inevitable company tie, tie pin and badge. On the following evening, a less formal introductory event was arranged for all the employees; of the 290 employees, all except one attended. These presentations formed a significant and lasting first impression of the Fast Car organization for the acquired employees, in particular the fact that it was a professionally managed results-orientated company.

In the first two weeks post acquisition, Greenside Motors was inundated with visits from Fast Car personnel. The installation of Fast Car's accounting systems and procedures being a major priority along with the commitment to reduce numbers, and prepare the way for the installation of their 'own skipper' at the helm. In the context of this acquisition, it was only managerial and administrative jobs which were vulnerable. From discussions with Fast Car, the decision to remove the top tier of management at Greenside had been made from the outset. Miss April began her retirement on the day the acquisition was announced. By the end of two weeks, Mr Charles and all but one of the previous directors had been asked to leave, including the director who had personally opened the negotiations with Fast Car.

Within days of becoming more familiar with the existing organizational structure, Fast Car decided that, in terms of middle management, Greenside was top heavy and needed extensive pruning. Decisions as to who they wished to retain and who they wished to displace were made very quickly and informally. Fast Car managers compared notes and first impressions of the managers they had met over lunch or travelling in the car. They all had a similar template as to what a Fast Car manager should be like, and existing Greenside managers were quickly matched or rejected against this template. Although Fast Car had a sophisticated method of managerial selection already available to them, one which incorporated the use of psychometric tests and other techniques, personnel decisions they made at Greenside were entirely subjective and based on the informal and intuitive evaluation of one or two of their managers.

During the early weeks post acquisition, Greenside personnel felt their personality and job performance were being closely scrutinized. It became a period in which it was important to create an impression of willingness to change, if 'one was to keep one's job'. There was considerable anxiety about job security and managers were especially concerned about the likelihood of geographical relocation. The anxiety about job security was endemic, even amongst the technicians on the shopfloor, even though Fast Car had no plans to reduce staffing in this area. Survival became an obsession. In the words of one manager interviewed in the week following the acquisition, 'People are desperately looking for clues – any clues from wherever, that tell them what they should do or say to reduce their uncertainty.'

At the time of this visit many employees were already wearing their Fast Car ties and badges. These employees overtly expressed more optimism than the others. The wearing of such items was seen as symbolic of their rejection of the past and a desire to become part of the Fast Car culture, and this seemed to be the message the bearers intended to convey. Interestingly, these were the managers who were still with Greenside twelve months later.

Employees at Greenside were unfamiliar with the very open and 'discussive' style of management characteristic of Fast Car. In the early days, this produced a major culture shock. At Greenside, if something was spoken of, it was certainly going to happen. Therefore, great confusion and uncertainty was generated whenever Fast Car personnel toured the premises suggesting a possible change here or there. To Fast Car, it was customary to float a variety of alternative suggestions for later discussion and evaluation; to the ever-listening Greenside personnel, however, these were interpreted as firmly decided actions, though they were often contradictory. In consequence, Fast Car personnel had to spend a considerable amount of energy dispelling rumours, of which unwittingly they themselves were the source.

The stark contrast between the 'closed' power culture of Greenside and the more open culture of its acquirer created an immediate problem for Fast Car. Prior to the acquisition, inter-departmental communication was poor; the positive outcome of the acquisition was that communication within the organization greatly increased. Consequently, the considerable anomalies in the pay and reward systems, of which employees were previously unaware, became widely known and became a major source of dissatisfaction.

The acquisition event had a noticeable effect on increasing organizational cohesiveness. As an organization in which employees were minimally informed, and few people knew anyone beyond their immediate work group, Greenside would hardly fit the description of a team culture. Yet, 63 per cent of the respondents who completed our initial questionnaire two weeks post acquisition considered the organization to have a strong sense of team spirit.

Princess Garage

In many respects, the timing of this acquisition so soon after the Greenside acquisition was unfortunate as far as Fast Car was concerned. Such a considerable amount of managerial time and effort was already being expended at Greenside that the acquisition of the much smaller Princess Garage came somewhat as an anti-climax. To the MD of Fast Car, the timing was particularly problematic, as he considered that he did not have a suitable Fast Car manager available to place immediately at Princess Garage.

In an organization in which personal status and reward were so strongly linked to financial results, persuading existing managers to relocate and leave the security of established dealerships was not easy.

As a stop-gap arrangement, the incumbent managing director, Mr Walters, was asked to postpone his intended retirement and assume the role of 'caretaker manager' until a suitable replacement could be found.

Originally, it was planned to stage an identical presentation on the day of the acquisition to that given at Greenside. At the last moment, for various reasons, i.e. lack of space, unavailability of the PR consultancy staff, this was not possible. An adapted and less well-synchronized version was presented entirely by Fast Car personnel. Fast Car were unhappy about this, and felt it was less successful in presenting the professional and dynamic image it would have liked.

The presentation took place in a local hotel in the evening of the day the sale was signed. All employees were invited and most of them attended. Unlike at Greenside, the news of the acquisition was not entirely unexpected. Rumours had been circulating for some weeks previously, and many of the managers had already been informed that a deal with Fast Car was about to be closed. Less well-informed employees suspected that the site was about to be sold for development as a Fast-way supermarket. They were therefore very relieved that it had been sold as a viable business to Fast Car. The general mood at this time at Princess Garage was considerably more optimistic than it had been at Greenside. Employees talked of the prospect of pay rises and modernization programmes rather than of fear of redundancies. They considered that as Fast Car had acquired both Greenside and Princess within a month, they were likely to be a rich and hence potentially generous employer. To quote one employee, 'Fast Car certainly have plenty of money to throw around!' At the presentation, Fast Car invited employees to submit written questions they might have about the acquisition and their future anonymously. Of the questions submitted, none related to the issue of workforce reduction but instead focused upon pay and reward comparisons with Fast Car's existing employees, and the continuation of existing benefits such as private health insurance.

Apart from experiencing an increasing demand for information on a daily basis from its new head office, in the first few weeks following the acquisition, Princess Garage was very much left alone. Mr Walters stayed on as caretaker manager, a role which, he confided, in many ways he had always occupied. During this period, nine employees voluntarily resigned and one accepted early retirement. In all other respects, business very much continued as usual.

Unlike at Greenside, there was little evidence of symbolic cultural adaptation, in that employees had not taken to wearing Fast Car badges, ties, logos, etc.

Integration Stage 2: the honeymoon period

Greenside Motors – seven weeks post acquisition

A new younger dealer manager, an existing employee of Fast Car, had been appointed and was now in place. He had managed previous dealerships within the group and he described his objective as being 'to make Greenside Motors like any other dealership within the Fast Car group'. Sales targets had already been set for Greenside for the next three years, and within the first year it was required to show a substantial profit. The new manager was still very much an outsider to Greenside employees, and he remarked that he felt that 'he still had to be careful with his coffee – as you didn't know what they might put into it'. He had installed himself in a new office. The old MD's office was left unoccupied, and remained so during the entire period of the research, becoming symbolic of the end of an era for Greenside.

Another Fast Car employee had also been brought in to replace the sales manager, a key organizational member, who had been poached by a nearby competitor in the early days following the acquisition. Fast Car were surprised and somewhat disappointed by his departure. He had been with Greenside over ten years and had some valuable contacts. His departure, together with the dismissal of two managers, seven administrative staff and a further ten voluntary resignations, had further heightened anxiety. Although Fast Car did not intend to carry out any salary review until the following year, it had graded all employees in line with its existing reward system. A formal company car policy had been introduced. Therefore, some employees had their cars upgraded, others had lost the benefit.

The structure and reporting arrangements had been substantially changed. A six-person management team had been formed which met regularly, initially on a daily basis, then as things started to settle down, once a week. Attempts were still being made to integrate Greenside fully within Fast Car accounting and budgetary systems. Plans were underway to move the accounting and administrative functions to a secondary location and introduce a fully computerized system. Managers were already being sent on training courses, etc., and were given detailed job descriptions, and new and wider responsibilities.

While initially every employee questioned had expressed concern about their job security, by now the remaining managers considered that the 'cull' was over. Having survived, they felt more optimistic. In particular, they considered their economic worth to the new organization had not only been proven but had effectively increased. They expected

Fast Car to recognize this by way of a pay increase, on the basis that since the takeover their responsibilities had increased, requiring them to work much longer hours.

Even at this early stage, there was evidence that employees had well-developed perceptions of the Fast Car culture – in particular its emphasis on cost efficiency and the speed with which it expected things to happen. In the words of one administrator manager:

> Things have happened very quickly – it's much tougher than it was. We were all very down in the first week or two. But we know what Fast Car expects of us. Younger people like me see it as an opportunity.

A parts manager similarly commented:

> Mr Charles made all the decisions – everybody else was frightened of doing anything on their own initiative. Important information, figures, profits, etc. were kept from employees. Before it was more relaxed, slower ... Now we know we have to do things the Fast Car way – that means decisions are made quicker and more is expected of individuals.

The questionnaire survey carried out at this time, to assess current attitudes towards the acquisition, found that the majority of white collar workers considered the takeover had resulted in beneficial and personal outcomes in improving the quality of work life and increasing self-esteem. They considered that the positive outcomes, in particular the more dynamic corporate image and the more open, informative organizational culture which was now developing, far exceeded the more short-term and hence temporary negative outcomes (e.g. the unsettling effects on employees/staff losses). Three-quarters of respondents considered their future job prospects were better now than they were before the acquisition. However, despite the positive attitudes towards change, renewed organizational commitment was not yet established and 54 per cent were still considering leaving the organization because they were dissatisfied with their current level of financial reward.

Also, this optimism did not appear to have permeated to the lower levels of the organization. At shopfloor level there was still considerable and, on the face of it, unnecessary concern about job security. Direct exposure to the new culture was limited. It was noted that while the new managing director maintained high visibility within the showroom and offices, his face was unknown in the repair and body shop.

The questionnaire data collected at this time validated the observational/interview data in confirming that managers and supervisory staff were generally positive towards the acquisition, and willing to abandon their old culture and adopt the new culture of their acquirer.

Princess Garage – nine weeks post acquisition

When we visited the organization at this time, Mr Walters was about to retire from his position as caretaker manager. Fast Car had been unable to find a suitable internal candidate to take over the running of the dealership, and had been forced to make an external appointment. Mr Walters was visibly relieved to be going, as he had found the pace of the last nine weeks extremely demanding, particularly the regularity with which he was called to attend management meetings.

Since the acquisition, there had been more staff movement than usual. It had become a standing joke that everybody rushed to get the paper on Thursday to read the job vacancies. In total, sixteen employees had left the organization; one had accepted early retirement, three had been made redundant and twelve had resigned voluntarily. The redundancies had occurred because Fast Car was in the process of computerizing the administrative department.

There was now widespread concern about job security, although the existing management structure was still intact. The majority of management and sales personnel had been interviewed by Fast Car personnel and detailed job descriptions drawn up. Similarly to Greenside, managers were now given more autonomy and decision-making power. They had also been presented with detailed target figures for the next twelve months. Employees seemed now to be considering how well they would match up to their new job demands and meet Fast Car's expectations. The personnel manager reported that she was increasingly finding herself in the role of stress counsellor, and felt that personnel at all levels were visiting her office on various pretexts but primarily to discuss their worries. Visiting Fast Car personnel were very much scrutinized, the consensus of opinion that their youthful and lean physical appearance was a reflection of Fast Car's corporate image.

All the employees commented on the change in atmosphere. Mr Walters was a popular and respected figure who took the welfare and personal development of his employees seriously. The pre-acquisition atmosphere was frequently described as being warm and rather cuddly; in contrast, the culture of Fast Car was considered to be extremely aggressive and 'pushy'. In the last few weeks, new and more rigid systems of control had been externally introduced. These had met with considerable resentment from employees, not only because they increased workload but because they changed the way in which work was organized. So long as their old managing director remained, employees felt to some extent protected from any wholesale change in their culture; therefore, his impending departure was an immediate source of concern. Employees very much had an eye on what was happening at nearby Greenside, and one manager erroneously reported: 'Since the appointment of a Fast Car man at Greenside, more than half the staff have gone – the same is likely to happen here.'

The questionnaire survey carried out at this time, to assess current attitudes towards the acquisition, found that employees despite their initial optimism expressed less favourable attitudes towards change than Greensiders, and were less positive about their future job prospects; 64 per cent of respondents, compared with 75 per cent at Greenside, considered that their job prospects were better now than they were before the acquisition. The questionnaire also suggested that employees considered themselves to be less well informed than Greensiders, and less well informed than they had been at the beginning of the process.

In response to the open-ended question, 'What (if any) positive/ negative outcomes have resulted from the acquisition?', the number of negative outcomes mentioned (in particular, the changed atmosphere and lack of communication from the acquirer beyond the initial presentation, and its creation of high expectations) far outnumbered any positive outcomes (such as increased investment and change in corporate image).

As Figure App. 1.3 illustrates, employees at Princess Garage were experiencing the events of the last six to eight weeks as slightly more stressful than their counterparts at Greenside. Work overload and pay levels were an important source of concern for both groups. However, employees at Princess Garage rated the item 'changes in work organization' as the second highest source of stress. At this stage, there was no widespread reporting by either group of ineffective or poor coping strategies, e.g. increased alcohol or nicotine consumption. The questionnaire data validated the observational/interview data in confirming that employees at Princess Garage were more apprehensive of the change they perceived to be imminent, once Mr Walters departed, than they had been originally. In the first nine weeks, the presence of Fast Car and its culture had been less overt than at Greenside. The only changes which had been introduced had been at the systems/procedural level, and these had become a cause of concern. With the impending departure of Mr Walters, employees were uneasy about the anticipated changes at the sociocultural level.

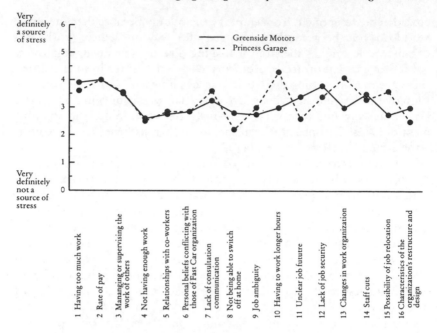

Figure App. 1.3   Sources of stress, 6–8 weeks post acquisition

Integration Stage 3: success or failure

Greenside Motors – one year post acquisition

In organizational terms, Fast Car considered Greenside Motors to be a successful acquisition. At the time of the takeover it had shown a profit of less than £30,000, and according to Fast Car, if it had adopted their accounting practices of levying market rents to owned dealership premises, it would have just broken even. A fairly ambitious sales target had been set for its first year at the time of its acquisition. In actuality, Greenside exceeded this target by 50 per cent and turnover increased in all departments.

There was notable change in the atmosphere of Greenside. It was positively frenetic, in comparison to the previous quiet stillness of our first visit. A considerable amount of modernization had taken place. Office partitions had been pulled down and plans had been drawn up to rebuild the main showroom. Computerized systems and procedures consistent with Fast Car's other dealerships were now fully operational.

The managers interviewed intimated that they were now totally committed to the Fast Car way. Many of the newer managers had seen the acquisition as a great opportunity to overturn many of the frustrating practices and become more involved in decision making. One of the managers interviewed, based in an adjacent building, said that while he had been working there for three years he had still been referred to as 'the new boy'. He confirmed the remoteness of the previous managerial style when he commented on his arrival at our interview, held in the former MD's office: 'I've never been in here before in the three years I've worked here. When the secretary told me where the interview was to take place, I had to say I had no idea exactly where Mr Charles's office was.'

Another considered that those who had previously felt oppressed by the old regime had now risen to the fore, and were enthusiastic in accepting and implementing the Fast Car culture. In his opinion, a good Greensider was an employee who always said 'Yes'. He commented that acceptance of the Fast Car culture was crucial, if one was to remain and develop within the organization. In his words: 'You can't remain a Greensider and survive. If you don't like the Fast Car way of doing things, there's no place for you here. The message is clear.'

At the managerial level, it was considered that the organization was now in a fairly stable state, although lower levels were still in flux. This was confirmed by interviews with supervisory staff, the level immediately below the managers. While they welcomed the improvement in intra-organizational communication, they were still uncomfortable and distrustful of the new managerial style. Complaints about work overload still continued.

The present culture of Greenside Motors

A substantial number of employees had been made redundant or voluntarily resigned from the organization in the last twelve months. The interview/observational data indicated that for those who remained the physical layout, procedural systems and dominant culture of the organization was increasingly resembling that of its acquirer – at least at the managerial level. This was also confirmed by analysis of the questionnaire data which found that the culture of Greenside Motors was now similar to Fast Car in respect of every key dimension of organizational behaviour and practices we measured.

More than 40 per cent of the technicians who had been with Greenside since its takeover also completed a post-acquisition culture measure. As we had suspected, their results confirmed that although Fast Car had successfully changed the managerial culture of Greenside, this culture had not yet worked its way through to lower levels of the organization, which still retained its original power culture. Interestingly, the only discernible change which had occurred was that it was now perceived as being more autocratic than patriarchal, with senior management now seen as more impersonal and remote than previously.

Employee response

The managers and other white-collar workers at Greenside clearly knew the 'new' culture, what was expected of them and how to behave in accordance with its values. However, overt behavioural change alone is an insufficient indicator that employees have fully accepted, internalized and are congruent with the underpinning values of the culture.

The measure of organizational commitment taken at this time found that white-collar workers reported a high degree of individual compatibility with the new culture, and there was a high level of renewed organizational commitment. In terms of individual outcomes, the managerial/white-collar group considered the acquisition to have been personally beneficial. In terms of personal success, 25 per cent rated the acquisition as being moderately successful, 42 per cent as very successful and 33 per cent as being extremely successful. As there had not yet been any salary reviews, any beneficial effects of the acquisition must be assumed to relate to improvements in the quality of working life, psychological environment and/or perceived opportunities for future job advancement. While manual workers were less positive and still expressed widespread concern about job security, neither group reported that things had worked out substantially worse than they had originally expected. A comparison of present levels of job satisfaction with similar occupational groups who had not undergone major organizational change found no evidence to suggest that the acquisition had an adverse impact in this area. Similarly a comparison of mental health scores over time and as compared with the 'normal' population generally, suggested that the mental health of employees had not been adversely affected by the acquisition.

However, the outcome of the Princess Garage acquisition was rather different.

Princess Garage – one year post acquisition

One year post acquisition, Fast Car considered Princess Garage to be an unsuccessful acquisition. At the time of its acquisition it was showing a financial loss. Fast Car expected that by the end of the first year's trading it would break even and in the following year show a profit. In actuality, at the end of the first year it showed a greater accounting loss than it had previously. When we visited Princess Garage, eight weeks prior to the financial year end, Fast Car personnel had indicated that 'there were some problems with Princess'. There had been considerable change at Princess Garage in the period since our last visit. The new dealer manager appointed to replace Mr Walters had resigned after three months. Mr Peters, one of the original directors of Greenside, had been appointed as his successor and was still settling in.

Within days of his appointment, the new manager had earned the title of 'hatchet man', when he made 25 per cent of the workforce, including eight managers, redundant. The redundancies had been widely reported in the local press and Fast Car had received a considerable amount of bad publicity. Ironically, despite having failed to record a profit for years, Princess Garage suddenly became known throughout the area as 'the loss-making garage'.

From the employees we interviewed, it was clear that all was not well with Princess Garage. Employees were still reeling from the shock of the redundancies; anxiety and confusion were endemic. There was a widely expressed lack of trust in Fast Car which was accused of insensitivity, and of introducing inappropriate changes to working practices. A growing sense of apathy and insularity had now developed.

All those interviewed commented on the longer working hours they were now expected to work. It was felt that this was acceptable in the short term, but suspected this was a norm within the Fast Car organization, which many employees were not prepared to accept.

Employees were still fearful and unhappy about the new systems which they considered Fast Car had imposed upon them without consultation. These were described as new and 'unproven'. That the systems had seemingly been proved effectively within Fast Car was irrelevant, they were still unproven to Princess Garage employees!

Some surviving managers did talk positively of the changes, particularly the move towards a more commercially oriented culture. The manager of the hire-car department said:

> Things are different. Business attitudes are different. Before it didn't really matter what or how well you did. Fast Car are successful, making profits is all important – it's good to be part of that. The last two months' figures have been better. Now everybody knows the monthly figures; before, occasionally a good month was mentioned.

However, the general consensus was that the organization was still in a state of flux and highly unstable. Having retained the same managing director for so many years, Princess found two new managers in less than six months extremely disturbing and confusing. In fact, many employees felt they had effectively been taken over twice. They had only just started to formulate ideas as to what the new manager expected of them, when he resigned and another 'new and unknown quantity' arrived, with possibly very different expectations.

In many ways, a year after its takeover, Princess Garage seemed to be at a similar stage of organizational change that had existed at Greenside six or seven weeks post acquisition. However, in contrast, employees seemed less optimistic and less willing to abandon their old culture and adopt any new culture. Because Fast Car had not introduced one of their own personnel, there was arguably no effective role model and their perception of the Fast Car culture was less developed than at Greenside.

The present culture of Princess Garage

When Fast Car acquired Princess Garage, there were eighty-eight employees, of which fifteen were managers. The organization now had fifty-one employees. The current workforce consisted of ex-Princess Garage employees (64 per cent) and new employees recruited since the acquisition (36 per cent). In total, fifty-five employees out of the original pre-acquisition population had been made redundant or had voluntarily resigned since the acquisition, indicating an attrition rate of 61 per cent.

Staff losses occurred at all levels, predominantly as a result of redundancy and early retirement. Of the original fifteen managers, only seven remained.

On the basis of our observations and interviews, there was considerable reluctance among the remaining employees to become culturally cloned with Fast Car. In particular, they found it difficult to accept a culture with a high degree of rules, regulations and standardized practices, because it was perceived to impose considerable constraints on them as individuals. While it was necessary to be seen to conform if one was to keep one's job, we were left with the strong impression that whenever and wherever possible, employees preferred to continue to do things the way they always had.

Throughout the period of the study, questionnaire response rates had been markedly lower at Princess Garage than at Greenside Motors; only 33 per cent of employees completed the post-acquisition measure of organizational culture, all of them either managers or sales personnel, and all but four having been with the organization less than six years. On the basis of their responses, while there was still significantly less clarity of role definition, in all other measured aspects of organizational behaviour and practices Princess Garage now more closely resembled Fast Car than it had originally (see Figure App. 1.1).

Employee response/individual outcomes

There was evidence of renewed organizational commitment and of respondents finding themselves compatible with the new culture, but to a lesser degree than their counterparts at Greenside. Levels of job satisfaction and mental health did not appear to have been adversely affected by the new acquisition. (See Figures App. 1.4 and 1.5.)

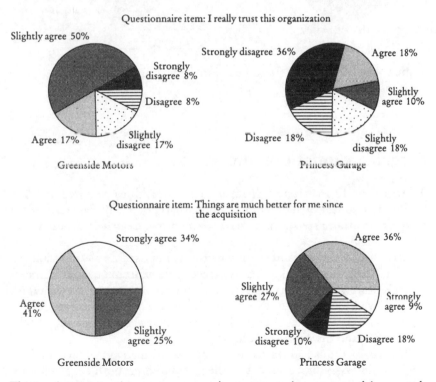

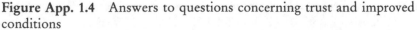

Figure App. 1.4 Answers to questions concerning trust and improved conditions

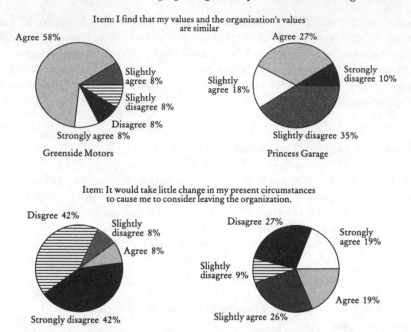

Figure App. 1.5   Answers to questions concerning values and propensity to leave

Organizational outcomes

In terms of financial performance, the acquisitions resulted in very different organizational outcomes. To the shareholders of Fast Car, prima facie, acquisition activity must have seemed to be 'at best an each way bet'.

Greenside, a power culture on which was imposed a role/task culture, was financially successful in that it exceeded its expected targets. Princess Garage, a person/support culture, on which was imposed a role/task culture, was unsuccessful. Not only did it fail to reach target, but it recorded higher losses than it had ever experienced before, to the amazement and dismay of its acquirer.

Both acquisitions had started to operate at the managerial level under a similar role/task culture to that of their acquirer. At both organizations, this culture change had not been achieved without certain financial and human costs.

Both organizations recorded above average rates of staff turnover in the twelve months post acquisition. Unplanned personnel losses occurred at all levels. Abnormally high rates of staff turnover and increased absenteeism were recorded among blue-collar workers, even though in actuality jobs at this level were never under threat. However, whereas at Greenside Motors the level of staff turnover was 35 per cent, at Princess it was a staggering 61 per cent.

There had been economies of scale and rationalization at both organizations which had resulted in job losses. But, at their own admission, Fast Car had deliberately chosen to accelerate the displacement of the existing cultures by replacing a substantial number of employees whom it considered to be resistant to change or unable to 'fit in'. Many employees who voluntarily resigned clearly made the same decision on the basis of their own appraisal of the situation. A larger percentage of employees remaining at Greenside is indicative of a greater willingness on their part to abandon their existing culture, and to accept and assimilate into the new culture of their acquirer.

As the integration process progressed, Greenside employees developed more favourable attitudes towards the acquisition as they began to learn and experience the culture of their acquirer. In contrast, the reverse appeared to happen at Princess Garage. (See Table App. 1.1.)

A comparison of the questionnaire response rates also supports this proposition. Response rates among managers and white collar workers at Greenside were as high as 90 per cent. The continuing lower response rate and lack of any response from blue-collar manual workers at Princess Garage can be taken as indicative of lack of trust and feelings of separation and alienation from the perceived dominant culture of the organization.

Organizational commitment/trust

Recent research in the area of organizational commitment has demonstrated the distinction between superficial compliance-based commitment, linked to the size of one's salary cheque or the prestige value of the company car, and deeper commitment based on identification and internalization of organizational values. In our assessment of the levels of renewed organizational commitment, we focused on deeper rather than superficial commitment as being indicative of cultural adoption and individual congruence, rather than adaptation or behavioural compliance. Levels of remuneration had remained relatively unaltered at both acquisitions, so there had been no attempt by Fast Car to 'buy' commitment.

Table App. 1.1 *Comparative experience of the process in terms of employee response*

Event	Greenside Motors	Princess Garage
Acquisition announcement	Great shock – clear message of Fast Car culture	Less shock, more relief. Less clear message
Early days	Increased cohesiveness. Initially 57% considered leaving	Increased cohesiveness. Initially 18% considered leaving
Introduction of change	Almost immediate change at physical, procedural and sociocultural level	Almost immediate change at procedural level, delayed change at sociocultural level
Effects of change	Increasing optimism. New culture experienced as less constraining – positive response to new managerial style. Renewed organizational commitment and less propensity to leave	Increasing apprehension. New culture experienced as exerting more pressure and control on its members. Lower levels of renewed organizational commitment than at Greenside and greater propensity to leave

As demonstrated (see Figure App. 1.5), levels of organizational commitment were significantly higher at Greenside than at Princess Garage, to the extent that the level of commitment of white-collar workers at Princess Garage was slightly lower than that of manual workers at Greenside.

Individual outcomes

At the individual level, employees at Princess Garage were generally less satisfied with the overall outcomes and were less positive in their attitudes to the acquisition than those at Greenside. In contrast, at the time of the acquisition announcement, it had been Greenside employees who had been the more anxious and concerned. Now, Princess Garage respondents expressed a greater inclination to leave the organization.

The levels of job satisfaction at both acquisitions were favourable as compared with normative data. However, again the managers and white-collar workers at Greenside were more job satisfied than their counter-parts at Princess Garage.

A comparison of mental health scores indicated neither group appeared to have been adversely affected by the acquisition, suggesting that fairly rapid change is preferable to that which occurs over a longer period of time and so creates uncertainty.

Summary

The case study demonstrates that these results did not occur by chance, but were the predictable outcome of the differing cultural dynamics they presented, and the mode of acculturation the acquirer elected to impose. In both cases, this was assimilation. Effective assimilation depends upon *shared* perceptions between both acquirer and acquired, regarding the unsatisfactory/unsuccessful nature of the existing culture and the attractiveness/superiority of the acquirer's culture. A greater number of Greenside employees appeared to share this perception, so culture change through assimilation was easier and more successful. This was clearly demonstrated in financial terms. Unfortunately for both parties, employ-ees at Princess Garage had different perceptions.

In the inevitable post-mortem discussions which followed, Fast Car themselves acknowledged that the poor performance of Princess Garage was almost entirely related to 'people factors', the importance of which they had seriously underestimated from the outset. It had been unfortunate that the acquisitions had been made during a period of market depression in the motor trade, but the market conditions had been the same for both acquisitions.

Getting their acquisitions 'to do things the Fast Car way' had been a more lengthy and difficult process than they had anticipated at both organizations. However, Fast Car confirmed they had met with greater resistance at Princess Garage. This was considered to be a continuing problem because 'they are still not doing things right!' In particular, the experience had highlighted to Fast Car the difficulties in managing two acquisitions and attempting to assimilate both cultures at the same time, without neglecting their existing core businesses – an experience they vowed never to repeat.

The energy they expended in the first acquisition was a likely contributor to the problems they experienced at Princess. Given their intention to impose their own culture, they communicated this with less speed and coherence. This would not necessarily have increased the attractiveness and acceptability of Fast Car's culture, but would have dispelled uncertainty and enabled employees to make a more informed and realistic cognitive appraisal earlier.

In making a horizontal acquisition, Fast Car stated that they considered they were effectively 'sticking to the knitting'. This assumption conferred a certain arrogance and to them affirmed the superiority of their culture. However, as Fast Car painfully came to learn, although the business activities were the same, their cultures, and hence their responses, were different.

References

Harrison, R. (1972). How to describe your organization's culture. *Harvard Business Review*, May/June, S/1, 119–128.

Appendix 2

Case Study 2: the acquisition of Fill-it Packaging – the challenge for the gang of four

This case study involves the acquisition of a power culture by a small management team. Despite a promising beginning, it illustrates how time pressures forced the acquiring management to rethink their attitudes to culture change and the problems which arose as a result of the inconsistency in the culture message which was then presented.

The team acquired an organization which had a history of labour problems. In continuing to reinforce, rather than change the existing culture, these problems remained largely unresolved.

The Fill-it Packaging Company

The Fill-it Packaging Company, a contract packaging business, was acquired by a small management team of four individuals. The company had previously formed part of a large UK organization, whose core business activities were in an unrelated area. Most of Fill-it's turnover was derived from labour-only contracts undertaken with large industrial giants such as Lever Brothers and Procter & Gamble for the packaging of household detergents, haircare and related products. Fill-it also marketed a limited number of its own products.

The acquiring team had previously worked together building up a similar business which had subsequently been the subject of an acquisition and resulted in their displacement. Three members of the team had at one time held senior positions within a large manufacturing organization that was a customer of Fill-it. One had been in marketing, one in production management and the other had a training/personnel background. The fourth member of the team was relatively junior and, unlike the others, had no financial stake in the business.

At the outset, they considered the future success of the acquisition was very much dependent on their ability to change its culture. Their ideas as to the way in which this change would be achieved were markedly different from the aggressive approach of Fast Car. In contrast, the buying team at Fill-it sought to achieve change more gradually through persuasion, and the adoption of a more sensitive conciliatory approach.

In the early days, this was evidenced in their pre-planning and the detailed attention they paid to the acquisition announcement itself. On the day the sale was completed, production was stopped and a group announcement was made to each individual shift. All four members were present and had spent a considerable amount of time rehearsing the content and style of their delivery. They were keen to achieve a balance between presenting an optimistic view of the future, while not appearing over-critical of past endeavours, and also demonstrating their sensitivity towards employees' concerns.

At this comparable stage, the acquiring team appeared to know much more about the workforce they were acquiring than Fast Car had. This perhaps may be because the negotiating circumstances were more amenable or more likely because, in contrast to Fast Car, one of the negotiating team members had a personnel and human resource background.

Before the deal was finally signed, the acquiring team familiarized themselves with the demographic composition of the workforce, their pay and conditions, staff turnover, sickness and absenteeism rates. Sickness and absenteeism rates were exceptionally high, particularly on Mondays, which led them to conclude that they were acquiring a very dissatisfied workforce. They suspected that a likely reason for this was that the majority of the workforce was employed on a temporary basis, even through many 'casuals' had worked for the organization over three years.

The management culture of the acquiring team

In the time spent discussing the forthcoming acquisition, the team expressed a consistent view of the culture they would like Fill-it Packaging to be or develop. All four members agreed to complete a culture questionnaire prior to the takeover, and again twelve months later, to compare the extent to which they had been successful in achieving/ creating their desired culture. The type of culture they wished to introduce at Fill-it was 'task', with strong support elements. Its main characteristics were:

1 An informal open managerial style.
2 An emphasis on the development of strong team spirit which allows autonomy and rewards employees in terms of their task contribution.

3 A nurturing rather than competitive environment, which places importance on treating and responding to employees as individuals, and is concerned with their personal development.
4 Features consistent with a 'task/support' culture.

The team considered their first step was to establish a clear understanding of the existing abilities and present responsibilities of each member of the acquired workforce.

At the time of the acquisition, they stressed to employees that their initial task would be to spend time 'getting to know their people'. In the first month post acquisition, each employee was extensively interviewed by the team member responsible for personnel, who drew up job descriptions for each individual. During this time, the team frequently toured the factory wearing badges bearing their first names. They asked employees similarly to wear badges to help them relate names to faces, and almost everyone complied.

They were keen to address the temporary/permanent issue and devise a more equitable reward system. They planned to do this by introducing a productivity bonus scheme, which rewarded employees on the basis of their team performance.

The culture of Fill-it Packaging Company

Fill it Packaging had been originally formed seventeen years earlier by a small entrepreneurial group of industrial chemists, one of whom was still with the company at the time of the acquisition. Unfortunately, their lack of financial expertise soon led to major cash flow problems, and they were forced to sell the company. The company had continued periodically to run into financial difficulties and had changed ownership twice since then. Despite several changes in management and a good customer base, Fill-it Packaging Company had failed to capitalize on its potential. It was widely considered that its present owners had been disinterested in the business activities of Fill-it, and had been extremely anxious to dispose of it. In the twelve months before the sale there had been a substantial investment in new machinery to increase its market attractiveness.

At the time of the acquisition, Fill-it Packaging had a workforce of 150 employees, most of whom were women. It operated a two fixed shift system of between 80 and 120 semi-skilled operatives, of whom only 20 were 'permanent' employees; 88 per cent of the workforce had been with the organization less than seven years. There had been little investment in the amenities and general housekeeping and maintenance of the factory, and it presented an extremely 'run-down', almost Dickensian, appearance.

Six years before, Fill-it Packaging had been acquired by the current sellers, when it was included in the sale of a divestiture. At that time, it had been in a loss-making situation and had continued to remain so as a rather forgotten asset of its large holding company. Eighteen months previously, a young, recently qualified accountant, Mr Campbell, was appointed as managing director. Mr Campbell was considered to be very much a rising star within the holding company, and was apparently charged with the responsibility of turning the company around. To this end he had been successful. He had appointed a new production manager from outside the company and invested heavily in new machinery. Output had increased by 25 per cent, and Fill-it Packaging had shown an encouraging profit in the last financial year.

At the managerial level, the acquisition announcement did not come as any great shock. Despite Mr Campbell's consistent denials, employees had become increasingly aware that Fill-it Packaging was about to be sold. Rumours had been circulating in the trade for the past six months, many unexplained visitors had toured the factory accompanied by Mr Campbell and staff were requested to take stock with unusual frequency.

On completion of the sale Mr Campbell was appointed to another post within the divesting organization. His removal was not a precondition of the sale. Indeed, the new acquirers were initially keen for Mr Campbell to join their 'team' because of his accountancy background, an area of expertise which they considered would have greatly strengthened their team. His secretary/PA also resigned on the day the sale was completed, and the company accountant left three weeks later.

Following Mr Campbell's appointment, 'getting the order at all costs' had become the first priority within Fill-it Packaging. There was general agreement among those interviewed that Mr Campbell was not a 'people manager'. The following description given by the production manager sums up the feelings expressed by those interviewed:

> Mr Campbell liked to keep people under the thumb. He was concerned with impressing the customer; not with impressing the workforce. His idea of motivation was to frighten people by threatening to sack them. He was very successful at uniting the workforce – against him!

Admittedly, the production manager was more bitter than most about the takeover. He had joined Fill-it on an unwritten understanding that, if successful, he would be appointed as production director within two years. He now considered he had very much been used by Mr Campbell. However, his remarks were confirmed less vehemently by other longer-standing managers. According to the transport manager, 'The atmosphere at Fill-it changed immediately the takeover was announced. A bad atmosphere had progressively developed over the last year and a half; people hadn't really wanted to come to work.'

Interviews conducted throughout the organization indicated that Fill-it Packaging had a strong 'power culture', the most consistent and salient features being the centralization of power, and the autocratic managerial style of its managing director. Both managers and operatives were little informed or consulted on organizational matters. The technical director, one of the original founders of the business, was not told of the acquisition until five minutes before the general announcement.

Managerial meetings were held once a week. There were no discussions; rather managers were told what to do. This was the only occasion when managers 'officially' met their departmental counterparts. All interdepartmental communication was expected to be channelled through the top. For example, according to the sales manager:

> If I have a problem meeting customers' requirements, say a technical problem, I couldn't walk over to John's office [the technical director] and talk about it. I would have to speak to Mr Campbell and he would talk to John and then come and tell me or speak to the customer direct. If you avoided the centralized system you got a good telling off. Not surprisingly, there were a lot of rows between certain individuals and Mr Campbell. People don't like being told to do things as if they were children.

One of the managers was not entirely negative in his comments about Mr Campbell. He considered that Fill-it Packaging in his words needed 'a good shaking up', and that Mr Campbell had the drive that the organization had previously lacked. However, his relative youth and inexperience in managing a difficult, and often apathetic, workforce had made him unpopular.

There were no clear role definitions, written managerial job descriptions, reward or appraisal systems at Fill-it Packaging. Salaries, holiday entitlement, benefits in kind, and the like, were a matter for personal negotiation. None of the managers interviewed had taken more than five days holiday in the last twelve months. Indeed, managers were encouraged to accept a cash option in lieu of time off. Managers were accustomed to working long hours, and a ten-hour day was not uncommon. Power cultures are associated with subjective and inequitable reward systems. This was well exemplified at Fill-it, in that all managers worked beyond official hours, though a select few were credited with overtime and financially remunerated.

The operatives interviewed had little contact with Mr Campbell, experiencing management as remote and little concerned with their welfare. They complained of a 'people are cheap' attitude, and that promotions or appointments to permanent status were made on the basis of favouritism rather than years of service or merit. Most stated that they only came to work for the money.

The division in worker status was a major issue at Fill-it Packaging. Permanent employees earned on average £30 per week more than the temporaries, even though they were working side by side on the lines. Worker status also affected holiday entitlement. At the time of the acquisition, there was no strong union presence at Fill-it.

The high rates of staff turnover, sickness and absenteeism had an extremely disruptive effect on production. Supervisors reported that it was difficult to plan weekly working schedules, as they were never sure how many employees would turn in for work on Monday morning. Often they would plan work around a listed workforce of 120 only to find that on Monday morning only 85 employees actually clocked in. This made it necessary to move employees from one production unit to another, a continual source of friction between supervisors and their workforce. Women who worked in the main unit considered a move to the smaller unit to be a punishment. Similarly, those in the smaller unit resented working with the main unit women, who they felt were 'clannish' and unfriendly. In that sense, there were different shopfloor sub-cultures operating between units and between temporary/permanent employees, and little social contact between the groups.

Managerial and supervisory response to the new management team, particularly to their highly visible and open managerial style, was initially positive if cautious. They were still very much an unknown quantity, described as having 'no proven track record but with big organization ideas'. At the shopfloor level, all expressed a positive desire for change, but were sceptical that this would occur. They were extremely distrustful of 'management' generally.

However, all of those interviewed at all levels commented on the immediate change in atmosphere since the acquisition, and on the interest and time the new management were taking to get to know people.

Operatives commented that instead of standing at the end of a line and watching them from a distance, the new managing director would walk over to them and speak to them direct. For the first time that anyone could remember, a managing director had accepted their invitation to attend the Christmas works outing.

Communications between management and operatives had previously always been confined to written communications on the noticeboard. It had now become the practice for members of the management team to brief the workforce regularly during comfort breaks, and then post written confirmation on the noticeboard. In the first few days following the acquisition, employees were invited to put forward any suggestions or concerns they might have. A large board was placed in the canteen for this purpose, but initially had produced little or no response. It was suggested that this was perhaps too public and was replaced by a box. Within a week more than forty suggestions were received, most of them relating to the temporary/permanent issue and the poor physical working conditions.

Summary

Employee responses to the culture measure supported the interview/observational data in confirming the type of culture operating at Fill-it Packaging as being an autocratic power culture. The main characteristics of the existing culture were those associated with power cultures:

1 Considerable reliance on formal authority.
2 Highly political environment.
3 Reward emphasis on favouritism rather than task contribution.
4 Non-person-oriented management, with little interest in organizational members as individuals.
5 Little autonomy or opportunity for risk taking, i.e. a culture in which people are expected to do as they are told.

The responses of managerial/administrative employees were compared with those of production/shopfloor workers. In contrast to the production workers, the managerial group reported the culture as having significantly more reliance on formal authority. Given the nature of managerial work, this is presumably because they encountered such situations with greater frequency and, being closer to the centre of power, experienced the autocratic essence of the culture more acutely and with increased awareness.

As the Figure App. 2.1 illustrates, there were considerable differences in organizational behaviour and practices between the existing culture of the acquisition and the intended culture of its acquirers. Given the cultural dynamics of this acquisition and the proposed direction of culture change from a power to a task/support culture, there seemed a strong likelihood that employees would be willing to abandon their existing culture and adopt the culture of their acquirer. However, at this

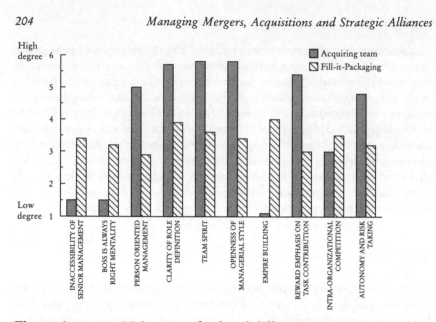

Figure App. 2.1 Main areas of cultural differences in organizational behaviour and practices between the acquiring team and Fill-it Packaging

stage, the mood of the acquired employees ranged from cautious optimism to deep mistrust, with the majority of employees unconvinced that a culture change was likely.

Fill-it Packaging – six months post acquisition

Following the takeover, the new owners embarked upon a major modernization programme. In the first few months, according to the new management team, everything was going well; productivity figures were up and absenteeism had declined.

Since our last visit, six weeks post acquisition, there had been many changes. Computerized systems had been introduced and the administrative and sales staff had relocated to smart new offices in the smaller unit. Of the original seven managers, only two had remained with the company; one had retired, four had left voluntarily and been replaced from outside the organization. The production manager had been dismissed and his position had not yet been filled. The organizational structure and reporting arrangements had changed; roles had been redefined and titles or functions renamed, e.g. the transport manager had been given wider responsibilities and was now logistics manager. Work teams had been introduced to replace the tiered supervisory system. The number of operatives employed on a permanent basis had remained unchanged, but approximately twenty operatives were now employed on a one-year contractual basis. These employees were still paid on the 'temporary' hourly basis, but were given the same holiday entitlement as the permanents. They were also allowed the opportunity to earn a productivity bonus and skills allowance to bring their wages in line with permanents. These two groups, forty employees in total, were designated as 'core workers'.

Stricter disciplinary procedures had been introduced to deter unauthorized absence and poor timekeeping. Workers were now required to wear company overalls and headgear – an unpopular decision, as the material chosen was uncomfortable.

The acquiring management team were in a despondent mood at the time of the visit. The acquisition had seemed initially to be progressing reasonably well. The work-team system had been introduced, together with a training programme, the aim being to enable operatives to develop additional skills, e.g. simple line maintenance to give them more task variety and to create a more flexible and efficient workforce. Then the organization had experienced a sudden and substantial loss of orders and was forced to lay people off. Almost overnight, the existing production workforce of over a hundred employees had been reduced to the forty core workers. Business was now starting to pick up and the size of the workforce had now increased, but the training programme had been temporarily suspended.

The primary responsibility for the lost business had been attributed to errors made by the production manager. Opinion seemed divided as to whether these mistakes were a result of incompetence or lethargy, or were a deliberate act of sabotage on his part. In any event, they had resulted in his dismissal eight weeks earlier. The 'official' version given to employees was that he had resigned. He was now working in a nearby factory, and the managing director suspected that some Fill-it Packaging operatives were 'moonlighting' there.

The present disillusioned mood of the management team was in sharp contrast to their optimism at the time of the acquisition. In recent months, a substantial number of employees had joined a union and taken their grievances, which the managing director described as 'tea and toilet' issues, to the area union representative. This had greatly upset the acquiring team, because they considered that they had worked hard to establish a communication system whereby employees could present their problems direct to management, without the necessity for union intervention. Productivity had now gone down and absenteeism was back almost to pre-acquisition levels.

The workforce of Fill-it Packaging had never appeared to be particularly communicative, perhaps because the culture had offered them little opportunity to express themselves. On earlier visits, there had been a noticeable 'them and us' attitude. At the time of this visit, this attitude towards management seemed as strong as ever, and the operatives interviewed were markedly less communicative than on earlier visits. They considered little had changed at Fill-it during the past six months. They admitted that they were now slightly better informed, but that this management were still 'playing the same old tune'.

Relationships between the two units were still poor, and the organization was more fragmented than before. Instead of two divisions, i.e. between temporary and permanent, the creation of a 'contracted worker' status had effectively split the workforce into three groups. Permanents complained because they were not entitled to earn a productivity bonus, and contracted employees complained that permanents did not pull their weight and, therefore, prevented them from earning their bonus. Suspension of the training programme meant that few operatives had been sufficiently trained to earn the skills allowance. Employees reported that they considered they had gained little financially from the takeover.

Members of the acquiring team admitted that they were perhaps less visible and less cohesive as a team than they had been initially. There were now regular arguments between team members, as everybody was tending to blame everyone else for their problems. They expressed their despair at being unable to change the inherent and ingrained culture of Fill-it Packaging. They had considered developing on a greenfield site as an alternative to acquisition, and were beginning to regret not doing so. They felt that the existing culture could only be displaced by replacing a substantial number of the workforce. As a result they were again tightening disciplinary procedures and introducing many rules and regulations, whereby unsatisfactory workers could be 'weeded out'. Many workers had already received final warnings.

The acquiring team seemed about to abandon their hope of creating a task/support culture at Fill-it Packaging. They were clearly disheartened that their values had failed to be accepted by the majority of the workforce. They recognized that they were still in the early days of culture transition, but suggested that because they were under acute financial pressure, they could not afford the luxury of a slow and gradual culture change. The culture the acquiring team were now developing was becoming ambiguous. The extent to which it was becoming dominated by functions, roles and formalized rules and regulations, made it now appear more a role culture than any other type.

At this interim stage, the culture of Fill-it was widely perceived to be incoherent and in a state of flux. The strong distrust of those in authority, inherent in the indigenous culture, had been difficult to overcome, frustrating the acquiring team, who interpreted it as unwillingness to change. In their definition of the situation, the vast majority of the workforce was obstructive, and they had responded accordingly by hardening their attitudes, with cyclic consequences.

It was observed that the acquisition team talked eloquently and naturally in the language of professional management. The chairman stated that he had consciously redefined almost all the existing terminology. He firmly believed that new cultures created their own language. In part this is true but, given the poor educational background of the majority of the workforce, such elaborated 'management speak', littered as it was with talk of 'benchmarks' and 'strategic missions', etc., may have seemed more like a foreign and hence incomprehensible language than a semantically different vocabulary.

Fill-it Packaging – twelve months post acquisition

Discussions were held with the acquiring management team to establish their assessment of the success of the acquisition. By this time, the more junior member of the team had left the organization.

In the intervening months, there had been further investment in factory hygiene. Many lost customers had now been regained. The concept of work teams was reported to be working reasonably well at present, and absenteeism had again started to fall. This was considered to have been achieved by the introduction of tougher disciplinary procedures. The team reported feeling more relaxed than previously, but there were still many problems with the acquisition. Although business was improving, on the basis of its financial performance during the first year the acquisition had been unsuccessful and failed to meet expected targets.

The acquiring team had continued to feel the necessity to impose tighter controls on the workforce. In contradiction with their original 'espoused' culture they were increasingly reinforcing the 'old' power culture of the organization. Initially stated commitments to increasing employee participation had been abandoned in favour of firm directives. The team now believed that the workforce was unable to think for itself, and constantly needed to be told what to do. As one member put it, 'Contrary to what we thought – this workforce likes to be bossed about!'

The initial practice of briefing all employees on a weekly basis had been discontinued.

The culture of Fill-it Packaging had changed little in the past twelve months, even seen through the eyes of the acquiring team. Their view of the existing culture differed considerably from their initial 'ideal' culture, in that there was markedly less team spirit, a less open managerial style, less concern for the personal development of employees and a higher degree of reliance on formal authority than they had originally intended. That their priorities now lay exclusively in formalizing communication channels and writing a rule book, was indicative of their growing commitment to increasing control, reducing autonomy and 'closing' communication systems.

The last twelve months had taken its toll on the team members. A comparison of their mental health scores pre/post acquisition found a noticeable deterioration in mental health over the last year.

On the previous occasions we had visited Fill-it, the team had always been keen for us to speak with as many employees as possible and welcomed any feedback. In contrast, they now felt that there was little point in conducting such an exercise. We did invite employees to complete a questionnaire to ascertain the extent to which they had experienced any culture change, and their general feelings as to the success of the acquisition and its implications on the quality of work life. This received a poor response. Less than 25 per cent of the workforce returned questionnaires. On the basis of the replies received and the general lack of response from the rest of the workforce, the experienced culture was little changed, and there was still widespread apathy and alienation amongst the workforce.

Discussion

On the basis of its existing performance, in financial terms, Fill-it Packaging was an unsuccessful acquisition. Nor, from the almost total lack of response to the final questionnaire, is there any evidence to suggest that it was successful in human terms either.

Once again, this study demonstrated that for the acquiring management culture change is experienced as a difficult and frustrating process. In common with Fast Car, the acquirers of Fill-it Packaging over-estimated the speed with which such change can be achieved. As was demonstrated, initial optimism and enthusiasm rapidly deteriorate into desperation when pressure is exerted to achieve short-term financial gains. Fast Car responded to this pressure by adopting 'machine gun tactics' and firing people; the team at Fill-it responded by questioning the wisdom and suitability of their culture. Paradoxically, by the end of this study, it was the acquirers who had abandoned their original culture rather than the acquired.

The experiences of Fill-it Packaging can be explained and understood within the context of the acculturation model. At the time of the acquisition, Fill-it Packaging had a power culture on which its new acquirers sought to impose a 'task/support culture'. The existing high rates of staff turnover and absenteeism suggested that many employees were already experiencing cultural alienation. Therefore, given the cultural dynamics, it would be expected that the majority of employees at Fill-it would be willing to abandon their power culture and perceive the new less-constraining task/support culture as being attractive.

The data collected within the early days of the acquisition confirmed that there was widespread dissatisfaction with the organization and its existing culture. Indeed, many employees were already effectively dismembered from it and had developed their own sub-cultures. The data suggested that membership of such sub-cultures assumed salience over any sense of wider organizational attachment. For many production employees, work was a passive experience undertaken in return for a pay packet. Employees 'attended' out of financial necessity rather than any feelings of attachment arising from a sense of active involvement or deeper organizational commitment. Therefore, while there was an expressed willingness to change, past experience appeared also to have created a widespread state of 'learned helplessness' – the belief that no behaviour on their part has any effect on the occurrence of an event. As a potential obstacle to culture change, it was only likely to be overcome with patience, consistent and continual reinforcement and feedback, and the development of trust.

In the first four months of the acquisition, the gradual process of culture change had been reported to be progressing well. But, at a time when employees were beginning to learn the 'new' culture, and trust was perhaps starting to develop, the organization experienced a substantial loss of orders and entered a period of crisis. It has been suggested that in times of organizational crisis task cultures revert to 'role cultures', which was consistent with the response of the acquiring team. Having introduced methods of increasing participation, the team then suspended these initiatives and retired 'behind closed doors'. This change of direction, coupled with the necessity to make over 50 per cent of the workforce redundant, is likely to have adversely affected employee trust and conveyed a confused and ambiguous culture 'message'. As was reported, relations between employees and the team developed into the kind of tangle or 'knot', characteristic of interpersonal perception, whereby one group's experience of the other was a function of the other group's experience of them.

As the new culture became ambiguous and then subsequently appeared more to resemble the 'old' culture, management were experienced by employees as 'still playing the same old tune'. It is suggested that the so-called 'new' culture was perceived to be as equally dissatisfying and unattractive as the old; employees became marginalized and deculturation occurred.

Having survived the crisis, the management team are still continuing to maintain a culture which is more constraining than that they originally espoused. In their assessment, the acquisition was a failure in its first year because they attempted to impose a new culture which was inappropriate to the business activity and the demands of the workforce. Whether their assessment is correct remains to be proven. However, if the culture of Fill-it Packaging continues to develop as a 'closed' role or neo-power culture, it seems likely that the quality of working life for the majority of its employees will remain unsatisfactory, and problems of high staff turnover will continue.

Appendix 3

Case Study 3: the Age–Nouvelle merger – a game of cricket or croquet?

This case study examines the early, essentially pre-combination stage of an Anglo-French merger between two large engineering companies. In particular, it focuses on the extent to which initial attitudes towards merger are revised as a result of the lack of or uncertainty of change rather than any actual change itself. In the context of this merger, this resulted in a 'pre-integration' drift in that 25 per cent of the managers we questioned left the organization prior to any sociocultural integration. The evidence suggests that rather than being 'resistant to change', they left because they were impatient for change. As most of the departing managers had been expensively 'bought in' to supplement existing talent developed within the organization, the findings challenge the assumption that those who voluntarily leave acquired or merged organizations are necessarily the less competent.

The study also illustrates how the problems of language difficulties and inherent national cultural stereotypes influence and may impede merger integration between organizations with different national origins. As the trend towards European cross-border alliances escalates, the historical reluctance of managers within British organizations to acquire a foreign language is likely to prove a serious disadvantage. The ability to speak another European language not only fulfils the obvious communication function but also facilitates cultural understanding; an essential pre-requisite to working together successfully.

Background to the study

Age Engineering formed the heavy engineering division of a large UK conglomerate. The division employed over 3000 employees. Because of a depressed home market, almost 80 per cent of its turnover came from export business. In recent years, numerous reports had appeared in the press linking it with several potential European merger partners. The announcement of its merger with the Nouvelle Compagnie was therefore not entirely unexpected, particularly as the organization had collaborated with Nouvelle on a number of joint ventures.

Six months after the announcement, the merger officially became operational. Its stated aim was to integrate the management of the two organizations to create a more flexible European-wide structure. It was envisaged that in the future this would involve regular staff movements between the UK and Continental Europe.

The merger was presented as an amicable marriage of equals but, in terms of the size of the workforce, Nouvelle had considerable numerical superiority. In press releases, organizational assets were quoted in francs. The new CEO was to be French and the operational headquarters were to be based in Paris.

Several months later, negotiations begun prior to the merger were completed and the newly merged Age–Nouvelle acquired a UK company. This acquisition distracted the attention of senior management and was considered to be a more immediate organizational issue than the merger.

Six months post legal combination, a series of interviews were conducted with a sample of senior/middle managers from Age. From the interviews it was clear that, while contact with Nouvelle was restricted to a small nucleus of individuals, all the interviewees had highly developed perceptions of Nouvelle and its culture, as being very different from their own. A questionnaire was subsequently distributed to a randomly selected wider sample of managers throughout the organization to assess more fully:

1 Initial reactions to the merger.
2 The existing culture of Age.
3 Managerial perceptions of the culture of Nouvelle.
4 Present merger attitudes and concerns.

Contrary to the predictions of the directors of Age, who seemed unconvinced that the merger was a 'big' organizational issue for their subordinates – after all, they were still at the 'helm' – the questionnaire achieved a very high response rate. Therefore, it seems reasonable to conclude that for the managers at Age who responded, the merger was considered important.

A French translation of the questionnaire was made available, but Age continued to resist any attempt to bring Nouvelle into the study. This is perhaps indicative of the quality of the relationship and degree of trust between the two partners.

Table App. 3.1 *How managers first learnt of the Age–Nouvelle merger*

Manner	%
Personally from superior	46
By group announcement	18
By memo or letter	9
From fellow employees	4
From outside the organization	
i.e. radio, newspaper or similar source	23

Initial reaction

News of the impending merger had been announced to selective senior personnel, and had then 'trickled down' throughout the organization, so that, by the time of the official announcement some months later, 60 per cent of our sample of senior/middle managers were already aware of the merger. Consequently, even at managerial level, there was considerable variation, not only in the timing but in the manner in which respondents first learnt of the event. (See Table App. 3.1.)

The majority of managers (77 per cent) reported that they were initially excited and entirely positive about the merger. Nineteen per cent of managers initially greeted the merger with cautious optimism. Only 4 per cent reported that they had been anxious and shocked by the news, either because they were unconvinced that the merger was beneficial to Age or they considered that their future job prospects were likely to suffer as a result.

When a merger is first announced it creates an expectancy of organizational change. At the individual level, this change is perceived as being either a threat, an opportunity, or an irrelevance. On the basis of their responses, the vast majority of managers at Age had initially made a positive appraisal of the situation and its potential consequences, but six months after the combination, and over a year since most managers had first been informed, attitudes had markedly changed.

Age Engineering – six months post legal combination

In contrast with the speed of acquisition, the pace of change had been slow and six months post merger the two organizations were continuing to operate separately under a joint organizational title. Beyond the introduction of a French language-teaching programme, the merger had had relatively little direct impact on the lives of the majority of employees, even at managerial level. There had been no widespread change, even at the system/procedural level, and overall merger-related employee issues were taking up little managerial time. In response to the question 'Has the merger affected your job and to what extent?', only 28 per cent of managers considered that it had.

Nevertheless, the merger, and most particularly the difference in culture between the two partners, were major sources of speculation. Whenever managers were asked about the merger, organizational names were dropped; Age was referred to as 'The British' and Nouvelle as 'The French'. Organizational characteristics seemingly had become undifferentiated from national stereotypes. One interviewee, discussing the differences between Age and Nouvelle, spoke of 'the British bulldog mentality' meeting head on with the 'arrogant and excitable French'. Another suggested an analogy between the gentlemanly conduct of cricket with the ambiguity and aggressiveness of croquet:

> The British and French have supposedly agreed to play the same game together. But they are playing different games. The British think they are playing cricket by the MCC rules but the French are playing croquet by their own rules. The British are just different from the French! . . . We understand the Germans, we should have merged with them.

A European industrial relations expert had been recruited to provide managers with detailed intelligence on the profile of a typical 'French manager', and how to deal with him or her. Age was particularly concerned with presenting a tough managerial image to its French counterparts, and managers were being encouraged to be more aggressive and assertive in their dealings with Nouvelle.

Consequently, everybody had a view about Nouvelle and its culture, or at least about the French and their culture, which to most amounted to the same thing, irrespective of how well informed members were to make that assessment. Those with any experience whatsoever of Nouvelle became key informants. Single experiences – an individual impression of one particular factory, say, on a one-day visit to France – were generalized as being typical. The possibility that the most visited site was Nouvelle's 'showpiece' was not entertained; rather, the conclusion drawn was that Nouvelle's factories were all superior and extensively equipped with the most up-to-date technology.

The new organizational structure and reporting arrangements were continuing to evolve and the organizational chart was still very much on the 'drawing board'. Joint policies on training, employee benefits and procedures were yet to be agreed. These matters were considered unlikely to be resolved for at least another twelve months. A number of joint working parties had been formed and regular meetings were held, mainly in France. These meetings involved a relatively small number of Age personnel, essentially directors and the most senior engineers and accountants. According to the questionnaire data, almost half of the respondents (48.8 per cent) had met less than ten Nouvelle personnel, and over 60 per cent had never visited France.

From the interviews conducted at this time, managerial integration was considered to be a remote and abstract issue. The more immediate concern was the numerical superiority of Nouvelle. As each new tier in the organizational structure was announced, a comparative headcount was made. Those interviewees who had attended meetings with Nouvelle reported that they frequently 'felt swamped' by the French. Whereas Age would only consider it necessary to send one representative to a meeting, Nouvelle would send at least five. Age was not accustomed to decision making by committee, and as an organization was known for its pathological hatred of bureaucracy. It was widely reported that Age delegates found these discussions and debates tiresome and frustrating.

There was a broad consensus of opinion among managers that, while British senior and middle managers would eventually be working in French plants and *vice versa*, wide-scale sociocultural integration would not be achieved for several years. Most respondents (91 per cent) stated that in the six months since the merger had become operational the existing culture of Age had not changed in any way, apart from the introduction of the language programme. Only 9 per cent of respondents, all directors, considered that the culture had already changed – notably that the firm decision making and delegation characteristic of Age's culture was rapidly becoming submerged.

A major problem to integration was language. It had become the policy for meetings between the partners to be conducted in the language of the country in which they were held. Most meetings were held in France, which again confirmed Nouvelle as the dominant partner and the language of the merged organization as French. This presented difficulties for Age. Most of their managers, and all but one of their directors, had an engineering background and so might be expected to have generally poor linguistic aptitudes. Those interviewed who had attended meetings conducted in French admitted that communication was a slow and laborious process, in which they frequently had to resort to drawing diagrams. At times this was extremely frustrating, particularly because their French counterparts, most of whom were professional managers, were linguistically competent in English.

Table App. 3.2   *Degree to which merger is a source of stress*

Not at all					Very definitely
1	2	3	4	5	6
48%	14%	14%	11%	10%	3%
Mean score = 2.26					

From the Age management team surveyed, only one was fluent in French, although 72 per cent were currently learning French. The personnel director indicated that the language programme provided for all managerial, clerical and secretarial staff was not proving to be entirely successful, primarily because students were expected to do a considerable amount of work in their own time. The drop-out rate was approximately 30 per cent and, among managers, around 12 per cent.

There was generally a high level of job satisfaction at Age and, at this stage, the merger was not widely reported to be a source of stress. (See Table App. 3.2.)

The cultures of Age and Nouvelle

The interview data, together with an analysis of questionnaire responses, strongly indicated that the cultures of Age and Nouvelle were perceived to be very different. (See Table App. 3.3.) The main areas of difference were perceived to be in size and staffing ratios, and in corporate philosophies.

Table App. 3.3   *Perceived differences in Age's and Nouvelle's cultures*

Very similar					Very dissimilar
1	2	3	4	5	6
2%	–	5%	21%	39%	19%
Mean score = 4.75					

Size and staffing ratios

Age was considered to be a small organization compared with Nouvelle, which received state support and was considered to be overstaffed. In contrast, Age had to survive by its own efforts in a very competitive market. It worked to a very tight budget and was considered to be a 'lean outfit'. Consequently, most of Nouvelle's turnover was generated from an almost guaranteed home market of government contracts, whereas Age was involved in more competitive tendering ex-UK.

Corporate philosophies

Age was a profit-motivated organization. Expenditure was related to short-term performance, and it only spent what it had already earned. High productivity was its most important organizational goal.

In contrast, Nouvelle was perceived to be long term in its thinking. To Nouvelle, the most important organizational goal was to achieve excellence in its engineering feats and the innovative quality of its products. Profitability was of secondary importance to sales and the prestige of tailoring new products to meet customer needs.

Decision making and general managerial style

Age prided itself on the speed of its decision making, usually made by the manager 'on the spot'. Subordinates were informed of decisions rather than participated in the process. In contrast, Nouvelle favoured decisions by committee.

The senior 'decision makers' of Age considered this made Nouvelle an excessively bureaucratic organization, stifled by its many rules and regulations. In contrast, many of the middle managers of Age felt the discussive style of decision making gave Nouvelle a more relaxed, flexible, team-orientated culture than Age.

There were major differences between Age and Nouvelle in their attitude towards management generally. Age boasted that regardless of function, with the exception of their financial director, all their directors were engineers, and that it had remained an organization in which it was still possible to rise from the shopfloor to the boardroom. All its managerial training programmes were strictly 'in-house'. In contrast, Nouvelle was managed by a team of professionally trained managers, qualified in their respective functions. Qualifications and the importance of Grande Ecole education were prerequisites for any managerial appointment. Their attitude towards management was considered to be more 'outward looking' and 'less insular' than that at Age. Many managers who had joined Age within the last five years described Age as being an 'old-fashioned' organization, still very much influenced by the outdated ideas of its founding chairman.

The influence of corporate philosophy, together with tough market conditions, i.e. a continuing recession in the home market, had powerfully shaped the culture of Age, the most salient feature of which was its competitive environment. Age was an organization in which people who 'get on' and do well, were those who were shrewd and competitive, with a strong drive for power; 42 per cent of managers described the situation with the statement: 'In this organization, it's the survival of the fittest'. The remaining 28 per cent tended to echo similar sentiments, in that they emphasized the short-term focus of the organization in maximizing profits, often at the expense of 'people' considerations. Examples include descriptions such as 'People don't count, only gains', 'Maximize short-term gains at any cost' or 'Get the job done and then sort out the problems'.

Age's decision-making style and emphasis on competitive individualism suggested it to be a predominantly 'macho' power culture. Senior and middle managers alike, irrespective of the length of time they had been with the organization, consistently, in both interviews and questionnaire data, presented Age as having a strong coherent and overarching unitary power culture, although, because of the nature of its business, in that it operated in a project environment, certain departments had developed 'task sub-cultures'. These were subordinate to the dominant values of the overriding power culture.

While the culture of Age was very much taken for granted and accepted as being 'right' and appropriate by those who had been with the organization a number of years, in contrast, managers with relatively less experience were less convinced of its appropriateness. 'Newcomers', i.e. those managers with less than seven years' service, experienced the culture of Age as being significantly more oppressive, more constraining and a less-satisfying environment in which to work than 'old timers', i.e. those managers with more than seven years' experience.

Current attitudes

The initial response of the majority of managers to the announcement had been positive, in that the merger initially had not generally caused any widespread anxiety. This indicates that it was perceived as an opportunity likely to result in beneficial organizational and/or individual outcomes, rather than as a threat. Yet, clearly, this was a marriage of opposites.

Assessments of merger outcomes at the time of the announcement are made on the basis of the likelihood and direction of future change. They may subsequently be revised as the cultural dynamics unfurl. Therefore, in cultural terms, the managers at Age were likely to be positive in their initial response, on the basis of two possible interpretive assessments of the situation, as illustrated in Table App. 3.4.

Although, since the announcement, there remained general consensus that the merger was in the best interest of Age organizationally, in individual terms current attitudes were now less positive than they had been initially. Respondents also tended to rate the feelings of their co-workers as being less favourable than their own.

Table App. 3.4 *Explanation of positivity of initial response to merger*

Assessment	Assumption	Expected mode of acculturation
Organizational members were happy with their existing culture and did not see its dominance or existence as being threatened by the other	Age assumed to be dominant partner	→ *Assimilation* – Nouvelle adopt the culture of Age
	Power is assumed to be distributed equally	→ *Separation* – Age and Nouvelle will retain their cultures and continue to operate independently
Organizational members saw the merger as an opportunity to abandon or change in part their own culture in favour of the other	Nouvelle assumed to be dominant partner	→ *Assimilation* – Age will adopt the culture of Nouvelle
	Power is assumed to be distributed equally	→ *Integration* – Age and Nouvelle will adopt the 'best' aspects of each other's culture

Although 77 per cent of respondents had described their initial response to the merger exclusively in terms of three adjectives – pleased, optimistic and excited – there had been a marked attitudinal change. Now, six months later, only 37 per cent of respondents still expressed a positive attitude; 49 per cent of managers were now 'uncertain or had mixed feelings'; and an increased percentage, 14 per cent, expressed entirely negative attitudes towards the merger. Furthermore, 37 per cent of managers indicated that they were now seriously considering leaving the organization, and within six months most of these managers actually did leave the organization.

What then had happened to cause almost half the managers to revise their initial attitudes? Given that systems/procedural change had been minimal, there had been no redundancies resulting from role duplicity and the culture of Age had remained relatively unchanged in the period since the merger, current attitudes were clearly not reflecting a negative response to any actual change experienced. Indeed, quite the opposite, as those managers who had originally perceived the merger as an opportunity for culture change, on realization of the long-term time-scale of such a change became increasingly frustrated and less positive about the merger. The differing attitudinal response between managerial groups was found to be explicable in terms of individual compatibility, experience and commitment to the existing culture, rather than any direct or increased exposure to 'the other' culture. Furthermore, attitudinal differences appeared to be little moderated by individual personal characteristics, such as enhanced career prospects or other demographic variables, such as age, tenure of employment, etc. These issues are now discussed in more detail.

Organizational culture

In terms of the culture measure, there were significant differences between the positive and the uncertain/negative attitudinal groups in respect of five areas of organizational behaviour and practices. The uncertain/negative group considered the existing culture of Age to be significantly 'less role or team oriented', 'less open', 'less concerned with its members as individuals' and 'more unwilling to allow individuals to take risks and be innovative' than the positive group. This group experienced the culture of Age as imposing more constraints on the individual than the positive group, irrespective of whether the managers concerned were directors, senior or middle managers. Nor was it found that those who still held positive merger attitudes considered the culture

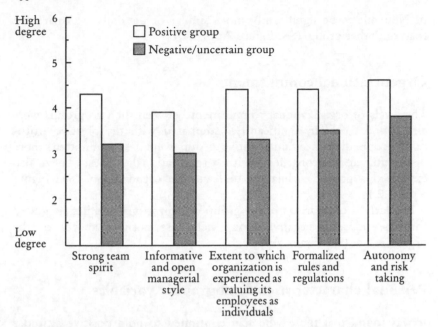

Figure App. 3.1 Significant differences in cultural perceptions between positive and uncertain/negative attitudinal groups in respect of culture of Age

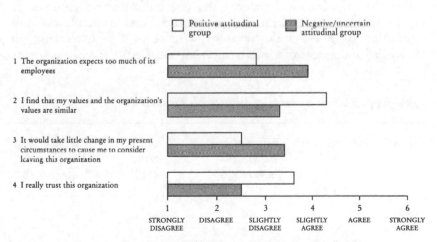

Figure App. 3.2 Significant differences between attitudinal group mean scores in respect of organizational commitment measure

of Nouvelle to be significantly more similar or dissimilar to their own than the other group. (See Figure App. 3.1.)

Organizational commitment

The levels of organizational commitment between the two groups were also found to differ significantly. Compared with the positive attitudinal group, the uncertain/negative group were less committed, more distrustful and incongruent with organizational values. They also expressed a greater inclination to leave the organization. (See Figure App. 3.2.)

Similarly, a comparison of the group organizational profiles suggested that the uncertain/negative group held less positive images of the organization. (See Figure App. 3.3.)

Personal characteristics/demographic variables

It was found that those who had continued to hold positive attitudes towards the merger did not differ significantly from the uncertain/ negative group in their assessment of their future job prospects. (See Table App. 3.5.)

It was also found that there were no significant differences between the groups in terms of the frequency of visits to France, amount of direct contact with Nouvelle, age, tenure of employment or occupational status within the organization. However, the uncertain/negative group were significantly less job satisfied; when asked to rate their overall level of job satisfaction on a 1–6 scale (whereby a score of 1 = Extremely job dissatisfied and a score of 6 = Extremely job satisfied), the mean score for

Table App. 3.5 *Assessment of future job prospects*

Attitudinal group	Better than before the merger (%)	About the same (%)	Worse than before the merger (%)
Overall	54	42	5
Positive	28	9	0
Uncertain/negative	26	32	5

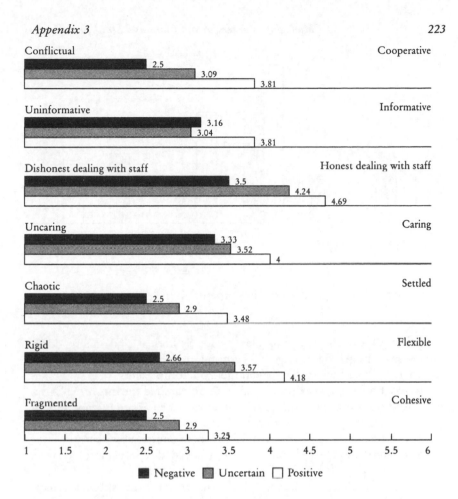

Conflictual / Cooperative
2.5 / 3.09 / 3.81

Uninformative / Informative
3.16 / 3.04 / 3.81

Dishonest dealing with staff / Honest dealing with staff
3.5 / 4.24 / 4.69

Uncaring / Caring
3.33 / 3.52 / 4

Chaotic / Settled
2.5 / 2.9 / 3.48

Rigid / Flexible
2.66 / 3.57 / 4.18

Fragmented / Cohesive
2.5 / 2.9 / 3.25

■ Negative ▨ Uncertain ☐ Positive

Figure App. 3.3 Age Engineering – comparison of organizational profile of attitudinal groups

the positive group was 4.95, compared with 3.84 for the uncertain/ negative group.

The uncertain/negative group also rated the merger as being more stressful, although they had experienced less change in their daily working lives as a result.

Mental health

The mean scores of the managers on the mental health measure were comparable with those of the 'normal' population generally, with the

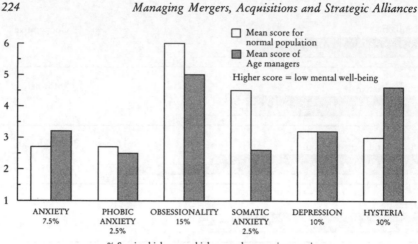

% Scoring higher or as high as psychoneurotic outpatients

Figure App. 3.4　Age Engineering – mental health scores

exception of one of the subscales – the hysterical personality scale. However, a larger percentage of respondents than normally expected scored as high or higher than psychoneurotic outpatients. It is suggested by those who have devised and extensively researched the measure (Crisp, 1977) that no more than 5–10 per cent of the normal population should score as high or higher than psychoneurotic outpatients; 15 per cent of Age's managers recorded obsessionality scores comparable with psychoneurotic outpatients, and 30 per cent recorded comparable hysteria scores.

Abnormally high individual scores on any of the subscales have organizational implications in terms of decreased performance and effectiveness. Highly obsessive individuals demonstrate excessive meticulousness, adherence to routine and dislike of sudden change. Behaviourally this manifests itself in compulsive repetitive actions such as a tendency continually to check and recheck details, and a reluctance to delegate effectively.

Individuals scoring high on the hysterical personality scale are considered to be over-dependent on others and emotionally unstable, with a tendency to over-dramatize situations.

Some doubts as to the reliability and validity of these particular scales as a means of clinical diagnosis have been expressed. In particular, it has been found that high scores on the hysterical personality scale tend to be associated with extroversion. However, in this context, abnormally high scores can be considered to be indicative of the exaggerated behaviour which mergers or acquisitions typically seem to produce in individuals,

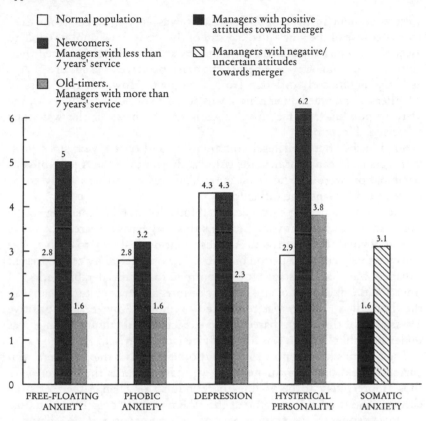

Figure App. 3.5 Mental well-being – a comparative group analysis of mean scores

i.e. in their attempt to appear outwardly 'merger fit', individuals become obsessed with the fear of demonstrating incompetence or being found to be 'sloppy' in their work and, in their efforts to maintain high visibility, affect or over-emphasize the extroverted aspects of their personality. As Figure App. 3.5 illustrates, poor mental health appeared to be associated with length of time with the organization, and to a lesser degree current attitudes towards the merger.

Summary

Despite the limited contact between the partnering organizations, Age's managers had formed clear perceptions of the culture of Nouvelle and were consistent in their opinions that it was very different from their own. Because of the 'one-sided' nature of the study, it was not possible to ascertain whether organizational members at Nouvelle experienced their culture in the same way or whether they also perceived the culture of Age as being significantly different from their own. However, regardless of whether this assumed dissimilarity was accurate or not, employees at Age were responding and making decisions on the basis of the way they perceived things to be.

Six months after their legal combination, and over a year since most managers had been informed, the cultural dynamics of the Age–Nouvelle combination were still far from clear. Any resolution was likely to be exacerbated by language difficulties.

There was increasing evidence that Nouvelle may be emerging as the dominant partner, but any implications this may have appeared not yet to extend beyond the boardroom. As these continued slowly to evolve, Age had effectively entered a period of limbo. The only certainty of the present situation was that this stage would continue for a considerable period of time, and the likelihood of any large-scale integration or cultural change in the immediate future was extremely remote. Any earlier positive assessment of the merger based on an expectancy of cultural change was understandably likely, as was demonstrated, to be revised.

The findings lent support to this hypothesis in that the managers who currently held uncertain or negative attitudes towards the merger were those more likely to be willing to relinquish or change their existing culture. The results demonstrated that the uncertain/negative attitudinal group experienced the culture of Age as oppressive and dissatisfying. Compared with those who maintained their positive attitudes, the uncertain/negative group were less committed and less deeply attached to the culture. Therefore, they were less likely to consider it worth preserving. Their awareness of cultural incongruence is likely to have been heightened by expectations of change and cognitive self-appraisals precipitated by the merger situation. This may have caused them to consider leaving the organization.

In contrast with the acquisitions, there was some evidence to suggest that merger events had adversely affected the mental well-being of respondents. Comparison between attitudinal groups on the basis of their mental health scores found the uncertain/negative group to be significantly more 'somatically anxious' but not yet abnormally so. This may be indicative of the effects of cultural alienation or merger uncertainty or stress more generally. In the absence of any pre-merger measures, no firm conclusions can be drawn.

Similarly, any explanation as to the abnormally high scores recorded by those who had been with the organization less than seven years is tentative. Given that 'newcomers' were fairly evenly distributed in terms of their age and position in the organization, a plausible explanation for their mental ill health is that socialization into a power culture is experienced as stressful, when one moves from a previously less constraining culture.

In organizational terms, it is too early to tell whether the Age–Nouvelle merger will ultimately prove to be successful or what will happen to the organizational cultures of the partners. What does appear clear is that in the period following a merger employees engage in a critical self-analysis of their present situation, in which they reassess their compatibility with their existing culture and their expectations of the likelihood and direction of future change. It becomes a 'sizing up' or 'wait and see' period. If the cultural dynamics unfurl contrary to initial expectations, assessments are likely to be revised. If eventually Age is to integrate or adopt the culture of Nouvelle, it would seem likely that by that time those more amenable to change will have left the organization and its remaining 'die-hard' members will have become increasingly resistant to change. The literature had tended to relate the 'post-acquisition' drift factor to fears of job security. On the basis of this study, decisions to leave the organization are likely to be made on pre-integration assessments as to what will happen to the organization and its culture at the macro level, and may override micro-level assessments of individual job prospects.

References

Crisp, A.H. (1977). Psychoneurosis in the general population. *Journal of International Medical Research*, **5** (Supp. 4), 61–80.

Appendix 4

Case Study 4: the Gable–Apex merger – a marriage of convenience

This case study considers the merger of two UK building societies. At the time of the merger, the Gable had approximately 1000 employees and the Apex had over 4500. As a result of the merger, the combined size of the Gable–Apex placed it among the ten largest UK societies and was considered to be of strategic benefit to both partners.

In organizational terms, the Gable–Apex merger was considered to be financially successful. Contrary to the initial perceptions of the middle managers of both organizations, the merger partners were more equal than indicated by their relative size in that both societies had an important contribution to make in the creation of a new 'better' organization. Integration was facilitated by the cultural similarity of the combining organizations.

This case study focuses on the response of middle managers to the merger and demonstrates how a misunderstanding of the terms of the marriage contract contributed to merger stress.

Background to the study

Approximately seven months after the announcement, the operations of the two partners were considered to be fully integrated. The old head office of the Apex became the headquarters of the new merged organization. More than six months later, this fact was still not fully recognized and accepted by those who had remained in the previous head office of the Gable, now deemed to be a satellite head office. Employees working there continued to describe and regard themselves as being 'head office', which initially caused considerable confusion for us in analysing the questionnaire data and identifying its point of origin.

As a result of the merger, there had been an overlap of branch networks in sixty areas, which resulted in the closure of thirty offices. While there had been no 'official' redundancies, role duplicity had resulted in a spate of voluntary early retirements and resignations. Many employees had been involved in merger selection interviews and many managers had been obliged to relocate.

This study is based on a survey of 157 managers conducted six months after the merger became operational. The sample consisted of middle managers (Grades A–F), i.e. from just below executive level, Grade A, down to the equivalent of first branch management appointment, Grade F. Of the managers studied, thirty-four were ex-Gable employees and 123 were ex-Apex employees. This closely approximates the ratio of Gable–Apex employees throughout the organization.

The respondents comprised twenty-six female (16.6 per cent) and 131 (83.4 per cent) male managers. This is a higher representation of women than might be expected, given the demographic composition of the whole sector. The building society industry, in common with the financial services sector as a whole, is a major employer of women. However, recent research (Ashburner, 1989) has found that only 2 per cent of all women employed in the sector occupy managerial roles. In terms of this sample, 11 per cent of the total number of ex-Gable managers were women, but none were employed at a level above Grade E; and 17 per cent of the total number of ex-Apex managers were women, the majority of whom (77 per cent) were also employed at the lower levels, Grades E and F. The few women who had achieved a Grade C or D status tended to be older and had been with the organization longer than their male counterparts.

Managers were asked to complete a questionnaire measure of the culture of their organization pre/post merger.

The pre-merger cultures of the Gable and Apex

Before the merger, the existing cultures of the Gable and Apex were basically similar. Both were predominantly role cultures, experienced as being cohesive. The salient features of both being, clear role definition and formalized rules and regulations and a hierarchical power structure. For both partners, head office was very much the Mecca of the organization. When compared in terms of seventeen key areas of organizational behaviour and practices, there were found to be no significant differences between the two. (See Figure App. 4.1.)

The only perceptible difference between the two partners was that of reputation. Whereas the smaller society, Gable, had a reputation of encouraging the 'buccaneering' or entrepreneurial, and was seen as more aggressive within the marketplace, Apex was considered to be more staid, ponderous and bureaucratic. Prior to the merger, 80 per cent of Gable managers considered that the organization's success depended upon the

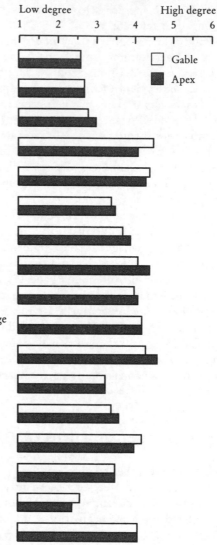

Figure App. 4.1 Managerial assessments of the pre-merger cultures of the combining organizations

ability of its members to pull together. Only 10 per cent felt that the Gable was an organization in which the political animal thrived. In contrast, Apex managers felt that success in their organization depended upon either always being seen to stick to the rules (32 per cent) or being a team player (43 per cent).

Low degree   High degree
1   2   3   4   5   6

1 Accessibility/approachability
   of senior management   □ Gable
2 Autocratic power   ■ Apex
3 People-oriented management
4 Clarity of role definition
5 Team spirit
6 Openness of managerial style
7 Value placed on organizational
   members as individuals
8 Formalized rules and regulations
9 Empire building
10 Free and unconditional exchange
   of information
11 Reliance on formal authority
   rather than task expertise
12 Reward system based on task
   contribution
13 Formally structured channels
   of communication
14 Intra-organizational
   competition
15 Autonomy and risk taking
16 Good interpersonal
   communications
17 Direction/interference from
   head office

Figure App. 4.2 Managerial assessments of the post-merger culture of the Gable–Apex building society

The post-merger culture of Gable–Apex

Again, there were no significant differences between the managerial groups in terms of their assessments of the 'new' culture of the organization six months post integration, and the direction in which it

Table App. 4.1   *Views on what sort of people get on in Gable–Apex*

	Gable managers' views (%)	Apex managers' views (%)
The Political, i.e. party liners, those who can 'talk' a good branch	45	34
The Competitive, i.e. those with good sales records, meet objectives whatever the means	13	35
The Competent, i.e. the quick, the clever and the qualified	23	21
The Committed, i.e. the hardworker, the 24-hour person	19	10

had changed. That members of both organizations presented consistent views of the post merger culture is indicative that a 'new' coherent culture had developed, one experienced as being different from the pre-merger cultures of both partnering organizations. (See Figure App. 4.2.)

While having retained certain role elements, e.g. a higher degree of formalization and regulation, the culture had become less cohesive, more competitive and power oriented. For the middle managers of both partners, the rules for playing the organizational game had changed. 'Getting on' in the new organization was now increasingly seen as playing a political game and maintaining high visibility. (See Table App. 4.1.) Both managerial groups now perceived the organizational culture to be more of a power/closed role culture than it had been previously. The senior management at both organizations had previously been experienced as being impersonal and remote – since the merger they were perceived by both groups as having become even more so.

Managerial attitudes expressed by those who completed the questionnaire at this time are a reflection of what was perceived to be an ongoing power struggle at the top of the organization. At the time of the merger, by virtue of its numerical superiority, Apex ostensibly appeared to be the dominant partner. By the time the merger became operational, the new senior executive was composed of equal numbers of Gable and Apex personnel. At the time the questionnaires were completed, six or

Table App. 4.2 *Areas of organizational behaviour and practices which managers perceived to have remained unchanged since the merger*

Gable	Apex
The dominance of formalized rules and regulations	The dominance of formalized rules and regulations
Degree of autocracy/democracy	Decision-making style
Degree of people-oriented management	The degree of autonomy afforded to employees
Level of team spirit	The degree of direction/ interference from head office
Openness of managerial style	
Extent to which the organization values its members as individuals	
Decision-making style	
Reward systems	
Formality and structure of communication channels	
Competitive nature of the organizational climate	
Degree of autonomy afforded to employees	
The degree of direction/ interference from head office	

seven months post merger, the power dynamics were still evolving and looked likely to change in favour of Gable. Apex managers were beginning to talk of a reverse takeover. Ultimately, this did seem to happen and within twelve months, at executive level, the ratio of Gable–Apex personnel was 4:2 in the Gable's favour.

An analysis of the questionnaire data found that both Gable and Apex managers reported having experienced culture change. However, Apex managers considered they had experienced significantly more change than Gable, contrary to the initial expectations of members of both organizations at this level. Given their increased size, Apex managers perceived their organization as being the dominant partner, and that Gable would be expected to adopt their culture. Conversely, Gable's middle managers initially had felt their culture to be threatened by 'the other'. (See Tables App. 4.2 and 4.3.)

Table App. 4.3 *Areas of organizational behaviour and practices which managers perceived to have changed since the merger*

Gable	Apex
Senior management has become less approachable and accessible	Senior management has become less approachable and accessible
Roles are less clearly defined	Management style has become more autocratic
Organization has become significantly more political	Organization now places less value on its members as individuals
Employees are less inclined to share and exchange organizational information	Roles are less clearly defined
Interpersonal communication between managers and staff and also cooperation between branches have deteriorated	Less team spirit
	More 'closed' managerial style
	Less people-oriented management
	Organization has become significantly more political
	Employees are less inclined to share and exchange organizational information
	Reward systems now favour those who sell well rather than those who are loyal
	Channels of communication have become more formal and structured
	Interpersonal communication between managers and staff and also cooperation between branches have deteriorated

Organizational commitment

The questionnaire measure indicated that organizational commitment had been renewed or at least had not been severely affected by the merger. Levels of organizational commitment were similar for employees of both merger partners, and were comparable with pre-integration levels at Age.

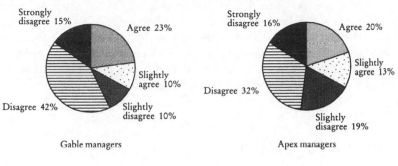

Questionnaire Item: It would take little change in my present circumstances to cause me to consider leaving the organization

Gable managers

Strongly disagree 15%
Agree 23%
Slightly agree 10%
Slightly disagree 10%
Disagree 42%

Apex managers

Strongly disagree 16%
Agree 20%
Slightly agree 13%
Slightly disagree 19%
Disagree 32%

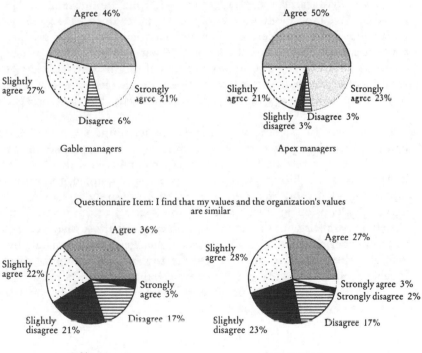

Questionnaire Item: I really care about the fate of this organization

Gable managers

Agree 46%
Slightly agree 27%
Strongly agree 21%
Disagree 6%

Apex managers

Agree 50%
Slightly agree 21%
Strongly agree 23%
Slightly disagree 3%
Disagree 3%

Questionnaire Item: I find that my values and the organization's values are similar

Gable managers

Agree 36%
Slightly agree 22%
Strongly agree 3%
Disagree 17%
Slightly disagree 21%

Apex managers

Slightly agree 28%
Agree 27%
Strongly agree 3%
Strongly disagree 2%
Disagree 17%
Slightly disagree 23%

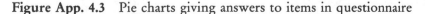

Figure App. 4.3 Pie charts giving answers to items in questionnaire

In contrast with Age, managers reported less inclination to leave the organization, suggesting that having survived the 'process', they now felt reasonably settled in the new organization. (See Figure App. 4.3.)

There was no widespread evidence of cultural incongruity on either side. The culture data suggested that there was actually no difference between the two cultures that was discernible by objective measurement. In their subjective assessment, members had experienced change but it would seem that in reality this change was not as great as it was perceived to be and, hence, had not seriously challenged core values.

General information

In terms of demographic characteristics, the two managerial groups were well matched. Typically, a middle manager was a married male in his thirties who had learnt of the merger from a group announcement. Apex tended to have more younger managers, i.e. under thirty-five years old.

Half the Gable managers considered that their future job prospects were better now than before the merger, 26 per cent rated them as being about the same and 24 per cent worse than before. In contrast, only 24.5 per cent of Apex managers considered the merger had enhanced their future job prospects, and the majority (54 per cent) felt their prospects had remained unaltered.

The merger had significantly more personal impact on the Gable managers than the Apex, with 62 per cent of Gable managers stating that they had been severely affected by the merger, compared with 22 per cent of Apex managers. However, this appears to have resulted in a positive outcome, in that those reported as being more severely affected by the merger also considered their future job prospects had improved. There are certain parallels with the situation at Age, in that those managers who reported experiencing more merger-related change in their working lives were also more positive in their attitude towards the combination. A possible explanation is that if the merger is experienced as affecting you personally, this is taken as a positive indication that you have a part to play in the new merged organization.

Job satisfaction

There was no evidence to suggest that the merger had adversely affected overall levels of job satisfaction of either managerial group. Managers completed the job satisfaction scale (Warr, Cook and Wall, 1979), which yields a global score between 15 (extreme dissatisfaction) and 105 (extreme satisfaction). The mean score for Gable managers was 73 and for Apex managers 72. These scores were also found to be comparable with the normative data available and the post-acquisition levels of managerial job satisfaction found in the earlier studies.

Stress

Clearly, the merger was significantly more stressful for the Gable managers than the Apex, with 75.7 per cent of Gable managers rating the merger as being very definitely/definitely a source of stress, compared with 20.1 per cent of Apex managers. Only 38 (24 per cent) of managers out of the total sample of 157 considered that the merger had caused them no stress whatsoever.

Although there had been reported to be a high incidence of stress-related absence among managers since the merger, this sample, which represented more than half of all middle managers, comprised perhaps the 'walking wounded' or 'worried well'. Only three managers (two

Table App. 4.4 *Stressors*

Gable	Apex
1 Having far too much work (Mean score 3.97)	1 Having far too much work (Mean score 4.37)
2 Not being able to switch off at home (Mean score 3.94)	2 Having to work longer hours (Mean score 3.74)
	3 Unclear promotion prospects (Mean score 3.72)
3 Lack of consultation and communication (Mean score 3.79)	4 Characteristics of the organization's restructure and design (Mean score 3.72)

Maximum score 6 = Very definitive sources of stress
Minimum score 1 = Very definitely not a source of stress

Gable; one Apex) reported stress-related absence as a result of the merger. Approximately 10 per cent indicated that they could have been absent as a result of merger stress but had 'soldiered on'. However, respondents were asked specifically about absence directly attributable to stress-related conditions rather than their general record of absence. Spells of absence due to physical symptoms such as influenza, stomach disorders, etc., not directly ascribed by absentees to stress but which may have been stress related, were therefore not picked up by the questionnaire. Unfortunately, absenteeism records were not available so it was not possible to ascertain the extent to which the organization had experienced increased absenteeism more generally since the merger.

Other than 'rate of pay' which Apex managers rated as a significantly greater source of stress than Gable managers, there were no significant differences between groups on any of the stressors included

Table App. 4.5 *Additional sources of concern*

		Apex (No. of mentions	Gable (No. of mentions
1	*Relationships with senior management* Perceived to be 'top heavy'; problems of empire building; senior management experienced as more aggressive and remote	12	4
2	*Lack of planning and forethought in decision making and communication*	8	8
3	*Changes in culture/problems with the other partner* Different levels of competence; the bureaucracy of Apex v 'favouritism' given to Gable; relationships between Apex HO and old HO of Gable	6	3
4	*Prospects of another merger*	3	2
5	*Changing market conditions* Increased sales pressure	3	–

in the questionnaire. However, the items were assigned different priorities. The responses drawing the three highest mean scores on the potential stressors included in the questionnaire are those shown in Table App. 4.4.

The item 'Personal beliefs conflicting with those of the organization', a likely indicator of cultural incongruity, was rated low by both groups (Gable mean = 3.09 – 13th out of 17; Apex mean = 2.99 – 15th out of 17).

For all managers, merger rationalization had increased individual workloads and, in common with managers at the two acquisitions, had become a major source of stress.

Other aspects/changes following the merger which were considered to have become a source of concern are shown in Table App. 4.5.

Coping strategies – Gable

Of the Gable managers who completed this section of the questionnaire, twenty-nine (88 per cent) considered that the merger had to some degree caused them stress, and eight of the affected managers (28 per cent) reported that they had coped badly with the situation, suffered from increased irritability, insomnia, etc., and had not developed any strategy for dealing with their stress. The other main strategies are shown in Table App. 4.6. Interestingly, the poor coping strategies (increased use of alcohol and nicotine) were those employed by women.

Table App. 4.6 *Strategies to combat stress – Gable*

Strategy	Number	%
Talking with spouse	6	21
Talking with colleagues/friends	4	14
Exercise/sport	4	14
Increased participation in family activities	2	7
Increased alcohol consumption	2	7
Increased smoking	2	7
Confronting the problem with superior	1	2

Table App. 4.7 *Strategies to combat stress – Apex*

Strategy	Number	%
Talking with spouse	19	26
Talking with colleagues/friends	16	21
Exercise/sport	7	9
Prayer/meditation	4	5
Increased participation in family activities	1	1
Increased alcohol consumption	4	5
Increased smoking	5	7
Increased eating	3	4
Confronting the problem with superior	2	3

Coping strategies – Apex

Of the 109 Apex managers who completed this section of the questionnaire, seventy-five (78 per cent) considered that the merger had to some degree caused them stress. However, in contrast with Gable, for the majority (48.6 per cent) the stress was perceived to be only experienced occasionally. Of the seventy-five managers affected, fourteen (19 per cent) similarly reported that they had coped badly and had not developed any strategy for dealing with the situation. The other main strategies are shown in Table App. 4.7.

Once again, the poor coping strategies (increased consumption of nicotine, alcohol and food) tended to be 'female' strategies. This may highlight the problems of dual career couples in that there is possibly insufficient time allocated in such a relationship for the woman to talk about her job, perhaps because the male partner's career traditionally remains dominant.

Several male respondents considered that their wives and families had suffered more than themselves, particularly as many managers had been obliged to relocate.

Mental well-being

Thirty-four managers (22 per cent) out of the total sample of 157 were not prepared to complete a self-report measure of mental health. Two reasons were given for this. Either managers considered it irrelevant as they had

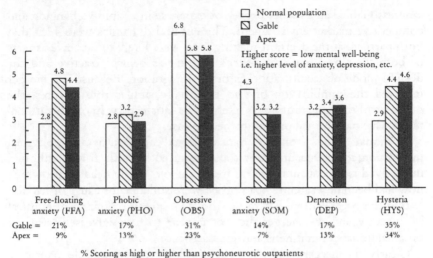

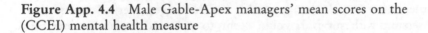

% Scoring as high or higher than psychoneurotic outpatients

Crisp (1977) suggests that no more than 5–10% of the normal population
should score as high or higher than psychoneurotic outpatients

Figure App. 4.4 Male Gable-Apex managers' mean scores on the
(CCEI) mental health measure

not experienced any stress, or they felt it to be contrary to their self-
interest, given the present political organizational climate.

An analysis of the results found that both Gable and Apex managers
(males) had significantly higher mental health scores than the normal
population on two of the subscales; free-floating anxiety and hysterical
personality. (See Figure App. 4.4.)

There was again evidence to suggest that the mental well-being of
Gable managers had been more adversely affected by the merger than
Apex. An abnormally high percentage of Gable managers scored higher
than psychoneurotic outpatients on all six subscales. In common with
Age's managers, Gable–Apex managers also displayed behavioural
characteristics associated with an hysterical personality. The data relating
to the female managers indicated a similar trend in that the scores of the
female Gable managers were observed to be considerably higher than
those of their Apex counterparts and compared unfavourably with the
normal population.

Summary

The Gable–Apex merger was a genuine collaborative marriage. Apex
provided the greater infrastructure and established branch network,

whereas Gable had a higher degree of expertise in a rapidly changing and competitive market environment. The cultural dynamics were such that both partners at the decision-making level were likely to perceive aspects of both their own and 'the other's' culture as being attractive and the desired mode of acculturation as being integration. Because the merger involved the combination of two essentially similar role cultures, the outcome of this integration was likely to be satisfactory. In organizational terms, this has already proven to be the case.

In human terms, from the data collected six months after physical integration, the merger appeared to have started to 'settle down', although unresolved issues, such as the future of the old Gable head office which now had become a satellite head office were still a major cause of friction within the organization. There was no widespread reporting of cultural incongruity and the merger did not appear to have adversely affected organizational commitment and job satisfaction.

Clearly, the merger had been a stressful life event for middle managers, particularly those members of the smaller partner. There was again strong evidence that it is the expectancy of change and fears of future survival, rather than actual change itself, which trigger merger stress. This obsession with survival would seem to continue for some time post merger and may be reflected in the high hysterical personality scores of both managerial groups. As already mentioned, the validity of the scale has been questioned in that scores on this scale have a high correlation with scales of extroversion and a low or zero correlation with other subscales. However, as this study again demonstrates, in the merger situation, personal survival appears to be equated with the ability to play politics and become noticed. Therefore, this obsession may cause individuals to affect or exaggerate extroversion and emphasize to others that they are 'merger fit'. The continued maintenance of such a pretence is likely to have detrimental psychological consequences.

It would seem likely that a repeated measure of mental well-being taken at the present time would show little differences in the mental health of the two groups. Since this specific study was completed, sixty-two senior managers (executive and Grade A) of Gable–Apex have completed the occupational stress indicator test (Cooper, Sloan and Williams, 1988). These results found no significant differences between the managerial groups on any of the items.

References

Ashburner, L. (1989). *Men managers and women workers: Women employees as an underused resource*. Paper presented to the Third

Annual Conference of British Academy of Management, Manchester, 10–12 September.

Cooper, C.L., Sloan, S. and Williams S. (1988). *Occupational Stress Indicator*. Windsor: NFER Nelson Publishing Company.

Warr, P., Cook, J. and Wall, T. (1979). Scales for the measurement of some work attitudes and aspects of psychological well-being. *Journal of Occupational Psychology*, **52**, 129–148.

Index

Chanch freehold

0208 - 8520991